Having traveled nearly everywhere searching frequently for exotic adventure, sometimes for intellectual challenge, occasionally for glitz and glamor, I've returned to Mexico and found the excitement, the wisdom and the elegance for which I'd been searching all along.

# MEXICO

# FOR

# LOVERS

## by *antoinette may*

WIDE WORLD PUBLISHING/TETRA

Wide World Publishing/Tetra
P.O. Box 476
San Carlos, CA 94070

Printed in the United States of America.
ISBN: 0-933174-96-9

**Library of Congress Cataloging-in-Publication Data**

May , Antoinette .
    Mexico for lovers  /  by Antoinette May ,
        p.   cm.
    Includes bibliographical references and index .
    ISBN  0-93317496-9 : $12.95
      1. Mexico- -Guidebooks .   2. Mexico- -Description and travel .
    I.  Titles .
    F1216.5 . M39    1994
    917 . 204 ' 835- -dc20                                            94-24160
                                                                           CIP

## *Acknowledgements*

I wish there was a way to thank the entire population of Mexico for its unique part in the creation of this *aventura de corazon.* Sadly, it must suffice to thank a few of the many talented and creative people who helped to pull this book together.

Who first? There are so many who did so much. It was Cecilio and Cecilia of the Mexican Tourist Office in Los Angeles who first opened doors for me as did Amy Bortz and the other dedicated staff members of Daniel J. Edelman, Inc., in Chicago, New York and Los Angeles. From there the list grows and grows. Since occasionally one must be a pragmatist as well as a lover the only possible means of crediting them seems to be alphabetically. My heartfelt thanks to: Dolores Avalos, Sharon Barlowe, Sue Brush, Irene Buchanan, Susan Devine, Jennifer Ehrman, Rosa Teresa Espinosa, John Gilruth, Ellin Ginsberg, Gracie Hamilton, Bud Lewis, Julie Mendez, Marvin Perton, Kristin Sandberg, Ed Strausberg, Elizbeth Vasey, Vickie Von Arx, Susan Wagner, Karen Wos.

But one especially warm *abrazo* to Frank "Pancho" Shiell, a true miracle man.

Baja California
Baja California Sur
Copper Canyon
Mazatlan
Las Cabos
Guanajuato
San M
Guadalajara
M
Morelia
Puerto Vallarta
Cu
Manzanillo
Zihautanejo
Ixtapa
Acapulco

Yucatan
Peninsula
Isla
Mujeres
o City
Cancun
Veracruz
Cozumel
vaca
Merida
o
Oaxaca

# CONTENTS

# INTRODUCTION

Having traveled nearly everywhere searching frequently for exotic adventure, sometimes for intellectual challenge, occasionally for glitz and glamor, I've returned to Mexico, that continental boy next door, and found the excitement, the wisdom and the elegance for which I'd been searching all along.

Now isn't that a love story?

Happily, our affair promises to be a true romance with many, many chapters for Mexico has enough variety to satisfy anyone. The choices are endless. Big city sophistication or small town intimacy? Sun drenched virgin beaches or snow covered volcanoes? In Mexico City one can enjoy 2lst century luxury in an ambience of high rises. Yet within a few hours or even minutes very different explorations beckon: colossal remnants of an ancient past in which great civilizations thrived only to mysteriously decline leaving alluring clues — temples, pyramids and steles that cry out to the Indiana Jones latent in all of us.

Looking for sun, sand and surf? The beaches and hotels at Acapulco or Cancun are world famous. A stay at either of these two posh resort areas can be as relaxing or as frantic as you desire. Rise at noon, languorously recline on sand fine and white as face powder then dance all night to the disco beat. Or sample a hidden paradise at hideaway beaches such as Yelapa or Rio Lagartos where the only foot prints you see will be your own. Admittedly some of the hotels described here *are* pricey. This book is clearly, unabashedly dedicated to romance and indulgence. The time comes for hedonism in everyone's life. These are places and events to be remembered always. A very special time with a very special person deserves a very special place. What price perfection? Only you can decide.

Colonial villages such as the mountain citadel of Valle de Bravo or the historic silver town of Taxco recapture the romance of another century, while striking scenic attractions like the spectacular and imposing Copper Canyon or the breathtakingly beautiful falls at Agua Azul offer unexpected thrills.

But there's something else as well, something even more essential. Mexico's greatest asset is its people. Nowhere will you encounter any more friendly. On all levels, Mexicans are proud of their country's rich, diverse history and its many attractions and delight in showing them off to visitors. Unlike the service personnel in many tourist oriented countries, they don't have to go to a "smile school" to learn hospitality. It just comes naturally.

That rich, layer cake atmosphere with its sudden, unexpected veins of lush sweetness, is the upside. Mexico has a downside as well. Prosaic souls quick to compare everything with the way it's done back home will feel it most.   Mexico *is*  different. Its people have their own concepts,  values, and ways of doing things or *not*  doing things.   There's a saying south of the border:   "It all happens at quarter to midnight."   That eleventh hour quality does flavor much of the life, seeming to blend with the magical realism so unique to Mexican art and litera- ture.

Of course magical realism is rarely on your mind when things don't work:   the radio in your car, the air conditioning in your hotel, the drain in your bath or per- haps even your waiter.  It does take a little time to accustom ourselves to the fact that Mexicans refuse to enslave themselves to clocks.

But then aren't surprises a part of the total "love" experience?  And if we want no differences we could always just stay home..... or maybe go to Disneyland.

*A street scene in San Miguel de Allende.* Photo by E. Monroe.

Mexico City

# MEXICO CITY
## A LATIN MANHATTAN

In Mexico City, a stroll down a street is a time trip telescoped into a single sun-drenched moment in a few feet of stone pavement.

First you may encounter a somber-faced campesino enveloped in a pon-

Today Mexico City is the largest urban center in the world, a megalopolis of 25.6 million people. But then it's always been big. By the early 1500s, its precursor, Tenochtitlan had a population exceeding 200,000 — more than any European city of that time. Added to

*A Latin Manhattan*

cho, wearing a sombrero and grinding his midday meal on a metate that hasn't changed since the Neolithic age. Next you notice the resplendent edifice against which the man leans, no doubt the townhouse of some feudal lord built during the colonial era. But this too is just another juxtaposition; the facade has been transformed into a store, and behind the plate-glass windows are displayed faxes and virtual reality computer games.

this, close to 400,000 more people lived on the lake bed, plains and foot-hills within a fifteen mile radius of the capital's epicenter.

From the mountain peaks, Greater Tenochtitlan must have appeared like a single sprawling metropolis linked by a complex network of causeways and canals. The 2700 square miles encompassing the whole Valley of Mexico was populated by as many as 1.2 million people, a figure all the more startling because it was not surpassed until the beginning of the twentieth century. It was an era of livestock and pack animals, trains and some motorized vehicles, rudimentary electrification and a health system equipped to cope with epidemic diseases.

The Aztecs, the great nation responsible for this vast mega city, were the last of many nomadic groups who arrived some 30,000 years ago wandering across the Bering Strait and drifting south through what is now Canada and the United States. This culture traced its origin to a garden spot called Aztlan, thought to be located somewhere in northwest Mexico. Archaeologists have long since abandoned efforts to match the fabled Aztlan with any locale in the arid, mountainous north. But then hasn't Eden always been painted in idyllic terms, the better to convey a sense of Paradise Lost?

It is surmised that a powerful civilization may have routed them — an event not likely to be recorded by the Aztecs who were acutely embarrassed by any mention of defeat. A chief deity, Huitzilopochtli, meaning "humming bird-of-the left," guided the migration.   If his chosen people tarried too long in one place, the single minded god invariably ordered them on to the promised land. They would recognize the place, he prophesied, when they saw an island in the midst of a lake where an eagle devouring a snake would be perched upon a cactus .

When the Aztecs finally reached the Valley of Mexico in 1280 A.D, they found the area in chaos.   Several cultures scrambled for supremacy. To the valley's inhabitants, the Aztecs must have appeared very primitive. Nowhere in their travels had the migrants seen such wealth and sophistication.   Fighting skill was the only commodity upon which they could trade, but that was formidable.    Anxious to deny their own nomadic, barbaric past, the Aztecs began the difficult transition from a hunting- gathering existence to a sedentary, agricultural life — all the while functioning as mercenaries, fierce fighters who quickly gained a reputation for cruelty.

Before long Huitzilopochtli, the Aztec's relatively benign hummingbird deity, had evolved into a war god who regularly demanded  the sacrifice of victims — rival  warriors captured in battle. Though blood sacrifice and cannibalism were also practiced by the neighbors, these peoples objected to the marked tendency of the Aztecs to elevate the practice from an occasional ritual to a regular feast.

A well fed Huitzilopochtli kept his word to his chosen people.  One day the divine prophesy — an eagle devouring a serpent on an island in the midst of a lake — unfolded itself before a devout Aztec. The lake, Texococo, was situated in the center of the Valley of Mexico and it was there that the Aztecs built their great city-state Tenochtitlan, the precursor of Mexico City.  The momentous event elevated Huitzilopochtli  to Lord of Creation, the all-powerful god of the sun.  Aztecs now considered it their divine duty to introduce him to the world.

With an inestimable geographic advantage over every other city in the New World, Tenochtitlan quickly flourished. The Aztecs devised a spectacular transportation system harnessing the full potential of the surrounding lake waters. Almost every street in the capital paralleled a canal, and every family owned at least one canoe. Through the use of barges and boats, the Aztecs compensated for the total absence of beasts of burden. Goods moved more efficiently within Tenochtitlan than in European cities with their narrow streets and animal-drawn carts. In less than 100 years, the island city was the glittering hub of an empire that provided the Aztecs with economic and military security beyond all other tribes.

It was from this dazzling stronghold that Moctezuma ruled most of Mexico by the early 1500s. Greatly feared as well as revered, the people considered him divinely inspired. Distinguishing himself militarily as a youth, Moctezuma rose to the rank of general. At the time of his candidacy for the throne, he served the terrible humming bird god, Huitzilopochtli, as high priest.

The combination of military prowess and religious piety raised him above all rivals in the eyes of the Supreme Council. Moctezuma frequently secluded himself in a dark chamber of Huitilopochtli's pyramid so that he might better commune with the deity. As Huitilopochtli's servant, he shared the god's nemesis: Quetzalcoatl. It was a heavy burden even for a ruler who was himself revered as a god.

Fabled Quetzalcoatl reaches across the centuries, a figure of romance, betrayal, illusion and eternal mystery.

Little is known, much conjectured of this Arthur-like figure, half man, half myth. The few existing facts merely add to the puzzle. According to legend, Quetzalcoatl descended from heaven and proceeded to introduce the concepts of love, penitence and exemption from the traditional rituals of blood sacrifice. The human embodiment of divine love and wisdom as well as an able administrator, he united and ruled the people under one large confederation.

As with the Arthurian Round Table, it was all too good to last. The high priests and warriors didn't take kindly to Quetzalcoatl's substitution of incense, flowers and maize for human sacrifices. There had to be a way of removing him. . . . .and, of course, eventually they found it.

Quetzalcoatl was known to be vigorous, sexually potent, and endowed with an enormous penis; yet he vowed to remain celibate, sublimating his considerable energies in good works. Finally the day came — naturally it would have to be a ceremonial day with an attendant cast of thousands — when the wily priests handed Quetzalcoatl a drink laced with magic mushrooms. While under the influence of this powerful aphrodisiac, he was tempted by a beautiful woman and made love to her.

Upon awakening, Quetzalcoatl was consumed with guilt. In his own eyes, he'd condemned himself by breaking his self-imposed vows. Leaving everything behind — palaces, kingdom clothes — Quetzalcoatl arrived naked on the shores of the Caribbean. Promising to return one day, he embarked on a raft of snake skins and sailed eastward until a tremendous heat ignited the boat and, in a burst of flames, his heart arose, flying upward to finally merge with the sun. Quetzalcoatl's spring time promise is familiar to mythmakers everywhere. He is the martyr who must inevitably suffer, then be driven away or killed before he can return to the kingdom of heaven — ultimately to be born again. This time the self sacrificing god returned as the Morning Star, a symbol of hope and regeneration.

Fact or fantasy? The glyphs in the Vienna Codex record this spectacular astral happening as a solar eclipse, an event verified by the Observatory at Greenwich as having occurred on July 16, AD 750.

The story of Quetzalcoatl's disappearance was told and retold, a legend that refused to die. Everyone knew that just as the god had been overthrown in the past, so he would return to overthrow his adversaries and usher in a new era of peace and justice. The hope remained for hundreds of years until the early 16th century when history and mythology united to produce a great tragedy.

Mighty Moctezuma had been waiting for the shoe to drop for several years. From his palace rooftop, the ruler searched the skies for portents each day at dawn, sunset and midnight. In 1508 he'd watched with apprehension as a tiny black speck crossed the face of the sun. The last time the planet Venus had transited the sun had been 300 years before. A devastating flood had followed. Now he felt certain that some similar disaster was pending.

When the first man, a lowly peasant, came to him with a strange tale about "a small mountain floating in the midst of the water, moving here and there without touching the shore," Moctezuma closed his ears to the account. The troublemaker was thrown into prison for spreading such ridiculous lies. But then messengers arrived from the king of Tulum, deep in the Maya country to the southeast, confirming the report. Two great mountains or towers were, indeed, floating in the sea. Worse yet, they contained tall, light skinned beings with beards and hair that came only to their ears. Moctezuma lowered his head. For a time he said nothing as thoughts of the Quetzalcoatl legend returned to plague him. Was the god not tall, fair, bearded?

Quetzalcoatl's return had long been foretold. He'd promised to appear before them again some Ce Acatl year on the day of his birth, Chiconaui Ehecatl. This combination, which came up every 52 years, was scheduled to occur in the spring of 1519 — only a few months away.

In Cuba, the Spaniard Hernan Cortes had never heard of Ce Acatl but hoped the year 1519 would bring something more rewarding than a job running a small plantation where the Carib Indians had to be watched every minute. The damn fools would rather commit suicide than work for a Spaniard. A short, ordinary looking man who walked with a permanent limp since falling from his mistress's balcony, Cortes had big ideas; but even he couldn't have imagined himself as a god incarnate. Yet destiny had drafted him for that role.

The 34-year-old adventurer was intrigued by tales of land to the west. Even if there was no gold, as had been rumored, there was at least a native population to enslave. He hoped they'd prove a more tractable bunch than the Caribs. The Governor of Cuba mounted an expedition but was delayed. Last minute finagling enabled Cortes to take his place. In the governor's eyes it was to be merely a reconnaissance mission; Cortes envisioned it quite differently.

Meanwhile, in Moctezuma's palace a great sadness had overtaken the court. The ruler's beloved aunt, Princess Butterfly, fell ill and died. Then three days later the noblewoman astonished everyone by sitting straight up on her bier. The joy that Moctezuma felt at her miraculous recovery was quickly shattered. In what appears to have been an out-of-body experience, Princess Butterfly had seen men wearing black stones and riding hornless deer. She went on to describe the capital city in flames, her nephew's murder and the subsequent reign of the most dreadful of the white-faced creatures.

Only a short while later Moctezuma received word that men of her description had disembarked from a "winged tower that floated across the sea." The date was April 21, 1519. The Spaniards called it Good Friday, but Moctezuma knew that it was Chiconaui Ehecatl, the birthday of Quetzalcoatl in the year called Ce Acatl.

A strange sense of fate overshadows much of Mexican history. Five centuries ago, two worlds, two dreams met. On one side was Moctezuma and the mighty Aztec empire, on the other

Cortes and 550 Spaniards. Could the conquest have occurred if the conquerors' dream had not fit synchronistically into that ancient dream of the Aztecs? Moctezuma considered his doom sealed. Who could fight a god? This sense of grim inevitability does much to explain the takeover of a mighty nation by so few men. By the time Moctezuma realized that they were merely men it was too late.

For Cortes, too, it was a date with destiny. As a sixteen-year-old law school drop out, he'd been slated for an expedition to the New World when a woman diverted his attentions. While attempting to climb into her bedroom window, Cortes slipped and fell breaking his leg. The ship sailed without him in 1502. Seven years later he was again scheduled to sail when a painful flare up of a venereal disease forced him to withdraw. It was not until 1511 that Cortes participated in the conquest and settlement of Cuba where he would languish unhappily for seven years.

When Moctezuma gifted Cortes with gold, he sealed his own destiny. The conquistador, Bernal Diaz del Castillo, an honest, plainspoken man, spoke for all of them: "We came here to serve God and the king, and also to get rich."

The carnage that followed was unbelievable, but even more devastating was the destruction of the Aztecs' sacred images. Moctezuma implored: "Throughout all time we have worshipped our own gods, and thought they were good, as no doubt yours are, so do not trouble to speak to us any more about them." It was useless. Moctezuma was murdered, his heir tortured to death. Thousands were burned alive, martyrs to the alien concept of Christianity, the rest were enslaved. To the Aztecs this  was truly the end, the conclusion of the cosmos.

The Indians faced yet another scourge: epidemics. Ailments to which the Spaniards were nearly immune proved fatal to the natives who, in the words of one conquistador "died in heaps like bedbugs." The canals of Mexico City and its surrounding lake filled with corpses. The fields around the capital were littered with Aztecs who dropped at they worked.

Epidemic disease helps to explain the unique success of the Europeans in gaining Christian converts there.  Asians and Africans who fell under European domination had already developed as much immunity to epidemic diseases as their colonial rulers and couldn't be fooled into believing that divine retribution in the form of disease awaited them if they refused baptism.

The fact that baptized Indians died as readily as those who'd not been "saved" eventually proved as puzzling to priests as to the dying Aztecs — and almost as disastrous.  Why were converts still stricken in such spectacular numbers?  Where would the necessary slave force come from?  At last the priests arrived at a secular solution:  it was the Indians' heathen habit of bathing daily.  By discouraging baths—already an anathema to Spaniards who thought once a year a bit excessive—the conquistadors and priests succeeded only in bringing Indian hygiene down to their own level.  The effect of their wisdom was invariably more epidemics.

Scourged by disease, weakened by malnutrition and warfare, the Indian population shrunk by more than two thirds. Possibly 70,000 thousand remained.  Reduced to docile survivors, the once proud Aztecs were set to work by Cortes leveling their former temples and palaces to make way for the reconstruction of their city, by now virtually destroyed by the conquistadors.

While taking advantage of what remained of the Aztecs' architectural genius — a grid pattern of streets and canals, flat roofed villas and plazas, blanketed with flowers and greenery — the citadel of Cortes evolved into a  city free of the narrow winding streets and claustrophobic walls that characterized most of medieval Europe.  By 1524, Tenochtitlan was known as Mexico City.  Mexic meaning the place of the Mexicas — one of several names by which the Aztecs were called.  Probably the Spaniards called their colonial capital "Mexico City" because they had so much trouble pronouncing Tenochtitlan

In 1547 Cortes died and his remains were buried in the chapel of the Hospital de Jesus in Mexico City.  They would be removed and hidden in  1823 by a conservative Mexican who feared their desecration by nationalists in the wake of the Independence wars against Spain.  The bones were discovered 122 years later in 1945 and returned to the chapel.  A small — very small — bust of Cortes was placed there in 1981.  Another statue decorates a Cuernavaca hotel — they are the only public monuments to Cortes in all of Mexico.  No streets bear his name and no date has been set aside to commemorate him.

The conquerors were awarded parcels of land for their labors to the crown and thus began the era of large land holdings. Silver discovered beneath the arid ground of Guanajuato and Taxco proved a bonanza for the Spaniards who thrived on the riches mined by natives. By 1550, Mexico had emerged as the New World's greatest source of precious metal. Silver poured into Mexico City where it was minted into coins or bars for shipment to Spain.

Despite the deaths of many thousands of Indians, the city emerged as a thriving urban center for white inhabitants starting with the second half of the 16th century and continuing for 300 years. During this time Spain sent 61 viceroys to govern New Spain, as Mexico was then called. Spanish speech, dress and customs replaced indigenous cultures but always with adaptations to the climate and the unique way of life in this vast new country. Many beautiful buildings were constructed which are still in use.

Colonial times were, for the most part, tranquil. The rich got richer and were so sumptuous in their dress, mansions, carriages and social extravaganzas that all who visited were impressed by their standard of living. Meanwhile the peasant, held firmly in place, did most of the work.

The population of mestizos gradually evolved into a new race. The status quo had its critics and among the most vocal were the young army officers, both criollo and mestizo. Still, at the turn of the 19th century, few observers could have imagined that "New Spain" was about to give way to "Mexico." The prosperity of the Mexico City based elite was at its apogee. Though the vast number of the colony's six million inhabitants were poverty stricken, that had always been the case. And though Spain was militarily weak in Mexico, allegiance to the Crown depended less on coercion than on the ingrained obedience of colonial subjects and the racial divisions between whites, Indians and castes which hampered a concerted opposition to the mother country.

Despite these factors, in 1821—exactly three hundred years after Cortes conquered the Aztecs—Mexico gained independence, its revolt part of the uprisings that swept Spain's New World colonies from California to the southern tip of South America from 1808 to 1825. Of all the revolts, the Mexican struggle was the most violent because independence was achieved in two phases. Initially, criollos and Spaniards based in Mexico City and other urban centers banded together to suppress a widespread rebellion by Indians and mestizos in the countryside. Only after this threat had been quelled was Spanish rule thrown off.

Leona Vicario, a young criolla socialite, was an early exception. An orphan, the nineteen-year-old Leona lived with her wealthy uncle, Augustin Pomposo, a successful Mexico City attorney. Like most upper class women Leona began her day by being dressed and made up by her several servants. A stroll, accompanied by her duenas, through Alameda Park followed, then some leisurely shopping under the arcade of the Plaza Mayor, luncheon at home, siesta until sundown, a gown to be selected, cosmetics to be applied before attendance at a theater or ball — again accompanied by chaperones, and home by midnight. Only Leona's education set her apart. The other young women of her set had attended the traditional schools set aside for girls of their class where they learned only rudimentary reading and writing. Leona had been privately tutored and was an avid reader, excelling in politics, philosophy and science.

Voluptuously attractive, Leona hadn't lacked for suitors and was engaged to Octaviano de Obregon, son of a million-aire miner and merchant who'd bought the viceroy's friendship and confidence. Unfortunately the liaison was ill-advised. When the viceroy fell from royal grace and was deposed, the elder Obregon barely escaped with his life. His son fled to the country, leaving Leona behind.

Leona was severely disillusioned by the affair, but her newly severed loyalties to Spain brought her into conflict with her uncle, a diehard royalist. Leona's sym-pathies with the insurgents fighting Spanish troops in the surrounding countryside found a kindred spirit in Andres Quintana Roo, a young lawyer in her uncle's office. The two fell in love, but when Quintana Roo asked Pomposo to break Leona's engage-ment to Octaviano de Obregon, her uncle refused. Quintana Roo left Mex-ico City and joined the rural insurgent movement in Oaxaca under Morelos.

Canny Leona persuaded her uncle that her ardor for both the revolution and Quintana Roo had cooled. In reality, she'd become an active rebel conspira-tor. It began with letters to the insur-gents describing political and military developments in Mexico City, but soon Leona was using her inheritance to pur-chase arms for the rural guerrillas and recruiting upper class criollo youths to their cause. One of them, her cousin, Pomposo's own son, was persuaded to run off and join the rebels.

A leading propagandist for the colonial cause, Pomposo never suspected. His home was a meeting place for vice regal officials and royalist officers who were charmed by the ardent monar-chist's pretty niece and spoke freely of their war efforts in her presence.

It wasn't until a rebel courier was caught with a pack of Leona's letters that her true sympathies were finally revealed. Warned in time, she fled to a small village west of the capital where eventually Pomposo tracked her down. Persuaded by his assurances that she wouldn't be prosecuted, Leona agreed to return with him to Mexico City. Instead, Pomposo had her incarcerated in Belen, a notorious prison established by the church in the late 1600s to exor-cise women believed possessed by demons. To Pomposo, certain that his niece was a satanic agent, it was a fit-ting place.

Repeatedly interrogated by royal jus-tices, Leona refused to reveal the iden-tities of the insurgent leaders. A few days before she was to be tried — and almost certainly executed — she was rescued by rebels who broke into Belen. After hiding in a Mexico city slum for several weeks, Leona dis-guised herself as a muleteer and fled to Quintana Roo in Oaxaca. The couple was married and survived clandestinely for several years before Independence brought them amnesty.

Unfortunately politics in Mexico City during the post-Independence era was marked by instability and corruption. Most of the criollo elite avoided politics. entirely. The poor remained disenfranchised while the presidency slipped from the hands of one general to another — changing hands 33 times in the period from 1833 to 1855. In an era distinguished by personal opportunism, one towering figure emerged: Antonio Lopez de Santa Anna.

Santa Anna, born in 1794 to a family that had emigrated from Spain to Veracruz, was well aware of the contempt that Spaniards felt for criollos — particularly those born in a tropical environment like Veracruz which, according to the racial theories of the day, hastened the degeneration of white European stock. Surprisingly, he eschewed the independence movement and chose instead to advance his social status by joining the Spanish army as a cavalry officer. Tall, thin, with piecing black eyes and a charismatic manner, Santa Anna early displayed a flair for leadership.

It was only in the waning days of the revolution with the outcome fairly assured, that he abandoned the cause of colonial rule and  switched sides. Santa Anna fought well and was elected president in 1833. His first debacle occurred over the issue of Texas. Mexico, who had once encouraged North Americans to move into Texas hoping to develop the vast, little inhabited province, was seriously threatened. By 1835, two-thirds of the inhabitants of the northern state of Coahuila (now Texas) were settlers from the United States who opposed Mexican rule and wanted a republic of their own.

Santa Anna quickly mounted an army and rode north. All 183 of the North Americans defending the fort at Alamo, were killed; and, after an engagement at Goliad, another 350 prisoners were massacred on his orders. Santa Anna's army won a succession of battles and the general was preparing for a triumphal return to Mexico City when he carelessly neglected to post guards around his camp, even though a large force headed by Sam Houston was reported to be in the vicinity. Houston's surprise attack (his men riding to battle with the cry, "Remember the Alamo") routed the Mexican troops.

Despite an effort at disguise, Santa Anna was captured. In order to save himself, he signed an agreement granting independence to the Republic of Texas, thereby reducing Mexico to its present size — almost half of its original territory. Returning to Mexico City in 1837 thoroughly discredited, Santa Anna was exiled to Cuba.

It took war with the United States to resurrect him. The Mexican government, having repudiated the agreement granting Texas independence, viewed the United States announcement of the admission of Texas into the Union as annexation which could not be tolerated. Santa Anna now played a double game. From his refuge in Cuba, he offered the United States the territories of California, Texas, New Mexico and

Arizona plus 30 million dollars in exchange for aid in recovering the presidency; while, at the same time, tendering his services to Mexico in exchange for his release from exile. Somehow he succeeded in convincing both governments.

An American blockade was lifted to allow his ship to reach Veracruz; but after arriving in Mexico City, Santa Anna took command of the army to face an American invasion force led by General Zachary Taylor. He fought Taylor's troops to a standstill, then retreated to prepare his defense against another onslaught led by General Winfield Scot.

Although Mexican troops in the capital heavily outnumbered their invader, Santa Anna in a supreme act of egotism withdrew his forces from battle following a personal dispute with another general. This fit of pique won the war for Scott who, encountering a much reduced force, was able to occupy Mexico City. The true heros were young boys — cadets from a military academy who fought to the death defending Chapultepec Castle, the last youth leaping to his death wrapped in the Mexican flag rather than surrender.

Unable to find refuge with his own people, Santa Anna, who'd once dubbed himself, "His Most Supreme Highness," surrendered to United States troops; and with their aid, fled to Venezuela. Meanwhile in a treaty ending the war, Mexico was forced to cede the northern half of its territory to the United States in exchange for 15 million dollars.

It was this debacle and the subsequent

*Maximilian, Emperor of Mexico.*

sense of disillusionment that brought about the confrontation of two vastly different leaders: Benito Juarez, Mexico's only pure Indian president, and the Archduke Maximilian, one of the bluest bloods in Europe.

Born in Oaxaca in 1806, Juarez was a Zapotec, directly descended from the people who had built the great city of Monte Alban a thousand years before. His integrity and concern for the poor are legendary. In 1858 Juarez, Mexico's first *indigena* president, responded to the challenge of a bankrupt government by halting debt payments to foreign countries for a period of two years. He seems to have had little choice. The country's financial condition was so critical that no one would take the job of secretary of the treasury.

France, having jumped at this excuse to mount an invasion with the intent of annexing Mexico, was soundly trounced on May 5, 1862 — an event celebrated yearly as Cinco de Mayo Day.  The French bounced back, capturing Mexico City and routing Juarez.

Conditions following the the Revolution had caused the Mexican clergy and other conservatives to openly advocate monarchy as the solution to the country's ills.  Now they welcomed the invading French army, setting the stage for a puppet to be selected by Napoleon III.

Ferdinand Maximilian, Archduke of Austria, had been born July 6, 1832, the younger brother of Franz Josef who would eventually rule the Austro- Hungarian Empire, the Hapsburgs vast family estate encompassing not only Austria, Hungary and part of Poland — from the Alps to the mountains of Transylvania — but the areas that would later be known as Yugoslavia and Czechoslovakia.

His mother was the Archduchess Sophie, his probable father the only legitimate son of Napoleon.  It appears to have happened this way:  Despite her protests that he was an "imbecile," Sophie had been forced to marry the Archduke Karl.  After a parting shot to her royal parents:  "I have resolved to be happy, and I am going to be," Sophie settled in with Karl and dutifully produced Franz Josef.

What followed was a close alliance with Vienna's most glamorous resident — or prisoner — a young man known as Napoleon II, to the French, and the Duke of Reichstadt, to the Austrians.

The son of Napoleon and his Austrian second wife, Marie Louise, the young duke was a political pawn kept in Austria to prevent any possibility that his presence in France might spark a Napoleonic restoration.  Though the duke's golden boy looks and winsome personality endeared him to everyone, he preferred the company of Sophie who was six years his senior.  The couple was inseparable; and, when the duke contracted tuberculosis, Sophie nursed him constantly.  He died sixteen days after Maximilian's birth.

Franz Josef was the heir, Maximilian the favorite.  Tall, lively, golden haired with striking blue eyes, the young Archduke was a dashing horseman who won every race and took every jump.  The people adored him, the uneasy Franz Josef was more than eager to get him out of the country.

Maxmilian's bride was the Princess Charlotte, born June 7, 1840,  Charlotte's mother was Queen Louise, daughter of King Louis Philippe and Queen Marie Amelie, who still occupied the French throne when she was born.  Her father, King of Leopold of Belgium, had written of his slender, petite daughter with her striking dark eyes and delicate features,  "I think she will be the most beautiful princess in Europe — if only it will bring her happiness."

With little else to occupy them, Maximilian and Charlotte devoted themselves to building their dream home — a castle, of course.  Located on a rocky promontory extending into the Adriatic, Miramar (view of the sea), was a dazzling palace of white limestone and Carrara marble.

Maximilian and Charlotte were not destined to languish long. Several elements had come together in a fateful pattern. The United States was divided by civil war, an event that evoked a rustle of opportunism in European capitals where the loss of American territories had been neither forgotten nor forgiven. When Mexican conservatives approached France they'd come to the right place. Napoleon III wanted more than his money back, he longed to see his country restored to the vigor it had shown under the reign of his great uncle. That illustrious ancestor had nearly conquered Europe, but he, himself, would extend the Second Empire to the Americas!

Napoleon plotted. . . .the coup required his backing of a handpicked sovereign. The choice of an unemployed Hapsburg princeling for Emperor of Mexico would make Austria beholden to him and a Franco-Austrian alliance would render him the strongest power in Europe. The choice of the Austrian Archduke was to his mind brilliant. What no one took into account was that Maximilian was naive. Am I truly the choice of the Mexican people? he wanted to know. Charlotte even asked for an independent survey of Mexicans. Napoleon was sanguine, such doubts were foolish, he assured them. Maximilian and Charlotte would go down in history as the saviors of Mexico.

The newly created emperor and his high spirited empress arrived in Veracruz on May 28, 1865. At thirty-two, Maximilian was tall, thin, dashing, his flowing, muttonchop whiskers hiding a weak chin, the only defect in an otherwise handsome face. Perhaps his greatest asset was his Viennese charm. Maximilian had made the effort to learn Spanish before moving to Mexico and would make use of it not only to converse with the elite but also to talk with impoverished supplicants whom he received daily at the National Palace.

Charlotte was Charlotte no longer. She had changed her name to Carlota, affected a mantilla, and decreed that the ladies of her court would all be Mexican. Interested in the arts and sciences, the young rulers established a national theater and used their own funds to offer substantial prizes for the best original plays. They founded the Academy of Science and Literature with its cornerstone, a 5000-volume library relating to Mexican art and culture.

Maximilian and Carlota threw themselves wholeheartedly into the task of bringing Mexico into the 19th century, as they perceived it, but the cultural and social chasm between the Europeans and their Mexican subjects yawned wider every day. Maximilian's meticulously annotated manual of court etiquette went unread. When the monarchs attended a gala performance in their honor, they arrived scrupulously on time, but found the theater empty. The Mexican elite drifted in an an hour or so late.

But there were much graver differences. Maximilian, who had arrived in Mexico firmly resolved to restore tranquility to his new country, was utterly unequal to the task. He hadn't the slightest conception of the troubles facing him or the huge nation that he had so optimistically adopted. Maximilian quickly alienated his only Mexican supporters. Conservatives who'd sought the removal of Juarez and support for their own programs, and the clergy who wanted their lands returned, were both horrified by Maximilian's announcement that he not only had no intention of returning the land but actually wanted more in order to finance his reform programs.

Maximilian was busy redecorating the Chapultepec Fortress which he'd converted into a palace when an event occurred that sealed his fate. The outcome of the Battle of Gettysburg was a mortal blow to Napoleon, who'd planned to control not only Mexico, but Central America. Realizing now that he'd backed the wrong side, the French monarch quickly withdrew his troops supporting the Confederacy. As the Civil War which had divided the country drew to a close, the United States turned its attention to Mexico. Aid was sent to Juarez and General Sherman was ordered to assemble an army along the US-Mexican border.

General Bazaine, Napoleon's true authority in Mexico, panicked at the new guerrilla activity sparked by this support and demanded that Maximilian sign a proclamation that all Juarez militants be shot upon capture. The emperor was appalled by the measure, considering it far too harsh. When eventually pressed into compliance, Maximilian was unknowingly signing his own death warrant.

By the end of 1865 Bazaine informed Maximilian that Napoleon now planned to begin the withdrawal of his troops from Mexico—a violation of an agreement signed the previous year pledging that France would never abandon the new Mexican Empire. Surely Maximilian realized by then that he could never retain his empire without French support.

By spring 1866, the pressure on Maximilian to abandon Mexico was coming from all quarters: Washington, France, his own family in Austria and of course Juarez. Only Carlota counseled otherwise. The memory of the forced abdication her grandfather, Louis Philippe, was a humiliation that had followed her from childhood. Now the woman who had lived with the dread of abdication persuaded her husband that such a course would bring dishonor to the Hapsburg name. "Abdication is only excusable in old men and idiots," she wrote her husband in a memorandum summarizing her arguments. It is not permissible in a young man of thirty-four, full of life and hope for the future, for sovereignty is the most precious of all possessions." She would go herself to Paris to plead their case.

No welcoming committee from Napoleon's court greeted Carlota's arrival at the French port of St. Nazaire, nor was there any French official to receive her at the Paris train station. Instead, Napoleon sent a message to Carlota's hotel pleading illness and suggesting that she go on to Belgium where her father, King Leopold, had just died. Indignantly, she barged in on him unannounced.

Initially, Carlota argued that abandoning the Mexican Empire would be a diplomatic disaster for France and that

Mexico's mineral wealth would eventually compensate for the costs of maintaining an army there. But when logic failed the distraught empress lost her temper and upbraided Napoleon for his profidity. Unmoved, he sent her away empty handed.

Carlota traveled next to the Vatican in hopes of persuading the Pope to use his influence on Napoleon. It was here that her mind was said to have snapped. Attempting to calm her, the Pope offered Carlota a cup of chocolate but she declined, saying it was poisoned. After an hour the pontiff managed to extricate himself from the painful interview, but the distraught Carlota, claiming that she was surrounded by potential assassins, refus-ed to leave. As a result Carlota was the first woman to ever spend the night in the papal palace. Broken at last, she returned to  her family in Belgium. Their message to Maximilian was that Carlota could never return to Mexico.

In February 1867, the French troops departed Mexico, a maneuver that required a safe conduct pass to Veracruz negotiated by Porfirio Diaz, Juarez's most brilliant general in the war for freedom. Diaz's men now controlled the southern and eastern regions of the country. Once again Maximilian was urged to abdicate and return to Europe. He refused, deciding instead to take personal command of his army.

Although he had no battlefield experience, Maximilian announced his intention to lead his men in the final clash against the Juariztas in Queretaro, some hundred miles north of Mexico City. Desertions had reduced his band to a bare sixteen hundred who faced an enemy army five times larger. The Juariztas laid siege to the city and three months later forced a surrender.

Juarez ordered Maximilian tried by court martial as a criminal, using the same standards that the emperor had decreed for Juaritzas who were captured in battle. The court found him guilty of violating Mexico's sovereignty and sentenced him to be shot. Requests for clemency poured into Mexico from the heads of European governments as well as from the United States, but Juarez was adamant. The naivete so typical of Maximilian is evident in a famous photograph taken three days before the execution. It shows Maximilian comforting the priest who had come to comfort him. On June 19, 1867 the former emperor was executed by firing squad. Maximilian's remains were shipped to Vienna for an imperial funeral, and burial in the family vault.

Carlota, remained in seclusion at Miramar, where she was said to have given birth to a son from her liaison with Colonel Van der Smissen, her favorite at the Mexican City court. Decades later, persistent rumors suggested that the child was General Jacques Weygand, a French officer who distinguished himself in both world wars. Weygand's family background was a mystery but he bore a striking physical resemblance to Van der Smissen.

Carlota survived Maximilian by sixty years, dying in 1927 at the age of eighty-six. Utterly deranged, she spent most of those decades in a moated castle belonging to her royal family in Belgium. One day at the beginning of every spring, she insisted on re-enacting her departure with Maximilian to their New World empire. With her attendants patiently looking on, Carlota would board a small rowboat anchored in the moat and announce, "Today we leave for Mexico."

In 1867 Juarez, restored to the presidency, returned to Mexico City. He separated church and state, established religious toleration, and reformed the land system. He died in 1872.

Porfirio Diaz, who succeeded him, looms so large in Mexican history that the era between 1875 and 1911, in which he served eight times as president, is known as the Porfiriato. A fierce commander — Juarez's most effective general against the conservatives — Diaz's forced marches criss-crossing mountains and jungles are legendary, his personal courage unquestioned. It was he who took Mexico City from Maximilian and welcomed Juarez back into power. It was there the two parted company.

Diaz tried twice to defeat his former commander in elections, then lost again in another attempt after Juarez's death. Weary of the democratic process, he overthrew the incumbent and grasped power.

A mestizo, born to unsuccessful, small innkeeper parents, Diaz was fatherless in infancy and studied for the priesthood at his mother's behest. Later he switched to law, the same path followed by his early hero Benito Juarez. There the similarity ends. A popular general, who initially appeared to embody the former's high principles, the people hoped that Diaz would institute true democracy. Instead, his amended constitution enabled him to govern as dictator for 34 years.

Rough, vulgar, provincial, far more comfortable in an army tent than a palace, Diaz was initially ill at ease in Mexico City. Then a year after the death of his peasant wife, he married Carmen Romero Rubio, the teenage daughter of an upper class crony. Under Carmen's tutelage, the 51-year-old warrior blossomed into a poised cosmopolitan. Before long his dining etiquette was impeccable. Diaz also learned to reserve his raunchier jokes for the military colleagues who'd ridden with him against Santa Anna and Maximilian.

Strategic alliances with loyal generals and wealthy, elitist Mexicans were quickly forged. In his eagerness to restore solvency to the impoverished country, Diaz sacrificed Mexico's natural resources to foreign developers. In the next third of a century capital poured in. New ports were built, older ones modernized, railroads criss-crossed the nation. Electricity powered factories and illuminated cities.

"Order and Progress" was Diaz's dictum and once his iron fist had grasped the country its economic advances were indeed remarkable. Those who matured during his thirty-five year dictatorship — longer than any leader since the Aztec empire — were the first since the colonial era to live free of uprisings, war, or bloodshed in the streets. Diaz aimed at nothing less than the modernization of his country; Mexico City was its showplace. His centerpiece was the rococco Bellas Artes, the Palace of Fine Arts where world acclaimed performers flocked. For the urban elite, this was a self-assured, gilded era — the Mexican equivalent of Paris's Belle Epoque. Rich aristocrats moved into grand mansions, opened offices in multi-storied buildings constructed with iron and reinforced concrete techniques imported from the United States and Europe.

For the rich, the Porfiriato was the best of times — still remembered with nostalgia. These lucky few — 500,000 out of an entire nation — displayed an uncanny ability to screen out whatever was poor, shabby or backward from their field of vision and to convince themselves that the Porfirian brand of progress would eventually wash away poverty. In reality, there were more poor than ever. In a population that had grown from 8.7 million in 1874 to 15 million in 1910, comparatively few shared the bounty reaped by a remarkable 350 percent rise in the gross national product.

More than 80 percent of the Mexican population remained tied to an agrarian existence. A concentration of land ownership greater than at any time in the country's history — one man owning an incredible 7 million acres in Northern Mexico — had transformed the rural populace into peons whose purchasing power at the end of the Porfiriato had sunk to the levels of 1800. For peasants who dared rebel against the confiscation of their land and water by great estate owners, Porfirian order meant state repression. For urban laborers, the industrial revolution translated into 14 to 16 hour shifts, six or seven days a week and wages that couldn't begin to satisfy their food, housing and clothing needs.

As old age crept over him, Diaz complacently meditated over his triumphs. In 1907, sanguine about his nation's political prospects, he carelessly mentioned possible retirement to an American journalist. An opposing political party instantly sprang up led by Francisco Indalecio Madero.

A teetotaler, a vegetarian and a spiritualist, the diminutive, mild mannered Madero was an unlikely revolutionary. Diaz refused to take him seriously, but a great many other people did.

In 1910, the eighty-year-old Diaz engineered his reelection simply by not counting the votes. Representatives from around the world attended his massive victory parade and grand ball at the National Palace. To the world, Mexico appeared at the pinnacle of peace and prosperity. Few could have imagined the strange group of dissidents who would rally around the cause of Madero or the ten year holocaust that was to follow.

The gentle, idealistic Madero was joined by a strange pair of bedfellows. The least likely ally was Doroteo Arango, better known as Pancho Villa, a hell raising bandit from Chihuahua, who shaped an unruly band of train robbers and cattle rustlers into an army.

The other, Emiliano Zapata, a brooding Indian freedom fighter, battling for land reform and an end to the prejudices out of which Mexicans had been born.

On May 12, 1911, Zapata seized control of Cuautla. Eight days later Villa captured Ciudad Juarez. As more state capitals fell into guerrilla hands, Diaz was forced to resign and was permitted to leave Mexico for France where he continued to plan an invasion until his death four years later.

Regarded as a savior by the people, Madero proceeded to institute an honest system for election and won easily. His first action as president was to grant freedom of the press and to encourage workers to organize unions. But before he could rectify another essential problem — land reform — Zapata· was on the march again. Unfortunately Madero had a far more formidable enemy in the United States. Fearful that the new president would reverse Diaz's open door policy on foreign ownership, Ambassador Henry Lane Wilson backed a coup headed by Victoriano Huerta. Madero was seized and the Mexican congress forced at gunpoint to accept his resignation. Wilson, when asked by Huerta what to do with the deposed president, replied: "Do what's best for the country." Madero died mysteriously, "Shot by a fanatic" — according to Huerta.

Few supported Huerta, who was drunk more often than sober. Chaos and anarchy were the dominant factors of the following decade. Factions united for limited objectives and then dissolved into internecine conflict that prolonged the bloodletting. Six million would die before it was over. At last Alvaro Obregon and Venustiano Carranza rose to prominence by besting Villa and Zapata.

Though Villa's "army" — for the most part bandits and army deserters — adored him equally for his macho image and the loot he made available to them, he was recognized by others as a brawler and a rapist, capable of gunning down a man he'd warmly embraced only moments before. Carranza and Obregon bought him off with a twenty-six thousand-acre hacienda in Chihuahua. There the former revolutionary guerrilla lived in feudal luxury for three years before he was ambushed while driving home from a rendezvous with one of his mistresses.

Zapata had been lured to his death. As he approached the counsel table to negotiate surrender terms, the hero heard a bugle call three times in his honor. As the sound faded, a soldier fired a salvo into his body at point blank.

The next chapter of the decade-long holocaust was a duel between the winners, Carranza and Obregon. The former's term as president was to end in 1920; Obregon fully expected to succeed him. When Carranza reneged, open warfare erupted between the two. On May 21, 1920, Carranza was shot by one of his rival's officers, clearing the way for Obregon's presidency. Following his term, Obregon supported Calles as his successor with the idea that he would later return to power.

Calles' first move was to order foreign owners of oil fields to release their titles in return for fifty-year leases. Calles honored his promise to restore the presidency to Obregon who was ree-lected in 1928, but three weeks later he was assassinated while dining at a restaurant.

The largest metropolis in the world, Mexico City is also one of the most exciting to visit. Like Paris, Madrid or Vienna, the city is laced together by broad avenues and breathtaking monuments; and, like New York, it's a city that never sleeps. The fashionable dining hour is 9 p.m. or later and dance clubs don't begin to pulsate until after midnight.

*Zapata with members of his staff.*

## HOTELS

Since its inauguration in 1968, Mexico City's **Hotel Camino Real** has been host to more than one hundred heads of state as well as royalty. The building conceived by Ricardo Legorreta, "1992 Architect of the Americas," blends modern concepts with designs inspired by prehispanic pyramids. His magnificent circular fountain at the entry way is an introduction to a veritable museum of modern art. In the vast lobby an Alexander Calder sculpture and a mural by Rugino Tamayo (with the all-embracing title *Man Encounters the Infinite)* set a mood of creative excitement. The hotel's splendid collection also includes paintings by David Alfaro Siqueiros, Jose Luis Covarrubias, Pedro Coronel and Leonard Nierman.

Rooms are large and bright. All have marble baths; many balconies overlook pools and inner patios. The hotel is also conveniently located next to Chapultepec Park. (Mariano Escobeda 700. Phone: 1-800-722-6466)

*The roof garden of Marquis Reforma has a commanding view of the city.* Photo by the author.

The **Hotel Marquis Reforma,** an art deco palace, which rises mirage-like from the one of busiest and most glamorous thoroughfares in the world. Historic links are stressed in the glistening marble lobby (which spotlights nightly jazz and classical quintets) and by Carlos Espino's impressive bronze sculpture — an Aztec couple performing a ritual fertility dance in homage to the rain god, Tlaloc.

The hotel's pink facade is comprised of marble and stone brought from many regions of Mexico. Among its attractions are the excellent **La Jolla Restaurant** and the **Caviar Bar.** The hotel spa also offers the perfect place to pamper yourselves with a steam bath, sauna and deluxe work out equipment. You can also survive the pressures of vacation life — shopping and museum hopping — with soothing massages. The blue glass and pink marble facade overlooks Chapultepec Park and is within easy walking distance to Zona Rosa restaurants and shops. (Paseo de la Reforma 465. Phone: 1-800-2-35-23-87)

Two very pleasant hotels located in the heart of the **Zona Rosa** are the **Westin Galeria Plaza** and the **Hotel Calinda Geneve.**   The former, very modern, with excellent food  (one of the best restaurants in town) is state of the art in every respect.   The location on the corner of Hamburgo and Varsovia couldn't be more convenient. (Phone: 1-800-226- 3000).

Still, for price and charm, you really can't beat the **Hotel Calinda Geneve.**  The place oozes atmosphere and possibly a few ghosts.  Pancho Villa once rode his horse into the lobby, a shrieking French receptionist —  he claimed she was "shy" — across his saddle. (Londres 130.  Phone: 211-0071).

Three thoroughly delightful hotels in the colorful **Zocalo** area are the **De Cortes, Gran** and **Majestic.**   My very special favorite is the **De Cortez.**  This charming lit-tle gem was originally built in 1780 as a hospice.  Its rooms are spacious and sur-round a lovely courtyard complete with fountain. Ask for a room on the second floor in the back.  The mariachi music every Saturday evening shouldn't be missed.
( Hildalgo 85.  Phone: 1-800-528-1234).

The **Gran,** once a turn of the century department store, is covered by a beautiful tif-fany glass art nouveau ceiling, probably the finest example of belle epoch art in the city.  Other pluses are caged elevators, rococco chandeliers and an excellent cen-tral location. (16 de Septiembre 82.  Phone: 1-800-654-2000).

The grand colonial style **Majestic** was built in 1937 and has been lovingly cared for.   Most rooms offer the city's best view of the teeming Zocalo and the rooftop restaurant is not to be missed.   Colorful handpainted tiles and exotic potted plants decorate the public rooms.   (Madero 73. Phone: 1-800-528-1234).

# RESTAURANTS

**Del Lago** is considered by many to be the most beautiful restaurant in the city. Elegant, architecturally spectacular, the French dining establishment overlooks the lake in the newer section of Chapultepec Park.  The ambience is romantic, the food delicious, prices high but worth it. (Chapultepec Park, Closed Sundays.)

**Fouquet's** is owned by the same bon vivants who operate the celebrated mecca on the Champs Elysees. This ultra chic Parisian restaurant, located in the **Camino Real Hotel** across from the park, is world class. (Closed Sundays, Phone:  545-6960)  The sautéed fillet of salmon with bell pepper sauce is outstanding.   After much begging and pleading. . . .well, here it is:

**SAUTÉED FILLET OF SALMON WITH BELL PEPPER SAUCE**

4 salmon fillets
1 red pepper, chopped into very small cubes
1 onion,  very finely chopped
half a cauliflower
4 small cherry tomatoes
5 mushrooms

Sauce:
I red pepper, peeled
I cup white wine
5 Tbsp. double cream
salt and pepper to taste

Cook cauliflower in salty water.  Cool it in ice.  Slice mushrooms and add to half the chopped onions and saute in olive oil.  Add the red pepper and saute further.  Cook the salmon in butter seasoned with salt and pepper.   Fill the tomatoes with half the mushroom/pepper/onion mixture.

Sauce:  Saute the remaining onions in butter, then add wine. Allow to boil for 15 minutes.  Add the cream.

Cover the salmon with sauce and sprinkle with half the the mushroom/onion/red pepper mixture.  Garnish the plate with the stuffed cherry tomatoes. Serves 4.

When shopping finally begins to pall, any number of fine restaurants may be found in the **Zona Rosa**.  Two favorites are the **Ile de France**  and **Anderson's** — as different as two restaurants can be.   Located in the *Galeria Plaza Hotel*  on the corner of Hamburgo and Varsovia, the former is world class.  Like Fouquet's or Del Lago, the Ile de France is justly proud of its subtle nouvelle Mexican approach.

**Anderson's** just around the corner on the Reforma, offers an amusing change of pace.  Here the atmosphere is warm and clubby.  Menu highlights include the "Moo, Oink and Peep," an excellent mixed grill; and a surprise selection, *pollo coca cola.*  The latter is a delicious chicken dish livened with cheese, a splash of coke and a flash of chipotle. It's very, very good. (Closed Sundays, Reforma 400.)

A trip to Mexico City wouldn't be complete without a lunch or dinner at **San Angel Inn** where gracious living from the past is recreated in an eighteenth century hacienda — a Mexico City landmark.   The menu lists many international dishes, but the specialties include tortilla soup and pampano baked in maguey leaves. (50 Diego Riviera. Open every day.)

**Fonda del Recuerdo** is a large and noisy family favorite with delicious fish and a fiestalike atmosphere — somebody's always having a party here — with musicians. Try a *toritos*, a tequila-based drink that has  a nitroglycerin punch.  The restaurant is specially busy on Sunday afternoons.  (39 Bahia de las Palmas.)

**Fonda del Refugio** is modest in appearance but localite gourmets consider it a shrine to true Mexican cooking.   House specialties are *carne asada* ( thin filet of boiled beef served with beans, enchiladas and guacamole) and *Mole verde de pepita* (chicken with green sauce made of pumpkin seeds and chilies.)  166 Liverpool, closed Sundays.

**Hosteria de Santo Domingo** is a popular restaurant that claims to be the oldest in Mexico.  Excellent Mexican food, colorful decor, romantic music.  The mole dishes are especially good here. (Closed Sundays.  Belisaro Dominguez 72.

**Cafe de Tacuba Centro** is the perfect place to begin or end the day.  It's a very old, traditional Mexican restaurant that serves good breakfasts, wonderful pastries and cafe con leche; but, conveniently located near the Palace of Fine Arts, it's also fun after the theater.  Tamales here are outstanding, but the restaurant is known for its enchiladas.  The *tacuba* is the house specialty.  (Open daily.  Reservations not necessary  Lively and reasonable. Tacuba 28.

**Maximilian's** Holiday Crown Plaza, an elegant French restaurant on the ground level facing the Paseo de Reforma specializing in nouvelle cuisine.  The beautifully prepared and served selections are all winners.  Romantic piano music in the evening.

**La Casa de la Malinche,** Tacuba 79 downtown near Plaza de Santa Dominga, a converted 19th century house on property once owned by Malinche, the mistress of Cortes.  Good food — an excellent buffet —  efficient service.  Reasonable prices. Open daily from l to 7 p.m.

Your last evening in Mexico City?  Enjoy an adventure.  **Cantina la Guadalupana** is raucous and wild.  Matador atmosphere and among the house specialities: *criadillas* (bulls' testicles).  Another lively favorite  with atmosphere, good food,  reasonable prices. (14 Higuera. Open every night.)

**A note:**  Mexicans eat dinner in the early afternoon.  Actually the big push starts about 2 p.m., so if you can get to the restaurant of your choice around 1:30 p.m.

you'll have no trouble finding a table.  Mexicans take advantage of these luncheons to meet business associates and clients which means it is often after 5 p.m. before the major restaurants begin to empty.  Many Mexico City restaurants remain open through the afternoon into the evening shifts so that you can dine as early as you like. *However*, most Mexicans work late and therefore eat late — they wouldn't be caught dead having their evening meal before 9 p.m.

## SHOPPING

The **Zona Rosa** is a mile or two up the Reforma from Chapultepec Park. Better known as the "pink zone," the Zona Rosa  got its name from the shop girls and secretaries who popularized the area by stopping at the chic bars and restaurants for a drink before going home.  Only a few years ago when "nice" unmarried women were supposed to be chaperoned, such behavior had a slightly shocking, demimondaine feeling about it.

Not bad enough for the red zone, but still considered naughty, the women and their habitat were highly appealing.  Today the Zona Rosa is a magnet for the five million North Americans who visit Mexico City every year.  Many of the smartest shops and restaurants in the city are located here along streets named for some of the other great cities of the world:  Niza, Copenhague, Londres,

*The Zona Rosa or "pink Zone" is a magnet for shoppers.*

Toledo, Tokio, Florencia.  A happy hunting ground occupying some fifteen blocks, the lively pink zone offers designer gowns, handbags, shoes at one-third off USA prices, plus rare antiques, exquisite hand-crafted jewelry and folk art collectibles.

If one is new to the concept of bargaining, an excellent place to begin is **Fonart** at Londres 136, a government agency charged with promoting handicrafts.  The quality here is outstanding and the the prices are fixed.  Having sampled the wares at Fonart, move on to the **Londres Market** at Londres and Florencia.  This is a typical neighborhood market — the kind that's existed since Aztec times — filled with fruit, flowers and vegetables, but that's only the beginning.  You can, if you choose, select a gift for literally everyone on your list in this colorful labyrinth of lavishly festooned stalls.  Whatever you're looking for can be found here, but be prepared to bargain.

Don't even think of bargaining at such quality jewelry stores as **Los Castillo** (Amberes 41) or **Joyas de Plata** ( Copenhague 31); prices are fixed.  Remember that gold and silver aren't any less expensive in Mexico, but the craftsmanship is

*Sidewalk cafes are part of the Zona Rosa's charm.* Photo by author.

Quality jewelry isn't "cheap," but it can be found at more affordable prices than most of us are used to paying at home.  The true dividend lies in the imaginative styling that goes into these one of a kind designs.

Another interesting place to visit is the **Mexican Opal Company** (Hamburgo 203).  Both set and unset gems are available as well as a wide selection gold and silver jewelry.

A delightful place to relax and people watch between forays, is in one of the many delightful sidewalk cafes that line Copenhague (off Hamburgo between Niza and Genova).

A special once a week treat is the famous **Bazaar Sabado** (Saturday Bazaar) at 11 Plaza San Jacinto in the southern district of San Angel.  Any tax driver is familiar with the bazaar, where some 100 well established artisans display their wares every Saturday from 10 a.m. to 4 p.m. Located in a stately colonial mansion facing on cobblestone streets and the lush gardens of Plaza San Jacinto, the bazaar features outstanding art work as well as jewelry, clothing, glass and stoneware, papier-mache items and pottery.

Lunch at the nearby (and previously described) San Angel Inn would provide the frosting for an afternoon viewing this must see collection of exquisite arts and crafts.

# TEOTIHUACAN

Just thirty miles north of Mexico City lies one of the greatest ghost towns of all times: **Teotihuacan.**

By A.D. 200, a complex, thriving culture with tentacles reaching throughout Mesoamerica, the once great metropolis was an abandoned ruin when the Aztecs arrived in 1215.   No one knew its name but the primitive migrants, awed by mysterious remnants of a highly sophisticated culture whose monumental temples and pyramids must surely have been built by giants, named the city Teotihuacan, "City of the Gods."   Today it is called the first great city of the Americas.

At its zenith Teotihuacan was the sixth largest city in the world, with a population of some 200,000 and covering eight square miles.   Perhaps it was *too* big and *too* grand.   Some l,500 years ago Teotihuacan was the  heart of an empire extending from Texas to Guatemala.  Today no one can really say for certain what caused its fall.

What we do know is that this was a planned urban complex with vast avenues and colossal pyramids close in size to those of Egypt and that it was *the* Mesoamerican trade center for more than eight centuries.  Then in A.D. 750 — quite suddenly — this magnificent culture came to an end.

A spiritual and intellectual center as well as a commercial one, Teotihuacan was both the Alexandria and the Rome of Mesoamerica.   Today the remains of such a super power are not to be missed.    Here as in Delphi, Luxor or Angkor Wat, art survives the society that created it.  All that may be seen is the visible tip of the submerged iceberg that every "lost" civilization represents:  a metaphor or transmutation of the original.

The massively imposing **Pyramid of the Sun** is the magnet that draws every visitor.  From a distance, you notice first a stream of movement, like a trickle of water — or could it be ants? — down the sides.  As you approach, you see that these are lines of people moving up and down the exceedingly narrow steps.  Soon you're part of that flow, jostled by children who leap up without a twinge of fear, by other visitors maneuvering to take photos or by families trying to keep their members together. The higher you climb, the narrower the steps and the smaller the crowd. Yes, it's worth it, the view from the top is breathtaking.

Nearly 2000 years old, the Temple of the Sun is the most awesome and impressive structure in the complex. The second largest extant pyramid after the Pyramid of Cheops in Egypt. It's 210 feet high and stands over a cave that Teotihuacanos believed to have been the center of the universe.

*Pyramid of the Sun.* Photo by E. Monroe.

Fabulous as this temple is, don't make the mistake of ignoring the smaller, but equally intriguing structures that line the **Avenue of the Dead.** Actually, the street is misnamed. What once were taken for tombs later turned out to be temples and priestly homes — perfect for hands on exploring. Of particular interest are the **Temple of Quetzalcoatl,** the only building featuring sculptural carvings of the plumed serpent; and the **Pyramid of the Moon,** a somewhat newer and more sophisticated structure.

The site is open from 9 a.m. to 5 p.m. daily. There's a minimal admission charge and English speaking guides are available. The small but interesting museum is closed on Mondays.

Tourist excursions to the site are expensive and frustrating. On site time is generally limited to two hours. With the other alternative — a taxi ride costing at least $11 an hour — there's really no excuse for not taking a Mexican bus. These leave throughout the day from the Terminal Central de Autobuses del Norte. For less than $4 (a round-trip ticket), you can spend as much time at Teotihuacan as you wish. Consider having your hotel pack a picnic lunch.

# XOCHIMILCO

In Aztec times when what was to become Mexico City was surrounded by a lake, land was at a premium. Flowers, fruits and vegetables had to be carried in from long distances on the backs of men and women, since there were no pack animals or wheelbarrows. Then somehow, someone hit on the idea of building rafts, covering them with soil and turning them into floating gardens in an area of the lake known as Xochimilco. It was done and it worked.

Today canals are all that remain of the lake but the name Xochimilco has stuck and produce is still grown in abundance in what has become a truck gardening center graced with lovely poplar trees and laced by waterways.

*Xochimilco.* Photo by E. Monroe

Xochimilco is a lovely setting for visitors who pile into gondolas to be poled up and down the canals while boats bearing flowers, mariachi bands, tacos and crafts float by. Does it sound touristy? Just look around. Foreigners are invariably outnumbered by locals enjoying a colorful day off. Don't miss it.

Sunday is the best time to visit Xochimilco, located southeast of the city proper, a short taxi ride. Once there, avoid the so-called, "guides." You don't need one. Gondola prices are clearly marked on the dock. There's an interesting craft market nearby and a good restaurant, **Manantiales,** designed by the much admired Spanish architect, Felix Candela.

# THE SHRINE OF GUADALUPE

On December 9, 1531 Tonantzin, mother of all the Aztec gods, is said to have appeared to Juan Diego, at the site of her former temple on Tepayak Hill. According to Diego, the goddess said she loved the people and wanted her shrine rebuilt, "For I am the Mother of all of you who dwell in this land." A recent convert to Christianity, Diego approached the bishop. . . .perhaps the vision was really another mother, the Virgin Mary.

The bishop doubted that it was anybody, but when Diego returned — this time carrying a bouquet of roses that the apparition had caused to sprout from the frosty, stony ground at the temple site — he examined the cloth in which the flowers were wrapped.  Imprinted on the Indian's tunic was the portrait of a woman.

Her wish was granted.  The miraculous tunic now framed in gold hangs over a marble altar at the **Shrine of the Virgin of Guadalupe**.

Today the Guadalupe Shrine is considered by Mexican Catholics to be the holiest place in the western hemisphere.  Catholic heads of state, such as presidents John F. Kennedy and Charles de Gaulle, have traditionally paid homage there. Located on the northern edge of the city, the present day shrine is part of a large complex that includes a monumental plaza.    By 1709 the original chapel was thought too insignificant to house such a holy relic and a massive basilica was constructed only to be replaced by another in 1976.

The new ultramodern basilica is considered an architectural marvel by many, though not everyone would agree.  The unqualified miracle is the tunic on display inside.    To this day, experts are unable to say in what medium the image was created, much less give any but a supernatural explanation as to *how* , nor has anyone been able to explain why the tunic itself has not deteriorated after more than 400 years.

# THE ZOCALO AREA

---

The heart of the city, the **Zocalo**, is the second largest square in the world — only Red Square in Moscow is bigger — and occupies what was once  the fabled Halls of Montezuma.   Today it's ringed by architectural and cultural treasures.

**The Great Temple of the Aztecs,** (Templo Mayor) actually the base of twin temples to the gods of rain and war, was the holiest shrine in the Aztec Empire. Reduced to rubble during the siege in 1521 and covered over by the foundations of Cortes's Iberian city, the structure was accidentally discovered in 1978 by workmen from the Mexican Power and Light Company who were laying cables.

The cables were quickly forgotten as a city street became an ongoing archaeological site.  The excavation continues, intensely exciting as archeologists peel away

*The heart of the city.*

*The National Palace.*

the rubble of centuries bringing ancient history to life. Artifacts on display include an altar to the moon goddess, as well as numerous masks and statues. The museum is open from 9 a.m. to 5 p.m.

**The National Palace,** next door, built with rubble left from the destruction of Moctezuma's palace was once the headquarters of Hernan Cortes. After serving as the official residence of the Spanish viceroys, it was used by the Emperor Maximilian during his brief reign and then by all the presidents of Mexico up to the present day.

Additionally, the palace houses the Finance Ministry, the National Archives and the Benito Juarez Museum. Over the central portal hangs the Liberty Bell rung by Father Miguel Hidalgo in 1810 to rally his followers, the event that marked the beginning of the struggle for independence.    The palace also contains one of Diego Rivera's most famous murals.  Painted in the 1930s, it depicts the stormy period of Mexican history from the War of Independence through the Mexican Revolution.    Open daily from 8 a.m. until 6 p.m..

**The National Pawn Shop** or Monte de Piedad (Mountain of Pity) stands in front of the National Place, across the street from the Majestic Hotel (don't forget that great rooftop restaurant that overlooks the whole panorama).  Once an 18th century palace, the pawnshop was opened by the Count of Regla in 1775, as a bank for the poor. It continues to serve in that  capacity and has many interesting items for sale.

**House of Tiles** (Casa de los Azulejos) at 4 Madero and Lazaro Cardenas on the western edge of the Zocalo, was originally built in 1596 by a scion of the Orizaba family.  A "no a count" son of a count, the ne'er do well had been told by his father, "You will never have a house of tiles," that is to say, "You will never make good."

The son, who surprised everyone by doing very well, made a statement with his home, a veritable palace.  Every square inch of the facade was covered with blue and white tiles.   The former mansion now houses a branch of Sanborn's — a very upscale drugstore with an excellent restaurant much frequented by politicians doing "power breakfasts" or enjoying coffee breaks.  There's also a charming boutique and a craft center upstairs.  Open daily 8 a.m. to 10 p.m.

**Palace of Fine Arts** (Bellas Artes) corner of Lazaro Cardenas and Juarez.  This lavish, wedding cake creation was begun in 1900 during  the Porfirio Diaz regime and completed 34 years and many presidents later.  Designed by the Italian architect Adam Boari, the palace is home to  the National Symphony and the site of performances by ballet and opera companies.  The Ballet Folklorico performs there on Sunday mornings and Wednesday evenings.  Prior to each performance, the 22-ton Tiffany Glass curtain is displayed.  The ultimate in Tiffany Glass.

Additionally, the lobby is adorned with art by Rivera, Orozco, Tamayo, Siqueiros and Gonzales Camarena.  The most notable is a Rivera mural that's a replica of the controversial mural that the artist did for Rockefeller Center in New York.  The original, which contained a portrait of Lenin, so horrified the Rockefellers that they ordered it painted over.

# CHAPULTEPEC PARK

Much of the history of the ill-fated Maximilian and Carlota is enshrined in Chapultepec Castle which now houses the **National Museum of History.** Gowns, carriages, furniture — even bathtubs — from their private quarters are on display.

Among the exhibits at the **National Museum of Anthropology** are the Aztec stone calendar, giant Olmec heads from the jungles of Tabasco and jade jewelry recovered from sacred Mayan wells.

Other treasures to be found in Chapultepec Park include the **Gallery of National History**, the **Museum of National History**, the **Museum of Modern Art** and the **Rufino Tamayo Museum**, which, in addition to the artist's own works, contains some 300 paintings of other world famous artists.

Another attraction is the neighboring **zoo** spread out over 700 acres along secluded paths marked by century old cypress trees. It's believed that the trees, now more than two hundred feet tall, were planted by the fourteenth century poet king Netzahualcoyotl. The zoo's superstars are the pandas, a pair of emigres from China and their two babies, first generation Mexicans. The state of the art zoo continues in the tradition of the fabulous menagerie maintained by the Aztec emperors.

# FRIDA KAHLO MUSEUM

Everybody, it seems, knew Frida and Diego. He was one the greatest artist in the world; she the frequently rebellious priestess in his temple. After more than forty years their fame — and mystique — is undiminished. But there *is* a difference: Frida has emerged as an artistic genius in her own right.

The story of Frida Kahlo begins and ends in the same place: the house on Londres 247, in Coyoacan. Open 10 a.m. to 3 p.m. and 4 to 7 p.m. . The exterior of her former home looks very much like any other in Coyoacan, a fashionable suburb on the southwestern periphery of Mexico City. But the inside is quite extraordinary — a woman's home with all her paintings and belongings turned into a museum. Each object on display is animated by the former occupants' presence.

A bright blue stucco structure marked by tall, many-paned windows with green shutters, it bears the name **Museo Frida Kahlo** over the door. Be warned: the one thing expected from a museum are facts. Better forget facts, this is a museum dedicated to myth and fantasy.

One of the first things one sees is a plaque that reads: *Aqui nacio Frida Kahlo el dia 7 de julio d 1910.* (Here Frida Kahlo was born July 7, 1910.) Another inscription proclaims, *"Frida y Diego vivieron en esta casa ."* (Frida and Diego lived in this house from 1929 to 1954) . That neither statement is true seems uniquely appropriate. Frida Kahlo's whole life was about myth — not only myth in the universal, artistic sense, but in a uniquely personal one.

It began with her birth date which was really July 6, 1907. Perhaps for Frida — a child of the revolution growing up in a decade when streets literally ran with the blood of rebels — it was only natural to perceive herself and modern Mexico as having been born together. The year of the war's outbreak would be her own birth year — so much more appropriate than the original one so easily forgotten.

*Frida Kahlo and Diego Rivera*

(But what an irony to her parents! For them, the revolution brought personal disaster not liberation. The father's frequent commissions from  the Diaz regime made possible the comfortable family home built in 1904. The demise of the Porfiate followed by a decade of civil war resulted in genteel poverty.)

The other dates aren't quite true either — ignoring as they do the fact  that Frida and Diego were separated, divorced and remarried during that  period and that even when they were together the couple lived much of the time in a pair of houses. But what difference does it really make? Frida Kahlo's whole world was itself a myth, myth lived as life and life as myth. Here was a woman who artfully succeeded in creating her own.

"I paint my reality," she once said and it's significant that most of the 200 or so paintings that Kahlo produced in her abbreviated career were self portraits. Fortunately she had dramatic material with which to work. On the edge of beauty, slight flaws only seem only to increase her magnetism.   Luxuriant eyebrows form an unbroken line across her forehead, the shadow of a mustache accents a sensuous mouth.  Dark, almond shaped eyes challenge the viewer, slanting upward at the outer edges.

Vibrant, tender and spunky, Kahlo attracted men and would take many lovers.  The first, Alejandro Gomez Arias, who remained a lifelong friend, later wrote of his teenage sweetheart,"To her sex was a form of enjoying life, a kind of vital impulse."

It was this young woman, who in 1922, first met Diego Rivera who had been commissioned to paint a mural in her school auditorium.  Looking for all the world like a loquacious frog, the world famous, fantastically fat artist loved to chat with students as he painted.  "I will have his baby as soon as I can convince him to cooperate," the fifteen-year-old Frida told her friends.  At the time, Rivera was busy juggling two mistresses, Lupe Marin, whom he would soon marry and his model, Nahui Olin, currently posing for the figure representing erotic poetry in the mural.

It was this same young woman, who three years later, while riding a bus home from school, was rammed by a streetcar.  Literally impaled on a metal bar in the wreckage, Kahlo's spine was fractured, her pelvis crushed and one foot broken.

In the dreadful days that followed, Kahlo's mother, in an effort to amuse her daughter, asked a carpenter to construct an easel that could be attached to the bed — the girl's plaster cast did not permit her to sit up.  In this way, painting became a part of her battle for survival. This was the beginning. It was the pain, the insistent, agonizing irritant that created the pearl of Kahlo's art.  A peculiar love of spectacle — perhaps a mask to preserve privacy and personal dignity — incredible charisma and an indomitable spirit in the face of both physical and emotional tragedy, and — above all — the insistence on surprise and specificity in life as well as art that characterized Frida Kahlo's central subject:  herself.

Such was her appetite for life, such was her intensity that it was not enough to simply endure, she had also to enjoy.   Recovering, relapsing, recovering again, Frida reinvented herself, creating a woman who could control her world.  In an effort to remain a part of the mainstream, Kahlo accented qualities she already possessed: wit, generosity, vivacity.  Dressed flamboyantly in floor length Mexican costumes, the public Frida was lively, fiery and fey, a character from an Isabel Allende novel sprung to life. Gradually she became a famous personality.

And then, quite by chance, Diego Rivera reentered her life.  At 41, the controversial artist had covered more walls than any other living muralist.  Born in Guanajuato in 1887 to a school teacher and a pious woman who owned a candy store, Diego was considered a prodigy from the beginning.  At ten he demanded to be sent to art school in Mexico City; the boy's parents, said to have been embarrassed by his outspoken criticism of the church, found a way to accommodate him.

In 1928, Rivera had recently returned from a tour of Russia.  His marriage to Lupe Marin disintegrating, he was on the loose and — despite an undeniable ugliness — had no trouble attracting women. In fact, it was said, that pretty American tourists regarded a tryst with the wild and famous Communist artist as *the*  thing to do in Mexico.

Frida and Diego met at a party given by Tina Modotti, the beautiful and talented protege of Edward Weston.  They talked of art and later he  dropped by to see her paintings.  A year later, on August 23, 1929, they were married.  He was six feet tall and weighed 300 pounds, she, five foot three, weighed slightly under a hundred.  Her parents called it a marriage of an elephant and a dove.  But, elephant or no, Rivera was an extraordinary man of enormous vitality and charm, a man who could be both tender and deeply sensuous.

Obviously Frida was aware of his womanizing proclivities, but would hardly be the first woman to fall into the age-old, self deceiving trap.  *I* will be the one to *hold*  his love, he will love me in a *different* way.  Actually, she did and  he did — but what a struggle!

In his favor it can be said that Rivera opened worlds to her.  Henry Ford was a friend, so were Nelson Rockefeller, Dolores del Rio, Paulette Goddard.  Marcel Duchamp was Frida's host in Paris, in San Francisco she was photographed  by Edward Weston and Imogen Cunningham.

Rivera admired strong and independent women.  The fact that Frida retained her own name pleased him.  He wanted and expected her to have her own ideas, her own friends, her own activities.  He admired her painting and encouraged the development of her unique style.  *But* he was a man determined to lead his own life in his own way and that included other women.

When Rivera built a house for himself and Frida, it was in fact two separate houses linked by a bridge. Though both technically belonged to Diego, when Frida was angry with him, she could lock the door on her side of the bridge, forcing him to go downstairs, cross the yard and knock on her front door. There, as often as not, he would be told by a servant that his wife refused to receive him.  There was nothing left for the world renowned artist to do but huff and puff his way back up the stairs, across the bridge and, plead for forgiveness once again before Frida's locked door.

Undeniably theirs was a stormy marriage.   Besides the physical pain that never left her, Frida had also to live with the anguish of being deceived and occasionally abandoned by the man she loved.   Inevitably she retaliated.   Vivid, intelligent, sexy, she attracted men and took many lovers, among them Leon Trotsky and Isamu Noguchi.  There's evidence that she had lesbian liaisons as well.  Rivera appeared not to  mind the latter, but objected strenuously to the former.   "I don't share my toothbrush with anybody."

In his autobiography Rivera confessed, "If I loved a woman the more I wanted to hurt her. Frida was only the most obvious victim of this disgusting trait." The result was a curious relationship of mutual independence and interdependence. They would be separated, divorced, ultimately remarried. In his own way Rivera was loyal and supportive. He was there to rally Frida's courage toward the end of her life when even the amputation of a leg could not stop the deterioration of her ravaged body. And he was beside her the night she died. In his autobiography Rivera wrote, "July 13, 1954 was the most tragic day of my life. I had lost my beloved Frida, forever. . .Too late now, I realized that the most wonderful part of my life had been my love for Frida."

Frida Kahlo's remains were cremated, a process that took four hours. During the wait, crowds of people cried and sang. Rivera stood by, hands clenched until the palms bled. At last the job was done, the oven door opened and the red-hot cart containing Frida's ashes slid out. For a few minutes the ashes retained the shape of her skeleton. Rivera took a small sketch book from his pocket and drew the silvery form until it was dispersed by air currents. Gathering the ashes in a red cloth, he placed them it in a cedar box.

Rivera's request that his ashes be mixed with hers after his death was ignored. It was deemed more fitting that the great muralist lie with Mexico's most famous citizens in the Rotonda de los Hombres Ilusrtres.

Rivera gave the Madero Street house, complete with its art collection, including his paintings and others that Frida had owned, and with all its treasure trove of Pre-Columbian and folkloric furnishings to the Mexican people. In July 1958, the Frida Kahlo Museum was opened.

A bronze cast of Frida's death mask has been placed on a pedestal there. Beneath it her ashes are contained in a pre-Columbian jar shaped like a rotund, headless female. The urn gives the sense of being pregnant with life, reminding one of the clay idol in *Four Inhabitants of Mexico* which Frida described as pregnant "because, being dead, she has something alive inside."

It is difficult to leave the museum without a sense of having known Frida Kahlo. So many relics — toys, photographs, jewelry, love notes — offer a vivid sense of her personality as well as of the ambience in which she lived and worked.

Kahlo's last painting, executed eight days before her death, hangs on the living room wall. Slices of luscious watermelon, the most beloved of Mexican fruit, like red flesh against a brilliant blue sky. Beneath it in blood red paint, the words **VIVA LA VIDA**.

## TIDBITS

Planes arrive and depart from the Benito Juarez International Airport. four miles east of the downtown historic center.  Airlines serving the capital include Aero California, Aero Mexico, American, Continental, Delta,  Mexicana, United, Northwest and US Air.

For transportation into town, look for signs just past the baggage claim area that say TAXI or *Transportacion..*  **Avoid all other airport taxi solocitations.**  Set rates apply to all areas of the city, with most fares running around $10 per trip.  Tip an additional 10% only if your driver handles your luggage.

**Around town**, it's best to remember that all taxis are not equal  Outside the more expensive hotels are unmarked sedans, usually black, with English speaking drivers and guides.  These are expensive, but sometimes worth it depending on your desired destination.  A good guide can make a trip, particularly if your time is limited.

Cruising the streets are taxis of three distinctions — orange and white four-door cabs offering comfort and metered rates; green and white new VW bugs with cheap, metered rates; and yellow and white older VW bugs, sometimes metered and sometimes not, offering the cheapest rates of all.   With the exception of the black sedans, none are really expensive and tipping is not expected.

Additionally, Mexico City has one of the finest subway systems in the world.  For slightly more than a dime you can explore the entire city in rapid efficiency on board quiet, French designed trains.  There are eight lines covering nearly 100 miles of track. Stations are attractive and clean,  some with special attractions: the **Zocalo station** features huge models of Mexico City during three historic periods: the **Bellas Artes station** has replicas of archaeological relics and the **Pino Suarez station** has an actual Aztec pyramid unearthed during station construction. ( Hours are from 6 a.m. to 12 p.m.  Watch your belongings and avoid rush hour.)

The bus is another option.  Once again, slightly over a dime will take you anywhere in the city.  A popular route connects the Zocalo with  Chapultepec park, two principal visitor areas.

A rental car?  Get real!  This is the largest city in the world.  Driving in it makes people a little crazy.  Or is it the ubiquitous image of the Virgin of Guadalupe dangling above the rear view mirror that causes native drivers to feel invincible?  Don't even think of it.

## MUSEUMS

There are so many historical buildings and museums in Mexico City that if you devoted one day a week to each of them, you'd be kept busy for well over a year. Unless otherwise noted, Mexico City museums are open Tuesday through Sunday. Most charge modest admissions, except on Sunday.

The Mexico City area code is 5. From the U.S./Canada, dial 011-52-5 and the local seven-digit number.

Temperatures in Mexico City range between 41 to 81.

### AN EXCURSION

One afternoon God felt sleepy. He lay down for a siesta and dreamed of perfection. While He slept some of His energy seeped into the land thus creating a power spot and — some say — paradise.

In 1963 Jose Luiz Chain also had a dream. His dream was a perfect health spa in paradise. What better location than God's power spot?

Well, at least that's the way the story goes at **Avandaro Hotel**, an elegant getaway near the picturesque village of **Valle de Bravo**. Beautiful and decidedly upscale, Valle de Bravo is to Mexico City what the Hamptons are to New York, Palm Springs to Los Angeles or possibly Carmel to San Francisco. Well, perhaps more like what they *used* to be. Valle de Bravo is still a quaint and charming colonial town. It has yet to be "discovered."

Founded in 1520, the colonial village is called "the Switzerland of Mexico" for good reason. The mountains and alpine forests are magnificent, the air cool and invigorating. All that's missing are the sound of cowbells and yodels. Enjoy instead mariachi tunes and the clatter of donkey hoofs on cobblestone streets.

Located 92 kilometers west of Mexico City, Valle de Bravo is a sports minded town. Fresh mountain breezes have made the area a sailing enthusiast's dream. The lake is full of trout and bass, the piney woods invite the hiker or horseback rider and enthusiasts insist that this is the best place for hang gliding in the world for the winds travel in a triangle.  Valle de Bravo also has a particularly appealing craft market filled with unusually colorful straw work and exquisite crocheted items.

The nearby Avandaro Hotel — (avandaro means dream place) — is where the movers and shakers of Mexico come to play.   In August of 1993 the golf and spa resort was host to the closing session of the Mexican state legislature. The exclusive getaway featured in *The Lifestyles of the Rich and Famous*, *Elle* and *Playboy* magazines was selected as the "reward" destination for top achievers in the Palmolive, Bacardi and Mercedes Benz companies.

What do you do there?  Enjoy state-of-the-art spa pampering, charming chalet style cottages with individual fireplaces, seven tennis courts (more than any resort in the state of Mexico) and an 18 hole golf course. If you're very lucky you may be there for butterfly season in the winter when hillsides and trees glow as if touched by a golden snowfall.   But this is a living blizzard — millions of monarch butterflies resting from their annual journey to Mexico from Canada.  An unforgettable sight.

For reservations call 1-800-654  DREAM.  Could anything be more appropriate?

*Mexico City zocalo.* Photo by the author.

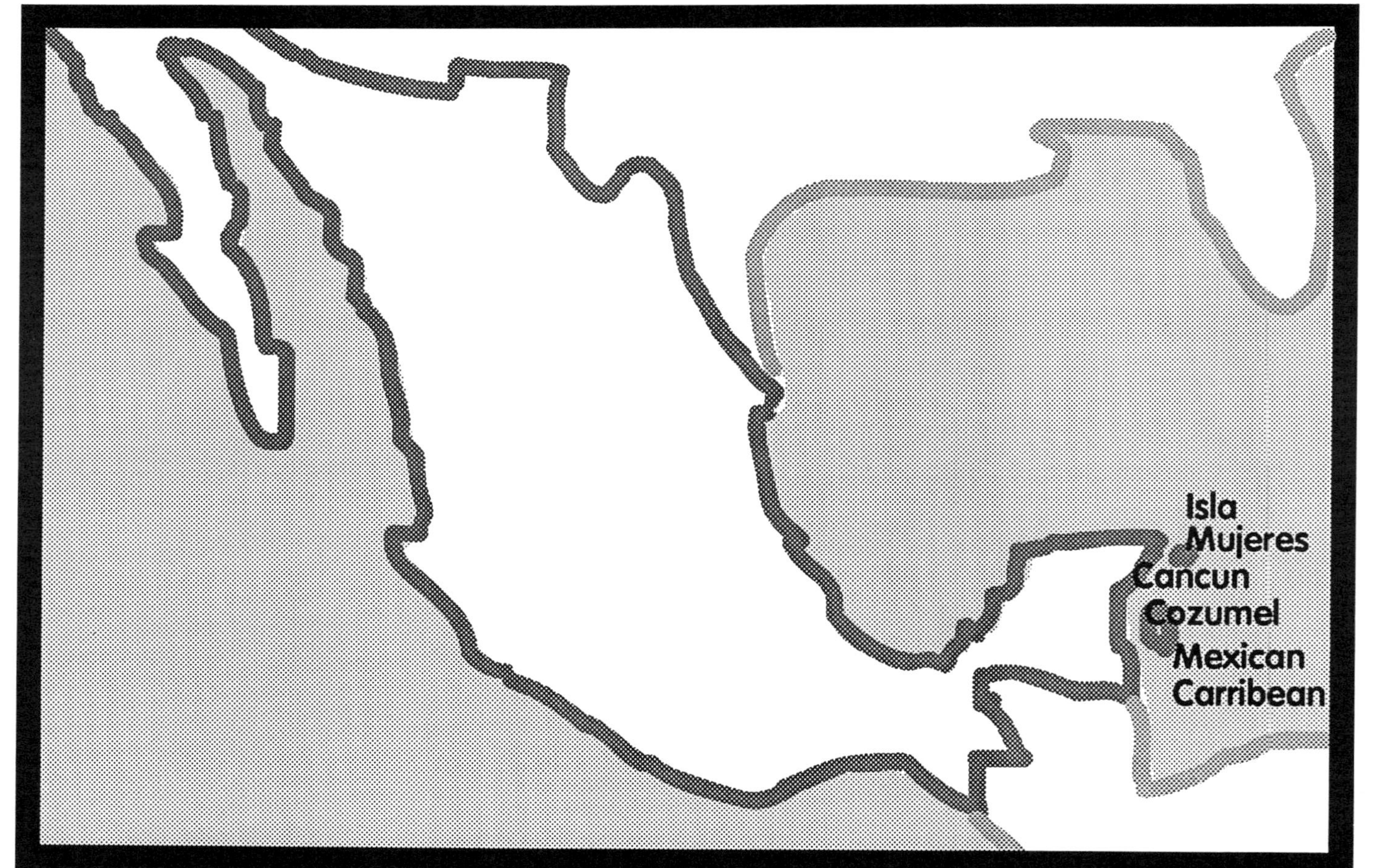

Isla
Mujeres
Cancun
Cozumel
Mexican
Carribean

# THE MEXICAN CARIBBEAN
## FROM RUINS TO RICHES......

Is it too surprising that Mexico's most popular honeymoon destination is the site of one of the most fateful romances of all times? It was a union that would eventually unite two warring peoples. Each possessed equally long records of achievement, yet both had been totally oblivious to the other. Their inevitable confrontation would result in a romance that presaged the genesis of a new nation.

It began in 1511 when seven Spanish shipwreck victims drifted to the shores of the Mexican Caribbean at what was then called Tulum, or walled city. Five of the men including their captain were killed by Mayan residents who'd been warned by an ancient prophecy of bearded men who would come from the sea to rob them of their land. The two survivors, Gonzalo Guerrero and Jeronimo de Aguilar, must have been fast talkers, somehow managing to convince their wary captors that they were strong and resourceful, potential assets to the community.

Aguilar was sold to a passing trader and taken to nearby Cozumel where he remained until freed by Cortes's invasion. Guerrero's destiny was very different. He remained in Tulum and learned to speak Mayan so well that he eventually won the heart of Princess Zazil, the beautiful daughter of a ruling chieftain.

Then, in, 1519 after pacifying the island of Cozumel, Cortes's men proceeded to invade the mainland. It was Guerrero who incited the Mayas to fight. He refused to give credence to the prophecy. The Spaniards were simply men like himself and could be defeated. Guerrero's battle strategies depended upon surprise attacks, ambushes and cunning. The modern day term "guerrilla warfare" gets its name from the tactics he introduced.

When the Spanish conquest of Tulum proved a dismal failure, Cortes offered Guerrero amnesty, sending his old comrade Aguilar with gifts and a promise that the prodigal son would be well received. Guerrero's reply has never been forgotten:

*"Brother Aguilar, I am a married man,*
*    I have three children,*
*They, (the Mayas) hold me as a chief*
*    and a captain during wars.*
*Go with God, for my face is carved and*
*    my ears pierced. What*
*would the Spaniards say about me,*
*    when they saw me in this*
*manner! You have seen my children,*
*    how lovely they are. For*
*your life, if for them you'd give me these*
*    green beads which you*
*have brought I shall say that my*
*    brothers have sent me from*
*    their land."*

The three children of Guerrero and Zszil, his Mayan princess, were the first *mestizos*, the first blending of Indian and Spanish blood.

About that time another Spaniard, Juan de Grijalva, sailed down the Caribbean coast and was so impressed by the view of Tulum that he literally wrote home about it: "We sailed a day and a night, and on the following day at sunset, we descried a citadel, or city, so large that Seville seemed to us neither larger nor better."

One might well say the very same today about a city only a few miles to the north of Tulum. The fabulous Cancun has acquired an international reputation. Visitors—not only from Seville—but Rome, London, Paris, Tokyo, Berlin, not to mention the United States are constantly writing home about it. But posh, polished Cancun, for all her glitzy allure, is not the only island in the sea. There are also her Cinderella sisters: Isla Mujeres and Cozumel. Which is fairest of them all? Only you can decide.

# ISLA MUJERES

Isla Mujeres, the least known of the islands, is for many the most romantic. With origins shrouded in mystery, it's believed that the island was a sanctuary dedicated to the Mayan goddess, Ixchel, an all powerful deity whose realm included the moon, prophesy, creativity, childbirth, medicine, shells and weaving.

A pilgrimage to the secluded southern coast of the island brings one to Ixchel's shrine which hugs a craggy cliff overlooking the sea. The small, windswept temple has an aura of mysticism, a sense of long forgotten secrets.

The Plymouth Rock of Mexico, Isla Mujeres was discovered March 1, 1517 by Her-nandez de Cordoba. The expedition had been beset by misfortunes, the seamen lost and adrift for twenty-one days before they at last sighted the island. What first confronted them were stone statues of bare breasted Mayan goddesses, presumably replicas of Ixchel, standing guard along the coast. Hence the name: Isle of Women.

*Isla Mujeres is casual and easy going.*

But there's another equally provocative story about how

the island got its name. Pirates once found the place a convenient retreat in which to hang up their cutlasses and stash their women. In l860, one particularly ardent buccaneer, Fermin Mundaca, decided to retire there. His incentive was La Triguena, a teenage beauty with hair the color of wheat. He built a lavish estate, *La Hacienda vista alegre,* for his favorite, filled the gardens with exotic plants and engraved the gates with her name.

Unfortunately, La Triguena preferred a local suitor and married him — a blow from which Mundaca never recovered. Year after year, she bore her husband another child while Mundaca slowly went mad. Today his tombstone may be viewed

*Snorkeling is a favorite pastime on Isla de Mujeres.*

at the Isla Mujeres cemetery on the west side of town. The headstone— complete with skull and crossbones— contains a cryptic message: *"What I am, you shall be; what you are I was."*

A five-mile by 1/2-mile wide wisp of an island, Isla Mujeres sits just off the coast to the northeast of Cancun, clinging tenaciously to its own identity as a fishing village. Fishermen mend their nets and patch their boats seemingly oblivious to the tourists disgorged daily from Cancun. Isla Mujeres is for those craving a glitz break will appreciate relaxed, unpretentious Isla Mujeres as a refreshing throwback to the days before Cancun even existed. Slightly raunchy, down at the heels, the tiny island is a beach town plain and simple

## HOTELS

Rooms at **Na Balam** are actually beach front junior suites with private terraces overlooking the sea—the best place in town for sunset watching. The hotel is also a pleasant rendezvous at happy hour, between 5 and 7 p.m.
Telephone: (987) 70-279.

**Posada del Mar**, at Avenue Rueda Marina No. 15, is an escapist's paradise. Spacious landscaped grounds provide a tranquil oasis while just beyond, the beach beckons. Bungalows and hotel with 46 air conditioned rooms.
Telephone: (987) 70-300.
Slightly funky, sea-worn **Hotel Rocamar** faces a beach just across from the plaza. A nautical theme livens this very affordable hotel:  seashell lamps, washbasins inset with shells, giant fishhooks hold up dressers.
Telephone:  (987) 20-101.

## RESTAURANTS

The quality seems about even on Avenida Hidalgo (restaurant row).  My particular favorite is **Ciro's.**  If you like lobster, it's difficult to resist a place that prepares a dozen variations.   But then there's also **Maria's Kan Kin** out on the El Garragon Road, an excellent French restaurant with a romantic beachfront view.   Or **Loncheria Miramar** (Avenida Rueda Medina, next to the ferry pier) which hangs over the water serving some of the best food on the island at reasonable prices.

## BEACHES

The western (leeward) beaches tend to have calmer water than those on the island's eastern side. Expect to swim through schools of flashing yellow sergeant-majors and parrot fish that flame light gaudy spotlights, but try to get there early before the party boats arrive, otherwise most of the fins you see will be made of rubber.

**Playa Los Cocos**, near the northern tip of the island, is the prettiest,  with calm, translucent waters.   International visitors often bathe sans suits here, a custom rarely observed in Mexico.

**Playa Lancheros**, near the southern end of the island enjoys a more secluded location. Added attractions are live sea turtle and shark pens and sheltered swimming.  Across the street, up the hill and down a winding path is the Mundaca Hacienda.   Remnants of the extensive gardens and the crumbling ruins of the mansion remain to be explored.

***Playa Garrafon***,  a snorkeling paradise just beyond Lancheros where  the under-sea life is dazzling.  Swimming and snorkeling are easy here even for beginners and there's easy access to the gigantic coral reef and sandy-bottom entry path.

## SHOPPING

Though prices are generally cheaper in Isla Mujeres than in Cancun,  shopping can be frustrating as few stores take credit cards or traveler's checks.   Forestall disappointments by being prepared to pay in pesos.

In the midst of the marketplace atmosphere it's surprising to spot a sunset pink building, ***Rachat & Rome*** , near the ferry landing at Avenida Rueda Medina or the azure blue ***Van Cleef & Arpels*** one block from the tourist pier.  Decidedly upscale with carpets and air conditioning, the glass cases of both stores enclose fine silver, gold and pink coral jewelry.

But an even rarer gem is ***Casa del Arte Mexicana*** at Avenue Hildalgo # 6  which offers some of the most unique and exciting batik and/or tie dyed T-shirts and shifts in all of Mexico.  The store also features temple rubbings that are truly stun-ning.   This place is a true find.

## TIDBITS

***Getting there***—Everyone in Cancun who isn't trying to sell you a time share will attempt to get you on a party cruise.  Unless you really enjoy loud noise, little time to do your own thing, high prices, watered drinks and an emcee trying desperately to be funny, consider instead the "people" ferry from Puerto Juarez (just four miles north of Cancun.) Luggage storage areas are provided there as well as restrooms. A warning:  these ferries are known to leave ahead of time if they're full — so get there  early.  There's also a car ferry that operates from Punta Sam, approximately five minutes north of Puerto Juarez.  There are always car  lines, so it's wise to arrive 30 to 45 minutes ahead of time.

In case you haven't guessed, dress in Isla Mujeres is very casual.

The area code for Isla Mujeres is 987.

You can get everywhere in town on foot, but to visit the ruins and more remote beaches, you'll want to rent a bicycle, motorscooter or golf cart.

# COZUMEL

The ancients believed that Cozumel (which means "Place of Swallows") was a Garden of Eden from which the Mayans burst forth "like bees from a hive of honey."

Not surprisingly the whole island was a shrine to Ixchel, that same goddess of childbirth, fertility, creativity, the sea and the moon. How could it be otherwise when every night the moon rose in the east — literally born from the sea? The goddess's effect on the tides was undisputable. When the moon was full or at its beginning, tides would soon be at their highest, bountifully spilling fish and crabs onto the beach — a lavish feast waiting to be enjoyed.

Obviously Ixchel was a deity worth cultivating. Pilgrimages from the mainland, considered a holy obligation, were particularly popular with pregnant women or women who wished to become pregnant. Supplicants came from as far as Tabasco, Belize, Guatemala and Chiapas.

When Cortes arrived with his eleven ships and 400 men on the way to conquer all of Mexico, he found an island of 40,000 inhabitants — more than twice the size of today's population. Unfortunately, it was this Mayan version of Mecca, Rome or Jerusalem that received the full thrust of his idol smashing crusade.

*Cozumel is one of the five best dive sites on this planet.*

Little of Cozumel's original grandeur survived his greed or penchant for vandalism.  Later when less hypocritical plunderers arrived—real pirates—they found slim pickings.  The once splendid center was then so desolate that it provided another convenient hideout similar to Isla Mujeres.  When piracy passed from vogue, the island was abandoned once again.

of the top five dive sites on the planet.  The island's surrounding sea teems with underwater life, colored reefs and the slumbering hulls of Spanish galleons.  Today one in six visitors to Mexico's largest island come to dive.  There are shore dives and night dives, refresher courses for intermediates and crash courses for beginners, all taught by experienced bilingual dive masters.

*Cozumel is a favorite cruise destination.*  Photo by Steve Lucas.

It took the growing popularity of chewing gum in the United States to  finally rescue Cozumel from obscurity in the 19th century.   The island became a port-of-call on the chicle export route from Central America.  Later a U.S. Air Force base was built there from which the Allies launched planes to hunt German U-boats.

Finally, a Jacques Cousteau documentary in 1961 ensured Cozumel a worldwide following of divers, who rank it one

What draws them?  About one kilometer off the southern end of Cozumel lies one of the natural wonders of the undersea world, Palancar Reef, second only to Australia's Great Barrier Reef in length.

A massive fortress of coral, six mile long Palancar is a linear shelf which drops steeply from the shallowest level of 10 meters to a depth of 400 meters.  Palancar — so heart-stopping in its silent immensity — encompasses an ever changing landscape of free standing coral pinnacles towering as high as 30 meters, blue grottos, dark caves suddenly lit by vivid pink sponges or lacy gorgonia fans, arches, tunnels, and meandering ravines.

But Palancar is not the only reef in the sea and each has its own personality and marine life. Nearby Colombia Reef has large schools of grunts and snappers, while Punta Sur contains an exciting network of deep caves filled with marine life. At Santa Rosa Reef, noted for its huge coral mounds as tall as buildings, big groupers wait for divers hoping to be hand fed.

Few places can match the island's incredibly clear waters where visibility is rarely less than 100 feet and often reaches 200. Because of the continuous ocean currents that run from south to north, all of Cozumel's diving is drift diving, one of the most thrilling ways to dive because it enables the diver to take advantage of the underwater "winds." By floating with the current, one travels farther and sees much more.

Once a drift dive is over, divers ascend to the surface to find their dive boat waiting. The boat has been tracking their air bubbles and is ready to take them aboard.

*En Route to Palancar Reef.* Photo by T. Pappas.

# HOTELS

Like Isla Mujeres, Cozumel is a one-town island.  Though unlike the former, it does have a name:  San Miguel.  Hotels cluster in and around the  small town located on the western side of the island.   One charming alternative to the larger, grander hotels is **Meson San Miguel**  near the downtown plaza.  The location is convenient, the walled garden an oasis, prices easily affordable—there's a good restaurant too, **El Pozo**.  (987) 2-02-33.

The style and grandeur of the Mayan culture receives modern homage  in the ten-story pyramid shaped "palace", that comprises the **Fiesta Americana Sol Caribe** two miles south of town.  You'll find a lobby area that's the most impressive on the island with a huge thatched palapa hut, marble floors, a large lagoon sized pool and lovely grounds.  Each of the 322 rooms has a breathtaking view of the sea, plus air conditioning, purified water and satellite TV. (1-800-FIESTA-1).

A favorite among divers is **La Ceiba Beach Hotel** at Paradise Point on the southern coast.  Here, boat trips to Palancar Reef, night dives and lessons are stressed. The opportunity to explore a WW II plane deliberately sunk 50 yards offshore during the filming of the movie *Cyclone* is an added attraction.  (1-800-777-5873).

My own sentimental favorite is the well preserved old timer, **Club Cozumel Caribe** (north of town).  Well located on the classically tropical coconut-palm-studded San Juan Beach, it offers, in addition to your basic paradise ambience, a wide variety of water sports. (1-800-327-2254).

# RESTAURANTS

**Casa Denny's**, just off the zocolo, takes a casual approach.  People drop by in the morning to tell the staff what they'd like to eat that night for dinner.  Empanadas are a house specialty, but the seafood's superb.  Autographed pictures of happy customers include Jackie Onassis, Placido Domingo and ex-President Bush. Approaching its Big 5-Oh!, Casa Denny's was launched when Miss Juanita took pity on hungry construction workers carving an airstrip out of the jungle and began feeding them.  Soon  Juanita's home kitchen wasn't large enough for everyone who wanted to to eat there and a restaurant was born.

For a more seductive ambience, try **Big Julians**, on the waterfront or **Morgan's**, (Avenida 5a and Calle Juarez).  Named for the pirate who used to hang out on the island, the latter captures the Caribbean influence that's so distinctively Cozumel. Lilting music has a Calypso beat, food a Creole tang.  A chic, air conditioned restaurant resembling a West Indian townhouse, Morgan's presents a treasure chest of entrees ranging from conch steak to flaming crepes to seafood stew.

**Santiago's Grill**, at the corner of Rosado Salas and 5th Ave., is a rustic open air spot that patrons like so much that they stand in line to get in.  Fresh shrimp is a specialty.

For Mexican favorites, try **La Choza** on the corner of Rosado Salas and 10th Ave., a family-run restaurant that serves three meals daily.  There's no written menu. Dishes served depend on what the cook feels like preparing.  Pizza and pasta lovers flock to **La Cosa Nostr**a tucked away on 548 5th Ave. Sur.  Though the building looks Yucatecan, the daily menu is definitely Italian.

## BEACHES

The whole 30-mile-long island is strung with beaches on both leeward and windward shores, but two have a special quality all their own.  *Punta Morena* (along the windward road south of Santa Cecilia) winds down from a small cluster of palapas where fishermen gather to barbecue fresh fish.  Wild, isolated, marked by fascinating rock formations, the beach has an overhanging grotto, *Cueva del Amor* (cave of love) reached by rocky stairs.

Also *Playa Escondida*, located in a hushed jungle about 12 miles south of San Miguel along the coastal road, a secretive beach flowing out of the shadows and wandering for several miles along limpid waters.  In the distance inviting smoke signals from half hidden palapas: barbecued fish for sale.

## SHOPPING

Excellent Pre-Columbian reproductions have traditionally been sold in Cozumel, but more recently the stock has been varied by whimsical masks and other examples of folk art from the Mexican mainland.

Personal favorites are *Bali-Hai* (Avenida Rafael Melgar 8) for tropical jewelry combining shells, pods, coins and tassels; *Casablana* (Avenida Rafael Melgar 21) a colonial art gallery with cases and niches of Mayan art, jewelry and silver sculpture; *Xaman-ek* (Avenida Rafael Melgar 149) named for the Mayan traveler's god a veritable jungle of papier mache, ceramic and leather birds and animals; and *El Arca de Noe* (Calle 2, No. 11) for masks.

## SIGHT SEEING

Little remains of Cozumel's former glory as a Mayan sanctuary.  There are 30 known surviving ruins, all but two inaccessible.

The ruins of **El Cedral** are easily reached by taking the main highway south out of town past San Francisco Beach. Turn left at the sign and follow a paved road just over 3 kilometers. Surprisingly, this small ruin dating back to 500 A.D., with a tree sprouting from its roof still bears a few traces of the original paint. The site is a study in contrast. The exposed roots of the living tree hold the ancient stones in a timeless embrace while nearby there's a tiny church where one can see among the artifacts evidence of the continuing compromise between Christianity and the Mayan religion.

Today's Mayas have endowed the saints with very human attributes— not always benevolent. Like the ancient gods, they can be capricious. Not only is deference to the saints' status demanded, but attention to their physical comfort. Garments must frequently be washed and worn ones replaced. Offerings of chocolate and tortillas may be found before the Virgin and other holy favorites.

**San Gervasio** , another lonely survivor, may also be easily reached by car or moped. Take Avenue Juarez eastward, until you reach the San Gervasio sign. Soon the ruin comes into view, a tumbled mass of raised platforms, broken columns and collapsing walls.

Restrooms and a tiny snack bar adjoin but the most frequent visitors are birds and butterflies. Sometimes the silence is awesome. These crumbling monuments to a dead civilization — only a few miles from a very lively one — possess a strange sense of power. The temples and tombs have a magic uniquely their own.

Chankanaab—meaning "small sea"—is a decided understatement for **Chankanaab Lagoon Park**, a natural aquarium with more than 60 species of tropical fish, crustaceans and coral foundations. An additional attraction is the adjoining botanical garden with 352 species of tropical plants brought from eleven countries in edition to 4l7 kinds of plants native to Cozumel. The park, which includes diving areas ranging from 6 to 45 feet deep, a beach, restaurant, dive shop, snack bar, shops, dressing rooms and restaurants is open daily from 9:30 to 5 p.m.

**Save a Turtle**—to the ancient Maya the turtle was a sacred creature signifying the earth's abundance and fertility. Today the great sea turtles are on the decline because of illegal harvesting and the shortage of undisturbed beaches. It doesn't help that legend has it that their eggs are an aphrodisiac.

## TIDBITS

Cozumel's area code is 987. There's frequent air service between Cozumel and Cancun via Aero Cozumel and Aero Caribe, an 18 minute flight. Also ferry service from Puerto Morelos and Playa del Carmen. Other airlines include Continental, Mexicana and American.

Since most hotels are located several miles to the north and south of town, your stay will be enhanced by renting a car, moped or bicycle for at least one day.

As opposed to Cancun—high heels, flashdancing discos and poolside piña coladas—Cozumel (like its siesta slow sister, Isla Mujeres) is flip-flops, hammocks at sunset and Jacques Cousteau-like underwater adventures.  The dress and pace are casual.

# CANCUN

The love child of Mother Nature and Father Computer, Cancun was transformed in just two decades from an isolated strand of sleepy beaches to one of the Caribbean's most exciting vacation playgrounds.  How did it happen?

The answer is as magical as any Mayan myth, but it's a magic created by modern science.  The island was discovered by electronic technology. When the Mexican government sought to create a state of the art tourist mecca it collected every scrap of information about what tourists want. When processed by computer, the result was Cancun — today the VIP of Mexican sun spots, luring one million visitors a year.

Shaped like an art nouveau seahorse,

*Cancun — the VIP of Mexican sun spots.*

the island — connected to the mainland by bridges — is almost fourteen miles long and a quarter of a mile wide. On one side is the Caribbean on the other placid Nichupte Lagoon.

Driving in from the airport, the resort area sparkles like a mirage spun of sea mists and trade winds, laced with jungle. It's a futuristic white city, where sky touching pyramids angle upward from talcum powder sands and sea so blue, the brilliance makes you squint.

If this is a starter trip to Mexico, there's comfort to be found in menus printed in English, water you can drink from the tap and a sense that you and your money are very much appreciated. Few places in the world can match Cancun for its combination of sophisticated amenities, stunning beauty, and spellbinding archaeological treasures. A mega resort with restaurants, outings and nightlife designed to please every taste, Cancun combines the best of Mexico and the Caribbean in one tidy package. While some may fault the resort for its gilded sandbox image and unabashed commercialism, there is no denying the area's seductive appeal.

*Some say Cancun is a gilded sandbox.*   Photo by Chuck Fishman.

## HOTELS

Each new hotel strives to outdo the last in luxury and esthetic amenities — swimming pools encircle the grounds like loving arms or bedazzle the eye by seeming to drop off into the sea; lobbies are extravagant shopping malls. With a strip of approximately 100 hotels, the choice is endless and hopelessly subjective.   These are personal favorites:

***Fiesta Americana Condesa Cancun***—one of the newest and liveliest on the row, this property features three horseshoe-shaped towers surrounded by lush, tropical foliage, cascading waterfalls and swimming pools.  The hotel's distinctive

*The Fiesta Americana Cancun has everything.*

architectural design creates an intimate ambience beginning with what must be the largest palapa in Mexico—115 ft. high—shading the expansive lobby to the hotel's extraordinary swimming pool with a swim-up bar and restaurant accented by a l35 ft. long waterfall.
(1-800-FIESTA-1)

***Camino Real Cancun*** —The modified pyramid structure designed by Ricardo Leoretta,

*A mega resort with the accent on fun.*   Photo by Chuck Fishman.

Mexico's most pre-eminent architect, seems to spring from the land.  Nothing's borrowed—no pseudo colonial, no Palm Beach deco, the evocative image being that of nearby Mayan ruins.  That sense of fantasy is further enhanced by a man made lagoon stocked with large turtles and exotic fish which meanders through the extensive grounds linking the Caribbean to the east with Nichupte Lagoon on the west.  Bordered almost entirely by water, the hotel has the feel of a private island with a sea or lagoon view guaranteed with each of its 292 rooms. (1-800-722-6466)

**Hyatt Cancun Caribe**—a replica of Chac-Mool, the Mayan messenger to the gods, gazes out to sea here—like any other sunbather.  And why not?  All 202 rooms in the crescent shaped high rise have a view of the Caribbean on one side, the lagoon on the other.  (1-800-233-1234).

**Omni Cancun Hotel**—one of the prettiest and most romantic of the state-of-the-art hotel complexes, with pink stucco walls and tile roofs, a charming blend of colonial and art deco.  The Omini also has one of the best shops in town—**Arodi**.  (1-800-THE OMNI)

**Fiesta Americana Cancun**—considered a "boutique" hotel among the highrises has an appealing "little Spanish town" feel to it.  One of the most affordable on hotel row, the Fiesta Americana Cancun has an excellent beach location, yet is adjacent to shops.  (1-800-FIESTA-1)

**Fiesta Americana Coral Beach**—at the other end of the spectrum,  a mega-glamorous hotel with 1000 feet of powdery white beach front and a 660 foot long free form pool with three swim up bars.  Each of the 602 rooms is a luxurious suite with a large jacuzzi, private balcony and step down living room. (1-800-FIESTA-I).

# RESTAURANTS

From continental dining, to fresh seafood, to traditional Mayan cuisine, Cancun offers a truly dazzling assortment of dining options with more than 200 restaurants from which to choose.  One way to begin an evening is to "hotel hop," taking in several convivial happy hours, a variety of live music and some incredibly beautiful settings.   Add to this sunset cocktail or dinner cruises, Mexican-themed Fiesta Nights and Las Vegas- style floor shows.  Competition is fierce among Mexico's resorts so  Cancun's independent restauranteurs as well as the major hotels vie with one another to keep their city in the forefront.

As many times as I've visited Cancun my favorite restaurant remains the **Blue Bayou** in the Hyatt Cancun Caribe.  The "blackened" lobster is divine and with it one of the great soups of the world, cream of artichoke with oysters.  A special treat is the "Sexy Coffee" after dinner—a warm and sensuous blend flamed at your table.   An orchestra plays for dancing,  service is impeccable. Yes, it's expensive, but worth it.

*Mariachis are part of the ambience at the Blue Bayou.*
Photo by Chuck Fishman.

Horst Walther, food and beverage director of the Hyatt Cancun Caribe shared the recipe for his award winning soup.

### OYSTER and ARTICHOKE SOUP

3/4 pound of butter
1T olive oil
1/2 cup flour
1/2 cup chopped onion
1/2 chopped celery
1/2 chopped green onion
1 pint chicken stock
1/2 cup sliced fresh mushrooms
3 cup cooked artichoke hearts
1 pint milk
2 dozen oysters
2 egg yolks
1/2 cup stock from cooked artichokes

In a saucepan melt the butter, add olive oil, stir in flour and cook until smooth. Add carrot, onion, celery, green onions and cook until vegetables are tender. Place mixture in a food processor, add I/4 of the chicken stock and puree until smooth.

Saute mushrooms in butter until tender. Add them with artichoke hearts and their liquid to vegetable mixture. Stir in milk and remaining chicken stock. Cook over low heat 5 minutes. Soup may be prepared a day ahead to this point. Add oysters and cook 10 minutes over a low heat.

In a small bowl, combine egg yolks with 1/2 cup hot soup and stir rapidly into soup. Cook over low heat 5 minutes. If soup seems too thick, additional stock may be added.   Serves 8.

Also to consider:  two marvelous selections at the Fiesta Americana Condesa Cancun's award winning ***Mirage Restaurant*** , the soft shelled crab (tender crab meat flavored with a hint of fresh garlic and served in  its original shell) and the mango sorbet. Both are creations of Jaime Madrano, the executive chef.

*Beyond the high-rises the mysterious jungle beckons.*

Another excellent dining option in the same hotel is **Rosato Ristorante** specializing in northern Italian cuisine.

Also in the same deluxe category is the Camino Real's, **Calypso** with its spectacular sea view. Not to be missed here is the lobster gazpacho soup.

At the other end of the spectrum pricewise is **Restaurantes Los Almandros** at Avenue Bonampak in Cancun City. This is one of those rarities in Cancun—an authentic Mexican restaurant. The building approximates a mammoth Mayan palapa. Background music is lively but not too loud, the glassed in kitchen immaculate.

A colorful menu shows pictures of the native specialities with explanations in English. Two can spend under $15 for a dinner that includes *sopa de lima* (lime and chicken soup), *poc-chuc* (broiled pork meat with tomato, onion, coriander and oranges) served with black beans and tortillas plus three bottles of *Montejo*, a hearty local beer.

## ON THE SEA

The ocean extends in bands of color: first jade, then turquoise, then the blue-green of sub-surface coral reefs and finally the deep marine blue of the open sea. If you've ever wanted to learn or perfect a water sport, Cancun is tailormade. The clear, year-round warm waters coupled with temperatures in the

80's afford perfect conditions. Most hotels have centers where windsurfers, sailboats, kayaks, scuba and snorkeling equipment may be rented and with English speaking instructors on hand to give fast and easy lessons to anyone desiring them.  Add to this a wide selection of deep-sea fishing opportunities.

But most unique of all is magical **Contoy Island**, Cancun's hidden treasure, a place where you can explore a bird sanctuary and enjoy an exquisite beach in perfect peace. That means no vendors selling "silver", no realtors hawking time shares.  Arrangements may be made at your hotel to visit this wild preserve where one can snorkel, explore pristine nature trails, see and photograph rare marine birds.  Most trips include a seaside barbeque.

*Trying on treasure at the Hyatt Cancun Caribe.*  Photo by Chuck Fishman.

## DAY LIFE

The Cancun area was the home of the ancient Maya, one of the first shores touched by the Spanish conquistadors, and the refuge of maurauding pirates.  To get a sense of this rich and varied history, a visit to the **Museo Arqueologica de Cancun** is a must.  The small but well appointed museum is located next to the Convention Center.  Hours:  10 a.m. to 5 p.m., Tuesday through Saturday.  To see one of the Mayan ruins first hand, visit **Pok-Ta-Pok**, at the 12th hole of the Robert Trent Jones Golf Course.

**Shopping:**  Most shopping safaris begin at **Plaza Caracol**, the largest and most elaborate of Cancun's shopping malls.  It's difficult to resist the elegant Mexican designer clothes at **Boutique Soqui**, the silver at **Los Castillo**  and the brass and copper or enamel belts and jewelry at **Las Palmeras.**   The **Costa Blanca Shopping Center**  in the Zona Rosa has two specialty shops well worth checking out: **La Iguana**, a mad menagerie of creatures made from papier-mache or brass and copper; and **Mayart**  with reproductions of museum sculpture plus carved masks and temple rubbings.  In most shops prices are established, but bargaining is expected at the booths at the **Ki-Huic** market downtown and **Coral Negro**  by the Convention Center.  Stores open between 9  and 10 a.m., close for siesta at 1; then open again around 5 with final closing at 9.


# NIGHT LIFE

The action in Cancun doesn't stop when the sun sets.  In fact, most say it heats up.   While several splashy discos dominate the scene, nearly every hotel offers live lobby music ranging from reggae to salsa to flamenco guitar.   You can begin your evening with a wonderful meal, dining on anything from regional specialties to prize winning international cuisine.

After dinner options might include a cocktail on a seaside terrace or dancing the night away at a disco.   Try the mysterious grotto like mystique of **Dady'O,** or the surreal special effects of **Christine**  (pink fog, silver mist, thousands of balloons) or the latter day pirate raunch at **Carlos 'n Charlie's** dancing pier.

Ready for the ruins?  An evening at any of the above should limber you up for the big climb.


# TIDBITS

Cancun is serviced by American, Continental, Northwest and Mexicana airlines. Its area code is 98, prices tend to run high and the dress is casual chic.

# THE CANCUN-TULUM CORRIDOR

Beguiling as Cancun can be, hopefully you'll view it as the perfect departure point, the first hint of more exciting adventures to come. Across the blue lagoon from glossy hotels and sleek condos, the mysterious jungle beckons.

Given Cancun's phenomenal success as a tourist destination, it's no surprise that the

*Folk buses take guest to Xcaret.*

pristine Quintana Roo coastline to the south is slated for development. Scattered hotels and condominium complexes already offer isolated glimpses into the future. Still, for the time being, the area remains largely untouched. Travelers along Highway 307 can still discover a beach to call their own. This stretch of well paved road—some 130 km. of it—from Cancun to Tulum offers a tantalizing array of options.

# XCARET

For ten centuries Mayan pilgrims stopped at Xcaret ("small inlet") to purify themselves in the turquoise waters of the sacred cenote, a natural well of

*The Mayan Arch of Labna has been duplicated at Xcaret.*

fresh water peculiar to the region, before embarking in dugout canoes for Cozumel, the sacred shrine of the goddess Ixchel.

Today Xcaret, 35 miles south of Cancun, is an eco-archaeological park, its centerpiece an underground river that leads swimmers through a series of spectacular caverns. Snorkelers can explore an idyllic inlet that teems with tropical fish, archaeology buffs can watch the ongoing excavation of a working site, while others swim with the dolphins, ride horses through the surrounding jungle or bask on the sugar-sand beach. The complex includes several restaurants, a snack bar and picnic grounds.

Though Xcaret is an easy drive by rental car, one may also take one of a

*Beneath the lagoon at Xel-ha is a vast labyrinth at Xcaret*

fleet of brightly painted "folk buses" which depart very day at 9 and 10 a.m. from the entrance of Playa Caracol, next to the Coral Beach Hotel.

# XEL-HA

This exquisite lagoon—a vast labyrinth of underwater caves and tunnels—was once sacred to the Maya. Today it's a national underwater park covering approximately ten square miles with a natural aquarium and a shallow lagoon perfect for swimming and snorkeling. Walkways with viewing platforms, surrounded by lush vegetation, circle the lagoon affording pedestrians with an opportunity to see the multi-hued marine life below. Some fifty or so different species of fish in every imaginable hue cry out to be admired.

But even if not a swimmer, you need only slip into the cool, crystal water and wait for the fish to come to you. It's an incredible experience. Besides, not only are the fish surprisingly gregarious, but the Caribbean's warm waters are cooled by currents from underground rivers—a refreshing break. The park also has a small zoo, gift shops, restaurants, shower facilties and a rental shop for snorkels.

Not far from the lagoon is an archaeological site recently opened to the public. The ruins here suggest that Xel-Ha was a Mayan port city; frescoes are well preserved, the wall paintings even clearer than the ones at Tulum.

Bus tours from Cancun to Tulum usually make a stop at Xel-Ha on the way

*Tulum — the most important of the coastal Mayan sites.*

back to Cancun.  This is a strong argument for renting your own car so that you can reverse the itinerary.    Both sites can get very crowded.

# TULUM

Mounted on a summit of limestone cliff 40 feet high, lies the fortress city of Tulum, one of the last strongholds of a dying civilization.

A strange fate enshrouds Tulum.  In 1517 when first spotted by a passing Spanish ship, the city was a showplace, every stone inscribed with brilliant paintings and carvings—stark white, deep red or vibrant blue backgrounds covered with multi-colored stylized figures.  At the top of the largest building — the castillo, or castle a beacon fire blazed.

The fall of of this fabulous city occurred fifty years after the Spanish invasion of the Yucatan Peninsula yet was unrelated to it.  The Maya inhabitants simply left the area, leaving their once bustling city  silent, deserted. Today the silence is broken.  Tulum is the most visited archeological site in the Maya world.

The origins of Tulum stretch back to earliest time, but the majority of its structures date from the Postclassic or "decadent" period, around 1000 A.D. For this reason, the site tends to get short shrift from classicists who're inclined to write it off as "bourgeois." This attitude ignores the strength of the architecture—said to have inspired Frank Llyod Wright—and the organizational skill of the people who built these massive structures without the use of draft animals or metal cutting tools.

Tulum's buildings share a unique architectural characteristic. Its walls are slightly flared upward. This inverted pyramid effect creates areas of light and shadow that not only enhance the sculptured relief but protect the painted stucco moldings from rain water.

Originally called Zama, or "place of the dawning," the city that became Tulum was the most important of the coastal ceremonial sites. It was from the sea beyond these walls that the sun rose each morning and began its sacred dance across the skies. The effect must have been awe inspiring.

Today there's very little silence or solitude to be had in Tulum at tour time, yet the setting is still stunning. Mounted on the edge of a cliff, the abandoned city towers above one of the most uniquely beautiful beaches in the world. Yes, it *is* possible to dodge the crowd, to find a quiet corner to yourself and to meditate upon the mysteries of the Mayan world — or your own world.

*Tulum.* Photo by author.

## CANCUN TIPS

The pleasure of this trip will be greatly enhanced by renting a car and driving there yourselves rather than taking a tour bus. Ask your hotel to pack a picnic lunch. Though many of the ruins have recently been roped off, nothing can destroy the beauty of the view or beach. Also consider hiring a guide for twenty minutes or so to point out the highlights which now are easily missed by lack of access.

Outside the site a few spiritual descendants of the pirates who once took refuge in the area operate a mini marketplace. If you're looking for replicas of Pre-Columbian ceramics, you'll find an excellent selection. Also featured are jewelry, blankets, embroidered dresses at better prices than in Cancun. Bargaining is expected. Offer half the stated price and go from there.

**Sian Ka'an Biosphere Reserve**—While Cancun is Mexico's primo Caribbean resort, the coastline of Quintana Roo, home of the Sian Ka'an Biosphere Reserve, is Mexico's Caribbean wilderness.

**Sian Ka'an**, which, in the Mayan language, means "where the sky is born", consists of 1.3 million acres of largely undisturbed tropical forest, wetlands and marine habitats. The area's shallow bays comprise Mexico's most important spiny lobster nursery. Scattered keys in the bays provide nesting sites for thousands of water birds including woodstorks, frigate birds and boat-billed herons. Rare jabiru storks nest in the reserve and the beaches provide safe havens for endangered sea turtles.

Manatee, monkeys, jaguars, ocelots and crocodiles are among the species protected in the habitat, which was established in 1986. Approximately 1,200 plant species can also be found in the reserve. The landscape includes beaches, dunes, marshs, savannas, lagoons and large tracts of tropical lowland forests. Sian Ka'an's barrier reef is one of the longest in the world.

Fewer than 1,000 people—mostly Mayan fishermen and farmers—live in the buffer zones of the reserve. Although hunting is regulated by the government, the Mayans, who only hunt for self-consumption and religious offerings, enforce their own rules. They believe that the forests and animals have a spiritual "owner" who permits each person to hunt only a limited amount of animals during the year. When a hunter reaches his quota, the "owner of the woods" advises him to stop killing. Should he disobey, according to legend, the hunter will suffer some catastrophe.

Tours are available through Amigos de Sian Ka'an0, a non-profit, Mexican conservation organization. Information may be obtained by calling 84-95-83 or 87-30-80.

*Drawing of the Castle at Tulum by Frederick Catherwood, 1839.*

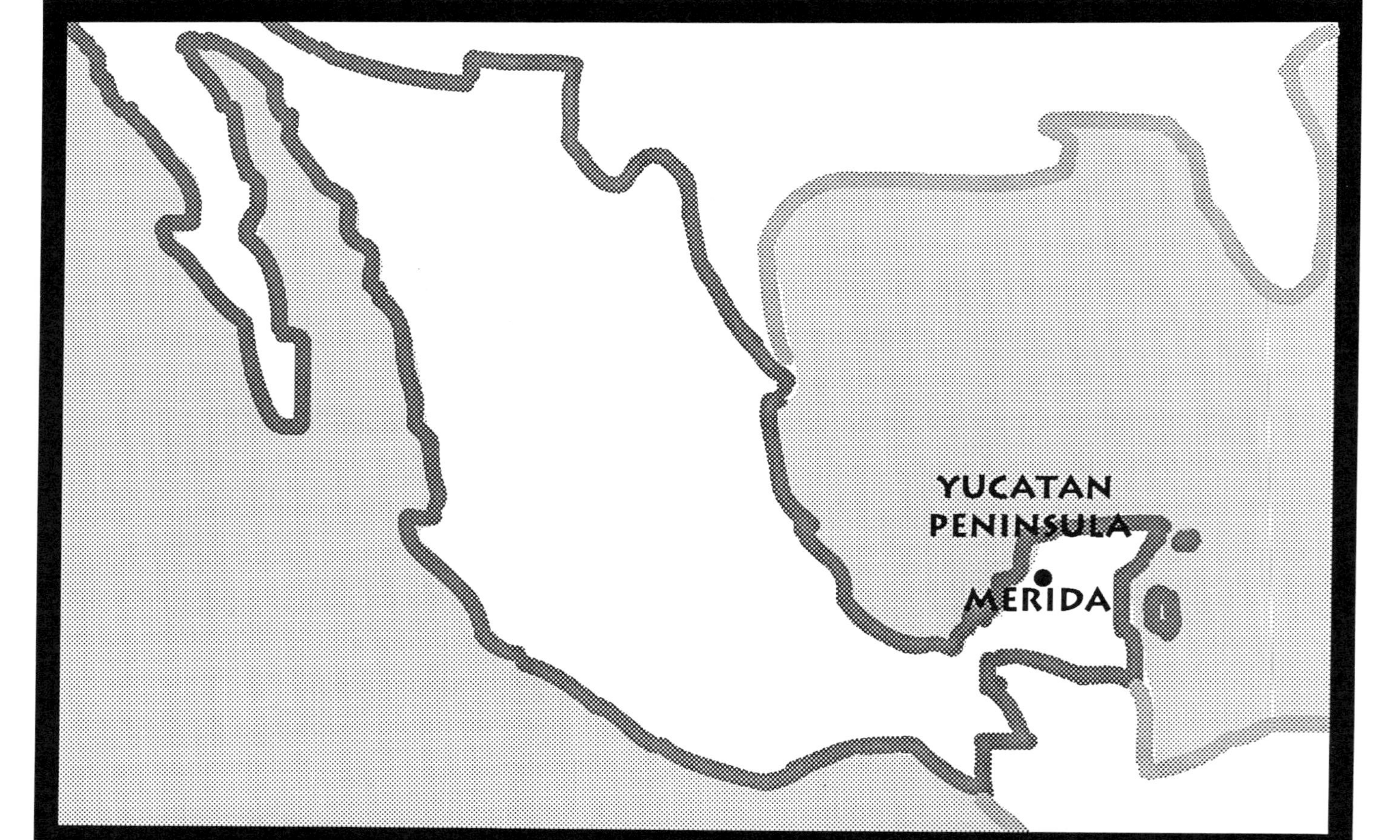

YUCATAN
PENINSULA
MÉRIDA

# THE MAYAN EXPERIENCE
## THE HEART OF THE MAYAS

A beautiful North American journalist was once invited to Mexico in recognition of an investigative series she'd written championing the cause of a Latino boy unfairly condemned to death. Fatefully, it would seem, she caught the eye of the handsome governor of the war torn state of Yucatan.

The governor commissioned a song for her—*La Peregrina*, the Wanderer. There were flowers, serenades, rides about the town in horse-drawn carriages. He told her of the land reforms he'd undertaken enabling the Maya Indians to enjoy a share in the vast wealth landowners had amassed at their expense.

It seemed they were made for each other. He proposed. She accepted. The journalist had returned to her native San Francisco to prepare for their wedding when she received word that her lover had been murdered by a cabal of jealous landowners.

His love ballad had ended:

> *"When you leave my palm groves*
> *and my land,*
> *Traveler of the enchanting face,*
> *Don't forget—don't forget—-my*
> *land,*
> *Don't forget—don't forget—my*
> *love."*

La Peregrina did not forget. Never marrying, she chose instead to devote the rest of her life to the fostering of Mexican culture.

The governor, Felipe Carrillo Puerto, known today as the Abraham Lincoln of Mexico, was shot by firing squad on January 3, 1924. The journalist was *New York Times* correspondent Alma Reed, who died in 1966. Reed's last request was that she be buried beside her lover, and that's where she rests today.

*Felipe Carrillo Puerto*

## MERIDA

The place, the city of their love, is Merida, capital of the state of Yucatan.

Evidence of a romantic past is very much a part of Merida's lively present. You feel it at night, when the white city turns to antique ivory in the lamplight. You feel it when you hear the carriages clopping around the plaza and down the broad Paseo de Montejo and most of all you feel it when they sing the love song *La Peregrina* — you can hear the words almost any night.

*Merida, the "White City."* Photo by T. Pappas.

At the hub of the Yucatan Peninsula, Merida was — until the advent of Cancun — the traditional gateway to the domain of the Maya. It remains a principal tourist headquarters and hotel oasis, retaining an ancient grace unlike any other city in Mexico.

It took fifteen years for Conquistador Francisco de Montejo to subdue the native inhabitants of Yucatan. He celebrated his final victory by "founding" Merida in January 1542. The stone buildings of the ceremonial center of T'ho reminded the conquering Spaniards of the Roman ruins in Merida, Spain. After they'd leveled the Maya stronghold, enslaved the local Indians, putting them to work building churches, mansions, and government buildings with limestone blocks from the ruins of their former temples and palaces, the conquistadors named their recycled city Merida.

Naturally, one of the first residences constructed was Montejo's. Generations of the conqueror's direct descendants lived in the grand mansion until 1980 when the family residence became a bank. Today you can admire the sweeping stairway, enormous courtyard and floors made of Carrara marble while cashing your checks there — Banamex gives the best rates in town. Outside, the Montejo family crest — a foot firmly planted on the head of a Mayan slave — repeats across the length of the building.

The natives, possibly because of their geographic remoteness, consider themselves Yucatecos first, Mexicans second. Nowhere is this individuality more apparent than in Merida. Their roots reaching more toward Europe than Mexico, the independent Meridians look and act different from their not-so-near neighbors. That marvelous montage of diverse cultural influences is obvious as you explore the colonial gem that is Merida.

The Regional Museum of Archaeology, one of Mexico's finest provincial museums, is a natural starting place and a delight on many levels.  The building, reminiscent of a giant wedding cake, is Montejo.  This eight-block, tree-lined thoroughfare, with its extravagant monuments and palaces—a street patterned after a Parisian boulevard—is one of the most beautiful in all of Mexico, perhaps the world.

The Plaza de la Independencia, Merida's town square, is the perfect place

*Rides in horse drawn calesas are popular with everyone in Merida.*

one of the beautiful mansions built along the fashionable Paseo Montejo by sisal barons during the nineteenth century when the fields of Yucatan furnished fiber to the world.  Here you'll see ancient treasures—displays of jewelry, artifacts, insightful explanations of how the Maya lived, along with an overview of the surrounding ruins which have made Yucatan famous throughout the world.

After exploring the museum, you'll want to take a carriage ride up the Paseo de to re-orient yourselves.  Prior to Montejo's conquest, the square was the site of the great temple of H-Chumcaan, surrounded on all sides by pyramids and lesser pyramids.  Today the only traces of them are the walls of the cathedral close by.

On the second floor of the neighboring Government Palace is a hallway with heroic murals.  They describe the grand sweep of historic events on the Yucatan Peninsula starting with the birth of the Maya and continuing through their victories and defeats, their gods, heroes and villains to the twentieth century.    Felipe Carrillo Puerto is prominently featured; Alma Reed left discreetly to the imagination.

*Alma Reed*

# CHICHEN ITZA

It was this ill-fated governor who first saw the potential tourist revenue in the ruins of **Chichen Itza**, a ninety-minute drive from Merida.   He not only invited archaeologists and reporters to visit the ancient Maya site but also built a road to take them there.  In 1923, while visiting the area with a team from the Carnegie Institute — the first scientific expedition to the area — Alma Reed

discovered that an earlier adventurer, Edward Thompson, had uncovered millions of dollars in gold and jade from a legendary sacred well in Chichen Itza and then smuggled them out of the country.   Her scoop made worldwide headlines, triggering legal battles only recently resolved.  Reed's tales of Maya mysteries and descriptions of sacred wells, plumed serpents, and towering pyramids established the Yucatan forever as a tourist mecca.

Today some resent what they view as Chichen Itza's commercialism.  They're disdainful of the colorful T-shirts and dresses, the families selling onyx chess sets and carvings.  Personally, I rather like all the activity, subdued yet vital.   Besides, Chichen Itza was both a commercial center and a ceremonial one, and Ek Chuah, the Mayan god of trade, was one of the most venerated deities. It's easy to forget that this great plaza, now a monument of cold stone, once pulsated with vendors hawking condiments, jewels, and slaves surrounded by cages of hairless dogs, birds speaking Mayan, and chattering monkeys.

Areas would also have been set aside for story tellers. Sadly, none are around today to tell us what really happened at Chichen Itza. The city reached a zenith between AD 300 to 900 and continued to thrive until its mysterious abandonment in 1250 —though it remained the site of religious pilgrimages until after the conquest.

The most impressive and intriguing structure on the site is the **Temple of Kukulkan**.  It's also the most romantic. Legend has it that Felipe Carrillo

*Chichen Itza with the Pyramid of Kukulkan in the foreground.*  Photo by C.J. Marrow.

Puerto had the temple on top filled with rose petals and it was here that he and Alma Reed made love for the first time.

Inside this massive pyramid, a narrow stairway ascends to a sacrificial altar encrusted with jade, thought to be Chinese in origin.  How did it get there?

Equally mysterious is the image of a giant snake, a shadow, that traverses the pyramid at exactly the same time each year.  At the spring and fall equinoxes, the shadowy reptile slithers along the balustrade and disappears just as the sun sets.  On March 21st and September 21st, for thirty-four minutes, the snake phenomenon created by a play of light and shadow moves from the top of the pyramid to its base.  For the ancients it must have been the ultimate fertility symbol.  The sun god had penetrated the earth.  It was time to plant.

Near the temple is the **Sacred Well,** where it is said that the most nubile but innocent maidens of the country were forced to sacrifice their lives to the rain god, Chac. The large pool of lusterless green water, like a gaping wound in the heart of the forest, was the source of the vast treasure smuggled out of Chichen Itza.  Edward Thompson, Alma Reed's unfortunate confidant, had guessed — rightly — that if the rain god exacted human tribute, the well's muddy bottom might yield offerings of another sort.  He smuggled out a a fortune in artifacts and jewelry culled from the pool's depths.  Today, visitors tiptoe to the edge, gaze wonderingly into the murky depths with a sort of fearful curiosity, then draw back to talk in instinctively lowered tones.  A sense of mystery — even of horror — pervades.

Among the most intricate and beautiful carvings at the site are those found on the walls of the **Nunnery,** an excellent example of Late Classic architecture. It was here that the English scholars, Alfred Maudslay and Annie Hunter, camped during the 1880's. Unfortunately, the two had hardly arrived before they each came down with malaria. A peculiarity of the disease is that it frequently strikes on alternate

*A temple with a view, Kukulkan's pyramid.* Photo by C.J. Marrow.

days. On one day a patient runs a high fever, while on the next he's exhausted but otherwise normal. As it turned out, Alfred and Annie were afflicted on opposite days, enabling them to care for each other in shifts. With the nearest water located a mile round trip up and down a precarious trail, it couldn't have been easy. Somehow the devoted couple put in six months in this fashion, all the while mapping, drawing and photographing the ruins.

Another remarkable pair were Alice and Augustis Le Plongeon, who despite a revolution going on around them, took more than 500 photographs of Chichen Itza and made 20 careful sheets of mural drawings. Precursors of Carlos Castaneda, the couple ventured deep into the jungle, encountering natives who practiced mesmerism, induced clairvoyance and used "magic mirrors" to predict the future.

More recent "legends" have evolved around the **Sweat Baths**. Did you see *Against All Odds?* If not, local guides will delight in briefing you on a plot that's steamy in more ways than one. Jeff Bridges and Rachel Ward got into the sensuous mood of Chichen Itza when they retired to the Sweat Baths for a torrid love scene. A rerun of this movie on your VCR does give an amusing, if slightly skewered view of the site. It's thought the Sweat Baths were once used for ceremonial purposes, probably by the participants who played the sacred ball game for whom the Mayas were famous. Today one can see the remains of a waiting room, a steam room, the oven and underground drainage canals.

If Chichen Itza seems too parklike for your tastes, there are other ruins outside the complex that wait to be explored in solitude. These are located in the area known as **Old Chichen**. To reach them, continue down the road to the south away from the main ruins and past the Hotel Hacienda Chichen, the original hacienda which Edward Thompson once bought for $75.

Follow the trail to the right. It isn't well marked, but that adds to the adventure. Most who venture here agree that the experience is worth the effort. After a half hour or so with the madding crowd far behind, you begin to have a sense of the mystery that has drawn so many explorers to this remarkable area.

Soon you'll come upon two Atlantean figures supporting a door lintel which contains a hieroglyphic of the year 879 A.D., the only proven date in Chichen Itza. Beyond this is one of the most intriguing of the Old Chichen structures, the **Temple of the Phalli.** The unknown sculptor of the objects protruding from the temple walls leaves little doubt as to what he had in mind. It's assumed that this was a temple dedicated to fertility. Some believe that couples who wished to have children may have frequented the sanctuary.

# UXMAL

For some, the ceremonial site of **Uxmal**, an hour's ride south of Merida, is even more spectacular than Chichen Itza. Both the founding and the demise of Uxmal are shrouded in legend. Like Chichen Itza, the once powerful city state of Uxmal was abandoned. We know that it was built over at least five times. But why was it built even once? There's almost no water in the area.

The city which flourished between AD 800 and 1000, is a stunning example of classic Mayan architecture. At night, the sound-and-light show at the scene of the ruins dramatically highlights the intricate geometric patterns for which Uxmal's architecture is famous. But under any lighting conditions, the place is a marvel: there were no mines on the Yucatan peninsula, no metal tools used in construction, and no draft animals; the wheel as we know it uninvented.

That the architecture of Uxmal should frequently be likened to the Acropolis seems appropriate for a ghost town haunted by parallels to Helen of Troy. Sac-Nicte, princess of Mayapan, was beautiful. Canek, the young king of Chichen Itza, handsome. When they met by chance it was love at first sight. Unfortunately there was one major drawback: the princess was engaged to the King of Uxmal.

Perhaps Sac-Nicte pleaded with her father. But her romantic preferences would have been of little importance to him. As the daughter of a king, hers was a marriage of state. The agreement had been made, a slight to the King of Uxmal unthinkable. The wedding plans continued and finally the nuptial ceremony at Uxmal.

People bearing lavish gifts came from all corners of Yucatan. Then a murmur arose. Where was King Canek's tribute? Where, for that matter, was King

*The Mayan site of Uxmal has been likened to Greece.* Photo by C.J. Marrow.

Canek?  The three-day marriage ceremony began.  One day of festivities, then a second day.  Princess Sac-Nicte walked through the rituals as though in a trance.  Then on the third day King Canek arrived with a large army and literally swept her off her feet.  In the confusion, the lovers eloped to Guatemala leaving the three armies of Uxmal, Mayapan and Chichen Itza to fight it out among themselves.

Today the **Great Pyramid** dominates the archeological site, stirring the imagination despite the forbidding, unapproachable aspect it presents from every angle.  A flight of 118 steps leads to its two platforms.  A chain was added in 1865 to facilitate the Empress Carlota's climb, and many are grateful for it today.  The pyramid is actually five superimposed temples, each built over the other, a synthesis in stone of centuries of continual occupation.

There's very little eroticism in Mayan art or architecture.  Uxmal appears to be an exception.  Ornamenting the building ironically named the **"Nunnery,"** is a frieze of naked men and the **Governor's Palace** contains a phallus of stupendous proportions.  Not far away (near the **House of the Old Woman**) is a sacred grove of stone known as the **Phallus Collection**.  Some are erect, others fallen, a kind of petrified forest of fertility.  And that's really what it's all about.  Fertility was all important in this drought-ridden agricultural area.

Nearby is the **Temple of the Phalli**, named for the unusual representations of this symbol.  Once they were used as water spouts to drain water.  Imagine the effect during the rainy season!

Which returns us to the crucial subject of rain.  The mask of Chac, the rain god is everywhere in Uxmal.  It pops out from friezes, fills in corners, and fits into the spaces above the doorways.  The god's features—sneering mouth,

*The Great Pyramid at Uxmal.* Photo by C.J. Marrow.

jutting fangs, horns, globular eyes, and snout—were designed to be awesome. And they are. Nearly one thousand years have passed since Uxmal was abandoned, but Chac remains very much alive. In this land of little rain, Mayan descendants believe that Chac continues to control their agricultural destiny. Despite the forcible efforts of the clergy to destroy him, Chac will not die, a deity still worshipped in secret ceremonies.

## A SPECIAL PLACE

After a few days of romancing the ruins, lovers most frequently head for the posh, polished resort of Cancun. An interesting alternative is **Celestun.** An easy ninety-minute drive from Merida, Celestun is destined for stardom in the high-priced tourist galaxy, but today it can be enjoyed practically for pennies. A luxury resort it's not, but for those who desire tropical beach atmosphere in an area that's really laid back, Celestun is paradise. It's one of those marvelous, good-for-nothing places that many of us dream about.

For true hedonists, doing nothing is what the village is all about. Its pristine beaches are often totally deserted. And Celestun is one of the few places in the western hemisphere where you can dependably see flamingo colonies. Bird watcher or no, the stunning sight of a group of flamingos melting together, a red-pink mist at the water's edge, is like nothing else in the natural world.

# WHEN IN MERIDA

The narrow streets of Merida were constructed for carriages, not trucks, taxis, cars or scooters. It can be noisy at night wherever you stay, so book a room as far from the street as possible.

## HOTELS

Favorite hotels are:

The **Casa de Balam** or House of the Jaguar.    A Moorish indoor courtyard transforms this well appointed, conveniently located hotel into an oasis of tropical foliage.  The staff is extremely pleasant and there's an efficient travel agency on the premises. (1-800-235-4079) .

**Hotel Calinda Americana** — white Corinthian columns, marble nymphs around a central fountain, crystal chandeliers, high molded ceilings — this former mansion helped to give Merida its "white city" reputation. An excellent band plays for dancing and a variety of Mayan dances are performed nightly. (1-800-228-5151).

**Montejo Palace**, a grand hotel on a grand boulevard, has a lively nightclub and a charming sidewalk cafe that spills out from the elegant veranda onto the Paseo de Montejo, a thoroughfare that has been compared to the Champs Elysees. (1-800-221-6509).

The most exciting architectural triumph to emerge on the Mayan scene since the Pyramid of Kukulkan is the elegant new **Hyatt Regency Merida.**  The 17-story, 300-room structure located in a quiet location close to the romantic Paseo Montejo has the whole town talking.

There's no question that Alma and Felipe would have loved *La Peregrina Bistro*, a cafe-style restaurant, named in her honor.  But surely they would also have enjoyed dropping into *Tutto Bene*, a themed fun-pub for entertainment and light meals.

The state of the art hotel also has a health club, outdoor swimming pool with landscaped sun deck and whirlpool, two outdoor tennis courts and a jogging track.

Reservations may be made by calling 1-800-233-1234.

**Portico del Peregrina** at 501 Calle 57, named for the song, is the kind of place that Alma and Felipe would have loved, a romantic restaurant with a courtyard bordered by arched walls, trailing vines and blossoms. The food is as good as the atmosphere is enticing.  It's so easy to get into the mood...... That absorbed couple at the next table....a reincarnation? Who can say.

*La Peregrina Room at the Hyatt Regency Merida.*

But a lively pair like Alma and Felipe would also have frequented **Pancho Villa's Follies** at 509 Calle 57.   The food is outstanding—try the lobster thermidor;  the decor pure funk, beaded lamps, a blaze of hot pink draperies clashing lustily with striped tablecloths.  And how could you not love a place where the bandido/waitors wear crossed cartridge belts and sombreros?  These guys are friendly, funny, nice and, that marvel in Mexico—fast.  The music's lively, the ambience upbeat. Photos of Pancho and his cronies amusingly macho.

Merida's an excellent shopping town with opportunities everywhere.  Many of the charming exhibits at the **Museum of Popular Art** are for sale.  Two other favorites are **La Canasta** (Calle 60, No. 500) and **El Paso** (corner of 60 and 59).  Both have a wide variety of distinctive jewelry, smart and wearable adaptatons of exotic clothing as well as unusual artifacts, well made and reasonably priced.

There's an outdoor concert every night of the week at one of Merida's many parks. Thursday night at **Santa Lucia Square** on Calle 60 is a particular delight. Hooks—twenty-two of them—where horses were once tied, remind the visitor that this was a stage stop for those arriving or departing the city.  Just across the street is a small stone chapel, dappled and gray, built some four hundred years ago for the use of mulattos and blacks brought to Yucatan as slaves by the conquistadors.

But back to Thursday evening when the place comes alive again.  An orchestra of guitars and brass begins to play.  Women in *huipals* and men in white cotton suits appear before the floodlit wedding cake facade of white arches that partially enclose the square.  They dance with trays balanced on their heads, they dance as matadors and bulls, they dance with woven ribbons.  It's very pretty and colorful; a wonderful place to catch the flavor of Meridian life as it was and  as it still remains.

Santa Lucia Square is also notable on Sundays as flea market.

To get a sense of just how good the good life really was during Merida's heyday, consider a trip out to **Hacienda Yaxcopoil** on Highway 261, the Merida-Uxmal Road.    Yaxcopoil, a Mayan word meaning "the place of the green alamo trees, combines the three great periods of  Yucatan history:  the Mayan era, the Spanish colonial period, and the boom years of the sisal cultivation cultivation during the late nineteenth and early twentieth centuries.  A colonial mansion built on the ruins of a miner ceremonial center, the estate was acquired in 1864 by Don Donaciano Garcia Rejon and his wife, Dona Monica Galera, ancestors of the present owner.

The 22,000 acre estate, one of the grandest of its time, is in great demand as a location for movies and television documentaries.  No question about it, the hacendados of old really knew how to live.  Today — when not overrun by TV cameras, stars and gofers — the place has a melancholy "haunted" quality.  It is difficult not to hear the echo of long ago laughter in the grand salon.

# AT THE ARCHAEOLOGICAL SITES

## HOTELS

**Hacienda Chichen**, a seventeenth century hacienda incorporating some of the Maya stones taken from nearby Chichen Itza, is a hotel that oozes history.  This was originally the home of Edward Thompson, Alma Reed's confidant, and the adjoining cottages are named for early archaeologists who lived there while excavating the site.

Another personal favorite is the **Hotel Mayaland**, which combines colonial architecture with art deco.  The grounds, literally a botanical garden, are dotted with cottages built like Mayan bungalows.  Inside,  guests sleep under mosquito netting, but in a bed, no longer a hammock.  The furniture is massive and exquisitely carved; there's a distinct movie-set feeling.  Not surprisingly, the place is a favorite of film stars, as well as presidents, dictators, and royalty.

Night time entertainment narrows down to the Sound and Light Show at Chichen Itza or strolling about the nearby village of Piste where there are always promenaders and often dances in the square.  Cap either with a bit of stargazing. After all, that's what the astronomical ceremonial site of Chichen Itza was all about.

At Uxmal, **Hacienda Uxmal** has delicious vibes.  Built originally as a headquarters for the archaeologists excavating the site more than sixty years ago, the hotel has been well maintained.  The large, airy rooms with their blocky 1930s furniture and ceiling fans, are built around an expansive courtyard.

Uxmal is even more remote than Chichen.  Aside from the Sound and Light Show, night life is left to the imagination.

*The grounds of the Hotel Mayaland.*  Photo by C.J. Marrow.

At Celestun, the best bets are **Hotel San Julio** and **Hotel Gutierrez,** both beachfront, clean, simple and cheap, but at present without telephone service.

## TIDBITS

According to a *Conde Nast Traveler* reader survey, the residents of Merida are the friendliest people in Mexico.

*   *   *

Merida is serviced by Continental and Mexican airlines.  Its area telephone area code is 99.

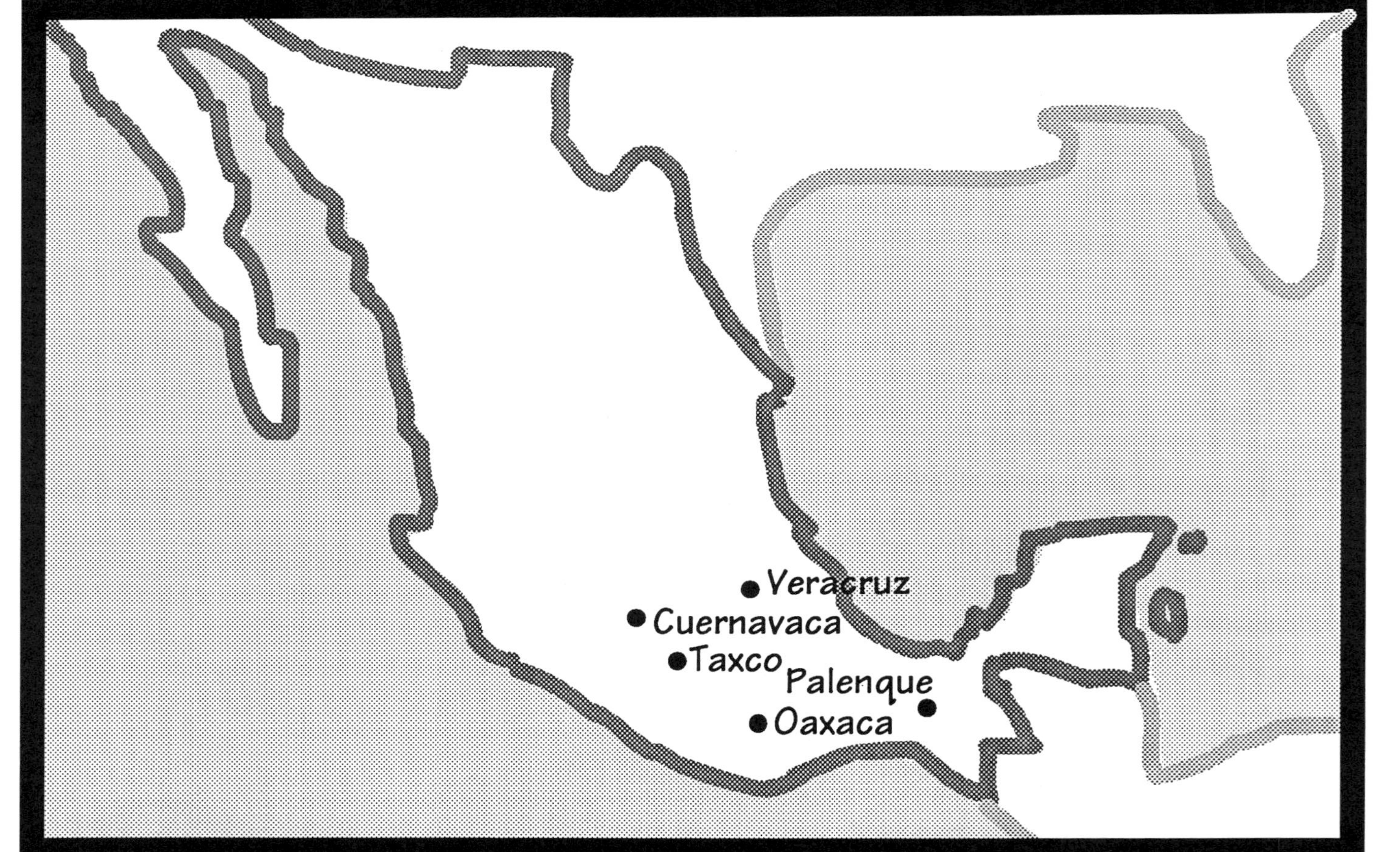

Veracruz
Cuernavaca
Taxco
Palenque
Oaxaca

## CUERNAVACA
### WHAT THEY DID FOR LOVE

It didn't take Cortes and his conquering compadres long to discover that vacation-wise, the Aztecs had a good thing going. From the earliest time, the court and anyone else who could manage it had been spending the chilly winters some sixty miles to the south over the mountains, but at a lower altitude, in a charming retreat with a perfect spring-time climate. The city was one of thirty awarded to Cortes by the Spanish king and he chose it as his retirement home.

The tongue-twister Nauhuatl name, *Cuahnahuac,* which meant "place of trees," sounded to his Spanish ears something like *cuerno de vaca,* "cow's horn." Not very poetic, but that's how today's town got its name. And that's also how this popular Mexican getaway got started. Today's Cuernavaca has a large permanent population of more than one million, but it's also a weekend retreat.

Climate is the town's largest attraction. About 2000 feet lower than Mexico City, Cuernavaca is an increasingly popular retreat for Mexico City's elite, a hangout for actors "between engagements," and home to a growing colony of retired North Americans who enjoy its springlike weather.

Drawn by the promise of the sun's caress, people go there for romance and relaxation. Cuernavaca has the distinction of having more pools per capita than any city, exceeding a million inhabitants, *in the world.* There aren't superlatives enough to describe yet another distinction — the restaurant in the Hotel Las Mananitas, judged to be one of the twenty-five best in the world.

*Cortes's palace was his statement.* Photo by the author.

A playground of the rich and famous even in pre-Columbian times, Cortes set the tone for the monument building that would follow in Cuernavaca. It was here that he chose to make his statement, erecting in 1530, the **Palace of Cortes**. It's rather difficult to imagine the conquistador and his Indian mistress, Malinche, playing hide and go seek among the dark corridors of the fortress-like structure.

Brutal conqueror that he was, Cortes was a man of his times, and should be viewed in that context. This was a larger than life personality, the consummate "envelope stretcher" of his day. But, as we all know, power and glory are fleeting accolades. Today the palace is the *only* monument in Mexico to the Spanish imperialist who changed the course of its history. The final irony is that the official name of Cortes's colossal palace is the Nahuatl word, Cauhnahuac.

A regional museum containing fascinating remnants of Tlauican pyramid which provided the original building blocks for the palace, Cauhnahuac also houses some excellent antiques and fascinating memorabilia from the colonial period. There are also superb Diego Rivera murals that must have Cortes spinning in his grave, depicting as they do the artist's preoccupation with the "tote that barge, lift that bale" aspect of Mexican history.

*  *  *  *  *

The murals were commissioned by Dwight Morrow, generally conceded to be the first, and possibly most, humanitarian and enlightened ambassador sent by the United States to Mexico. Arriving on the scene in 1927 following the torment of the Revolution, Morrow awakened Mexican interest in regional handicrafts and probably did more than any man in this century to keep the industry from dying. Though *gringos* are rarely commemorated with street names, an exception was made in Morrow's case. There's a thoroughfare named for him one block off the *zocalo.*

Yet it was not Morrow but his daughter, Anne, who put Cuernavaca on the map. She frequently spent weekends in the town with her parents. And when she did, a shy young man with a world-famous name came to call. Miss Morrow eventually married him, becoming Mrs. Charles Lindberg.

*  *  *  *  *

*The gardens that silver built.* Photo by the author.

If Cortes's palace is a monument to dominance, the beautiful **Borda Mansion and Gardens** are a temple to silver. Joseph de la Borde was a wandering Frenchman who arrived on the scene in 1718 and struck it rich in the silver boom. Though the lucky vagabond changed his name to Jose de la Borda, he kept many of his fancy French ways; among them a penchant for gardens in the Louis XIV tradition. Like Cortes, Borda was intent on making a statement. Much of his fortune went into the creation of a private park, a showplace by the time he died in 1778.

But once again time proved a cruel leveler. Jose La Borda, one of the wealthiest men of his age, was reputed to have spent a million pesos on his gardens, yet by the time the Emperor Maximilian visited them in the 1860s, they'd fallen into ruin.

The crumbling verandas, statues and fountains overgrown with roses, lily pools choked with weeds and tangled groves of oranges and mangoes appealed to Maximilian of Austria, recently become Emperor of Mexico.

Architects and gardeners summoned from Mexico City soon returned the mansion and gardens to their original glory. A showplace once again, the country house became the Emperor's favorite retreat. "Here," he wrote his mother, "we lead a really tropical life, surrounded by handsome, friendly and loyal natives." Much of Maximilian's pleasure undoubtedly came from his liaison with one of them.

The legendary Concepcion Sedano was the beautiful Indian wife of one of the gardeners busily transforming the gardens.

One need not imagine how Maximilian's wife, Carlota, felt about that. The memoirs of Colonel Blanchot, a young captain in attendance, fill in the gaps: "Cuernavaca was poisoned for the Empress by the knowledge that, in those enchanted bowers dwelt an Armida who had cast a spell over her husband's volatile affections." The emperor's valet was less poetic, describing in detail a small door in the garden wall through which a nocturnal visitor could pass unseen into the Emperor's apartments.

It's said that Concepcion, today referred to as "La India Bonita," (the pretty Indian) gave birth to Maximilian's son in August 1866 and then died of grief a year later on hearing of the Emperor's execution. The child is thought to have been taken to France under the protection of the Bringas family, close friends of Maximilian's.

Carlota was not without consolation, or so the story goes. The royal couple was rarely in Cuernavaca at the same time. When in residence there, and in other places too, Carlota's devoted cavalier was the brilliant and daring Belgian commander, Lieutenant Colonel Baron Alfred Van de Smisson.

Many believe that a few months after Carlota's impassioned plea to Napoleon III on her husband's behalf, she gave birth to Van de Smisson's child. Van de Smisson never married, rose to great heights in his profession and finally died by his own hand. The reputed child of their union, later General Weygand, was a French hero in both World Wars.

Curiously, during the World War I, a man claiming to be the son of Concepcion Sedano by the Emperor Maximilian, turned up in Paris where he was accused of spying for the Germans and was executed in 1917.    Ironically, in view of mysteries surrounding Maximilian's own birth, the man sentenced as a German spy may well have been the greatgrandson of Napoleon Bonaparte.

Don't miss the rather charming allusions to the double triangle in the form of murals that accent the mansion walls adjoining the gardens.  One depicts the emperor astride his prancing stallion, a riding crop jauntily at his hip, as he eyeballs the lovely Concepcion who returns his gaze demurely.

Another shows Maximilian and Carlota strolling in the garden. Ahead of them is Van de Smisson, gallantly kissing the hand of a lady-in-waiting. Maximilian seems to be calling his wife's attention to the action in an almost taunting fashion.

Cuernavaca's awesome chain of lifestyle statements contains a more and equally dazzling recent link. Barbara Hutton's exquisite **Sumiya** represents a monument to wealth and privilege, still another brilliant strand in the city's romantic history.

One of the great robber barons of the last century, Frank Winfield Woolworth, a former farm boy from upper state New York, opened his first five-and-ten-cent store in 1879.  Fifty years later there were 2,l00 red- fronted stores scattered across the United States, Mexico, England, France and Germany.

The favorite of his three daughters, Edna, beautiful but fragile,  married Frank Hutton, an ambitious stockbroker.  His handsomer brother, Ed, had married the most prominent heiress of the day, Marjorie Post, of Post Toasties fame.  The union of Edna and Frank resulted in one child, Barbara, born November 14, 1912.

It was a classic mismatch.  Frank was a heavy drinker and a compulsive wom-

*Sumiya—another monument to wealth and privilege—now a charming hotel.* Photo by the author.

anizer, Edna, a shy, homebody, very like her farm girl mother. Loneliness drove her into the arms of Bud Bouvier, the youngest brother of John Bouvier, eventually the father of Jacqueline Kennedy Onassis. The affair ended dismally when Bouvier married a younger woman, then sailed to France and the Great War.

Edna's revenge on both men was flamboyant and final. Donning her favorite evening gown—a straight chemise of white charmeuse, embroidered with gold irises from waist to hem—and a double strand of pearls, she consumed an adequate number of strychnine crystals. The body was discovered a few hours later by the four-year-old Barbara, thereafter often referred to as "the poor little rich girl."

At least that was *one* name for Barbara. The five and dime heiress described by Truman Capote as the "most incredible phenomenon of the century," was also known as the "million dollar baby." Someone even wrote a song about it.

December 1930 was *cold.* Four million people were out of work, forty percent of the nation's farms were mortgaged. It was inevitable that Barbara's debut, one month after her eighteenth birthday, would make headlines such as one in the *New York Evening Post.*

> ***Million dollar baby from the
> five & ten cent stores
> introduced to 'stuffed shirts'
> tonight at $100,000 bash.
> Rudy vallee will sing and
> Argentine dancers will
> perform amidst a bower of
> orchids and gardenias.***

It was the beginning of a gold-plated life. Hadn't Grandpa Woolworth told her, "'Barbara, you're going to be able to buy the world'"? She worked hard at it. Barbara's parties, clothes, jewelry and furs made her the envy of women around the world. As famous as Hemingway and Hitler in the '30s and '40s, her extravagances were fabled.

And so were her romances with royalty and celebrities. Originally a plumpish girl with large blue eyes and a winning smile, Barbara Hutton transformed herself into an aristocratic beauty whose looks alone would have attracted men. Her immense fortune was a sweetener that invariably turned sour.

There would be seven husbands: the Russian prince, Alexis Mdivani; the Danish count Kurt Haugwitz-Reventlow; the American movie star, Cary Grant (the press called them "Cash n' Cary"); the Lithuanian prince, Igor Troubetzkoy; the Dominican diplomat, Porfirio Rubirosa, former son-in-law of the dictator ("Rubi's" marriage to Barbara lasted 73 days and cost her $2 million); the German baron, Gottfried von Cramm, and finally Raymond Doan, a Vietnamese chemist, who Barbara elevated to the title of Prince Doan Cinh Na Champassak by purchasing the title for $50,000.

Barbara became Princess Doan in a civil ceremony by the pool at Sumiya, the Japanese mansion she had constructed in Cuernavaca. Spread over thirty acres of land within sight of the snowcapped peak of Popocatepetl, an inactive volcano reminiscent of Mount Fuji in Japan, the $3.2 million showplace had been completed in 1959, one of the most heralded architectural projects in Mexico.

The name Sumiya (The House on the Corner) was adopted from the original in Kyoto, built for an early day Japanese courtesan. However, Barbara's "house on the corner" looked more like an emperor's palace than a discreet lovenest. Materials, craftsmen and landscape gardeners had been imported directly from Japan and the house was filled with authentic fourteenth century imperial furniture, brightly colored silks, priceless Oriental screens, interior rock gardens and a jacuzzi for ten. Peacocks and cranes strutted about the grounds that included flower bedecked moats and bridges that served as passageways connecting one wing of the house to another. There was also a kabuki-style theater that seated forty where Barbara showed films — many of them sent by Cary Grant — and staged productions by Japanese dancers and musicians.

A guest tells of an evening when he was one of an audience of three watching sixty musicians perform on stage. The following day he sat on the lanai with Barbara as they watched twenty-five gardeners dressed as Japanese peasants working in a distant field.

Barbara married husband number seven on April 7, 1964. The civil ceremony was repeated the following afternoon for her friends. Both bride and groom wore Laotian finery—Barbara in a green caftanlike garment, Doan in a white suit, a colorful shawl slung over his shoulder. In true Buddhist fashion she wore gold rings on each of her big toes, bells around her ankles, and red paint on the soles of her feet.

Despite these concessions and the double sevens, the marriage was yet another failure. Barbara's health was going and so, unbelievably, was her money. She died of a heart attack on May 11, 1979. Ironically, it was the hundredth anniversary of the opening of the Woolworth stores.

In January 1994 the Sumiya opened its doors once again. Now known at as the **Camino Real Sumiya**, the former Hutton estate has been incorporated into Camino Real's modern l63-room hotel which contains many of the luxury trappings the heiress would have loved. The atmosphere is tranquil and lovely as an oriental painting: acres and of graceful gardens and fountains, picturesque walkways, sweeping views of snow-capped Popocatepetl. Dining is at the hotel's signature restaurant with a sprinkling of Japanese specialties. Traditional Mexican fare, an excellent poolside snack bar and a variety of lounges and bars are additional attractions. For reservations and information: 1-800 7-CAMINO.

# HOTELS ________________________________

In Spanish **Las Mañanitas** means "little mornings." Secluded behind vine-covered walls, the hotel of that name is perfect for treasured moments of lazy togetherness. A staff of 130 discreetly and smilingly sees to the needs of guests in the 22 rooms.

Eighth-generation royal crown African cranes stroll the undulating lawns of the five-acre estate which also includes a restaurant judged to be one of the twenty-five best in the world.

The common rooms are filled with whimsical paintings, the rooms decorated with fabulous antiques. The grounds contain Mexico's most important col-

*Las Mañanitas, tucked away behind stone walls in the town center, is an exquisite hotel on five acres of ground.* Photo by the author.

lection of Francisco Zuniga life-size bronze sculptures. Guests receive a key to an additional private garden and pool. The hotel is distinguished by being one of Mexico's two member hotels of Relais & Chateaux. Warning: Las Mananitas is pricey (but well worth it!) with no credit cards accepted. Ricardo Linares 107. Telephone: (73) 14-14-66.

The **Cuernavaca Raquet Club** at Francisco Villa 100 in the Rancho Cortes area, once a sumptuous privately owned estate, still attracts its share of Beautiful People. There are 59 rooms, many with fireplaces, parlors and terraces. The property includes nine hard surface tennis courts as well as a large pool and sauna facilities in a lush garden setting.
Telephone: (73) 11-24-00.

**Maximilian's,** at Galeana 125, is as romantic as it sounds. Recently renovated— with stunning results—the hotel oozes colonial charm. Telephone: (73) 18-20-04.

**Hacienda de Cortes** looks like a movie set and has served as one several times. A historic monument located in the Altacomulco area on the outskirts of town, the Cortes has 23 suites awash with flowers, fountains, art and history.
Telephone: (73) 15-88-44.

**Hosteria Las Quintas** is another popular retreat, a sprawling villa with 63 elegant rooms overlooking lush, perfectly kept, semi-tropical gardens with a large swimming pool.  Avenue Diaz Ordaz 107.  Telephone: (73) 18-39-49.


# RESTAURANTS

**La India Bonita**—a romantic restaurant named for Maximilian's sweetheart is located at Morrow l06-B, in "Casa Manana," the former home of Ambassador Dwight Morrow.  The atmosphere is Mexico at its most delightful.   Specialties on the exciting menu include pre-Hispanic favorites as well as excellent grilled meats.

**Las Mañanitas**—an unassuming door off Ricardo Linares l07 leads to unexpected pleasures hidden by plain, unadorned walls.  Guests relax on an elegant veranda overlooking lush gardens while flamingos, peacocks and cranes saunter by.  The menu is brought on a board, selections made and prepared while one sips  margaritas.   Having sampled nearly everything, including the luscious calves' brains, I can assure you that it's all marvelous.   Las Mananitas has been honored with the Travel Holiday Magazine Award every year since l968 and was selected by the Franklin Mint to be part of its "Demi-Tasse Collection" featuring the 25 best restaurants in the world.

**La Arboleda** in the Camino Real Sumiya.   Enjoy a drink in the bar, formerly Barbara Hutton's bedroom, then drift into the dining room overlooking a tranquil Japanese garden. For the adventurous, there's a dried seaweed omelette. The Vietnamese soup is excellent but I prefer the shrimp gazpacho, which to my taste is the best in Mexico.  *Pechuga de Pato a la Mandarina Mikan* (breast of duck marinated in tangerine sauce) is another delicious specialty.

**Marco Polo**, Hidalgo 26, across from the Cathedral, is a special favorite.  A fine Italian restaurant with a Mediterranean feel to it serves "trattoria Italiana" specialties prepared with home-made fresh pastas and delicious garlic sauces. It's particularly pleasant to dine there at night on the balcony overlooking the lighted cathedral.   A glass or two of excellent wine tends to invite introspection on the passage of time, the old stones below, the teeming street.....a kaleidoscope of centuries.

**Casa Grande,** Morelos Sur 807, in an elegant colonial mansion, serves  top quality Mexican food.  A guitar trio plays romantic music on weekends.  **Ma Mason** at Francisco Villa 58, is another lovely converted house with beautiful gardens. In addition to outstanding French cuisine, chef-owner Roberto Thomas uses Mexican ingredients to produce light, delicate sauces and luscious taste combinations.

## SHOPPING

The works of **Carlos de Villa** are showcased at his home/studio at Avenue Actores 111, Col. La Jolla. Villa, whose painting "Iconoclasta" hangs in the Jose Luis Cuevas museum in Mexico City, works in a style he calls "buffo hyperrealism," a mixture of surrealism and hyper-realism.

**Roman's Mexican Folk Art,** Ruiz de Alarcon 7, near the cathedral, is one of Cuneranavaca's pioneer handicraft shops with an exceptional selection of popular art from all over the country.

Three exciting stores are located directly across from Las Mananitas on Hidalgo street. **Primavera** offers top quality crafts and **Harms Joyeros** has truly gorgeous jewelry, paintings and sculpture. The sculpture of Victor Hugo Castaneda along with the works of a number of fine painters are displayed at **Citlalli.**

**Con Angel,** San Jeronimo 410, Col. Taltenango, is a special treat. An original boutique dedicated to angels offers fanciful replicas in every conceivable style, color and material—wood, clay, silver, ceramic, glass and bronze—on display in the beautiful colonial home of Patricia Garita. By appointment only, Monday to Saturday. Telephone: 13-22-08.

**Magadalena Cuillery**, an internationally known artist and designer, lends new dimension to silver with her exciting jewelry. Her workshop and showroom may be visited by appointment only. Telephone: 13-51-27.

**Bio-Art,** Blvd. Diaz Ordaz and Alta Tension, is a treasure trove of Mexican arts and crafts where truly exceptional items may be found along with authentic antiques. Across the street, check out **Girasol**, a branch of the popular chain specializing in sophisticated women's fashions incorporating unique Mexican motifs.

## SIGHTSEEING

A focal point of a visit to Cuernavaca is the **Cathedral** begun in 1529, ninety years before the pilgrims set foot on Plymouth Rock. The massive, fortresslike exterior is somewhat dour, possibly off-putting to some; but once inside the heavy wooden doors the interior comes as a revelation.

Revolutions and politics have robbed the church of its former elegance. The gold and grandure were long ago stripped away. In their place is a far more impressive simplicity.

The Cathedral also reveals a poignant story of the missionaries who stayed there before their departure from Acapulco to the Far East.  During the course of restoration in 1959 a mural was uncovered beneath layers of ravaged gilt.  It depicts the martyrdom of Mexico's saint, San Felipe de Jesus and his fellow missionaries; striking paintings executed by the mission Indians in 1597.

The fathers had been en route to the Philippines when blown off course by a hurricane.  When they arrived at last on the shores of Japan, the priests considered it an act of providence and began proselytizing.  The Japanese thought otherwise and warned them repeatedly to desist.  The zealots were eventually crucified.  The Indian's interpretation of the tragedy is touching as is their fanciful depiction of Japan, a land of which they knew nothing.

Another reason to visit the Cathedral is to attend the Mariachi Mass which is famous all over Mexico. It begins at 11 a.m. on Sundays, but you'd be wise to go early.  Corner of Hidalgo and Morelos.

**El Zocalo**—is actually a double plaza.  The larger is the Garden of Heroes (Hardin de Los Heroes), the smaller one the Garden of Juarez (Jardin Juarez) with an old fashioned bandstand.  Both are pleasant for strolling and people watching.

To find the **market**, walk five blocks north on Guerrero.  When you reach the footbridge crossing a ravine, turn right and there you are. Besides colorful produce, you'll find a variety of strawwork and ceramics.

Behind the Cathedral is the **Brady Museum**, housed in the former friar's convent of San Francisco.  The collection of art objects and antiques displayed there belonged to the late Robert Brady, who lived in the building until his death in 1986. The 1,300 items, ranging from pre-Hispanic to 20th century, include functional objects, modern paintings and toys.  A cantina, old style tiled Mexican kitchen and walled gardens make for an interesting place to visit. Seen by appointment, Thursday, Friday and Saturday.

## TIDBITS

A six lane toll highway links Cuernavaca with Mexico City.  Buses for Cuernavaca leave every hour on the hour from the southern bus terminal in Mexico City.  One could easily just come for lunch.  Delightful hotels, large and small, cater to the out-of-town visitor. In many cases, restaurants, amid gardens and terraces, have suites and rooms built around them.  A very good idea!  If you know you can stay, you very well might.  But don't count on room availability on weekends—the only time when busy Mexico City executives can escape for 48 hours in paradise.

The Cuernavaca area code is 73.

# TAXCO
## THE TREASURE OF SIERRA MADRE

Not long ago a Mexican comedian drew laughs in a film by declining a trip to Taxco with the explanation, "I don't speak English." Though it isn't *quite* that bad, anyone who's ever been to Taxco readily understands the joke.

Taxco exemplifies colonial Mexico. Its white-washed buildings evoke the *pueblos blancos*, white villages that dot the craggy mountainsides of southern Spain. Narrow cobblestone lanes — some of them less than 13 feet wide —

*Taxco exemplifies colonial Mexico.* Photo by Vern Appleby.

Visiting Taxco is a bit like entering a time machine that can't quite make up its mind. Past and present circle one another, sometimes clashing and sometimes blending. Aladdin's magic genie couldn't conjure up a more charming destination than this ancient village of silversmiths perched on a mountain. One of the finest examples of Spanish colonial architecture in the New World, the city itself is the most lasting monument to centuries of workers and artisans.

twist their way through Taxco's hillsides like drunken sidewinders, but that doesn't stop cars from moving through town with the insidious insistence of cholesterol in the clogged veins of a heart patient. Designated a National Treasure, Taxco is simply too beautiful for her own good, but does that make her any less desirable?

To understand and truly appreciate the Taxco of today, one must begin with the Taxco of yesterday. Origins of the tiny hillside town are lost in antiquity but it's known that silver was mined there long before the coming of the Spaniards.

In 1522 — just one year after the Aztec empire was destroyed by fire and sword, Hernan Cortes arrived.    He'd heard that the Tlahuica Indians living in the area had paid an earlier conqueror, Moctezuma I, in blocks of solid gold. Cortes couldn't quite manage the original name Tlachco ("place where the ball is played"), but he had no difficulty identifying precious metals when he saw them.   The first claim filed bore his name and the town's name was changed to a word that he could pronounce: Taxco.

That was the end of the ball game. From then on the Tlahuicans were kept far too busy digging holes and tunnels to ever play again.  In 1534, the huge *Hacienda del Chorillo* was completed near a large waterfall.   The flow powered massive water wheels which in turn channeled water over a colossal aqueduct, portions of which still exist. The old hacienda complex had great buildings in which the Spanish dons lived, below was a smelter built by Cortes to work the tons of gold and silver extracted from the mountains.  The approach to Taxco from the north passes under one of the aqueduct's ancient arches.

Later arrivals to the town lacked Cortes's Midas touch.  For years it was thought that all the precious ore had been mined.   Two centuries passed while the town slumbered.   Then in 1744, a wandering Frenchman, Joseph de la Borde (later Mexicanized to Jose de la Borda) came along.  Like Cortes,

Borda had an intuitive sense, an internal dowsing rod that enabled him to detect precious metal from a distance. He was also very lucky.

Jose's brother had been working a small mine with no success for years — finally dying penniless.  It would have been so easy to give up, to move on; but then, so the story goes, Jose's horse slipped on a steep hillside and dislodged a stone.  Beneath it was a vein of silver — the famed St. Ignacio vein — far richer than that originally discovered by Cortes.

It was the beginning of Taxco's golden age.  Borda built one of Mexico's most beautiful churches, Taxco's Santa Prisca, in gratitude to God for his good fortune.   "God gives to Borda, Borda gives to God," he explained and perhaps he was right.  After Borda's death, in 1778, the silver boom died.

Once again Taxco slumbered.   Residents were quiet and conservative, *very* conservative.   They remained fiercely loyal to the Spanish crown and fought on the side of the royalists in the war for independence, successfully repelling a fierce attack by revolutionaries in 1811.

Despite the fact that the cobblestone streets that once felt the wheels of carriages echo now with the loud squeals of taxis and the gentler squeak of Addidas, despite the fact that one *does* sometimes hear more English spoken in the stores than Spanish, Taxco is still conservative. The town holds on to its old ways.

Never is this more apparent than during

Holy Week, at Easter Time, when, beginning with Palm Sunday, daily parades are held. By Holy Thursday the event has be-come a spectacle that involves the entire town from noon until after midnight.

The forecourt of the Santa Prisca Church is transformed into the Garden of Gethsemane with guardian angels, Roman centurions and Hebrew elders. There is an enactment of the Washing of the Feet, the Last Supper, the betrayal of Jesus by Judas and Jesus' imprisonment in Nicholas Temple. At 11 p.m. Pontius Pilate reads the fatal sentence condemning Jesus and washes his hands. Concurrent with all this, candlelit processions enter the town from surrounding villages. Crowds, many of them masked, black-garbed penitents bare to the waist swell to up to 5000.

Some of the marchers carry heavy wooden crosses, others have their arms and backs laced with thorn branches. Many carry metal thongs with which they flagellate themselves. On Good Friday, Jesus, bearing his heavy cross, passes through the zocalo on the Road to Calvary. The "Crucificion" takes place at the Convent of San Bernardino where Christ is tied to the cross at noon. He remains there all through the long afternoon. The day ends at midnight with a Procession of Silence in which hooded men dressed in black flowing robes and women clad in rags, their bare feet bloody from the cobblestone streets, parade in total silence. The only sound is that of the heavy chains dragging from the ankles of the women.

*Taxco still clings to its old ways.* Photo by Vern Appleby.

On Saturday morning, church bells ring out after two days of silence to mark the Ceremony of the Resurrection. Sunday, there is a final procession at 5 p.m. Nowhere in the world will you experience anything quite like Taxco's Holy Week, a spectacle surpassing even the better known celebrations in Spain. It's an unforgettable — if a bit sobering — experience.

Actually, the rest of the year — let's say from Easter on! — Taxco is a joyous place. Almost every night somebody shoots off fireworks to celebrate a wedding, a birth, a birthday, or a saint's day. Some say each one is a prayer going up to heaven, *a lot* of prayers.

Though by 1570, Taxco was established as a world center of silver craftsmanship, that artistry didn't receive the critical acclaim it deserves   until this century. Oddly enough it was an American — a tourist before there even were tourists — who put the city squarely on the map. In 1930, just after a modern highway finally linked the long isolated mining town with the rest of the world, William Spratling wandered in.

Don Guillermo, as he was soon known, was an architecture professor from New Orleans' Tulane University on sabbatical. Possibly inspired by his good friends, William Faulkner and Sherwood Anderson, he'd come to Mexico to write a book.  Taxco seemed to provide exactly the peace and quiet he needed for such an effort — particularly after a local peanut vendor offered to sell him a charming little house just above the zocalo, practically for peanuts.

Spratling finished his book, *A Small Mexican World*, but the publishers went broke leaving the would-be author stranded in Mexico, a country that had claimed his heart.  How to finance the love affair?  Fortunately, Spratling had formed a close friendship with the then U.S. Ambassador to Mexico, Dwight Morrow, who suggested that his vast knowledge of design be put to use in Taxco.  Looking about, Spratling noted that the supposedly played out mines were still yielding enough silver to allow people to smelt in backyard furnaces. What they produced, they sold to whomever they could by the pound.

Another of those classic risk takers who crop up again and again in Mexican history, Spratling gave up his teaching post at Tulane and decided to design silverware in Taxco.  He opened shop on June 27, 1932.  It turned out to be a most auspicious date, a kind of economic independence day for the entire town. Unlike Cortes, Spratling returned far more than he took away.

Studying the ancient Indian designs, he retaught them to five eager youths, undoubtedly descendants of those early native craftsmen. It was the beginning of the flourishing silver industry that has given Taxco its reputation as the Silver Capital of the world. During World War II when jewelry supplies from Europe and the Orient were cut off, buyers from Nieman-Marcus, I. Magnin's and Bergdorf's literally fought over his designs.  Spratling moved his operation to what had once been the old smelter of Hacienda del Chorrillo; and, with five hundred employees, created a thriving factory.

Today the narrow cobblestone streets which radiate out from the central Santa Prisca Church like ripples on a pond pass a seemingly endless array of silver shops.  On the hill above is the modern Solar silver mine which still extracts the rich ore. Spratling's trainees and their sons and their sons' sons are the owners of these shops — more than 300 of them.  Silver furnishes Taxco with 90 percent of its income.

# HOTELS

**Los Arcos**, a gem of a small hotel that was originally built as a convent in 1620, has 25 rooms and three two-level suites.  There's a pretty little pool, a good restaurant and a lively bar with entertainment on weekends.   Just one block off the zocalo at Juan Ruiz Alarcon 12.  Telephone  (762) 2-18 36.

The **Hacinda del Solar** sprawls across some 80 acres of lush gardens but still manages to feel like an intimate country inn.  Each of its 22 elegant bungalows is named for a female friend of the owner.  Check out "Isabel" which has a lovely private garden.  Two miles out of town on Taxco Viejo.  Phone  (762) 2-03-23.

The Spanish colonial decor of the **Posada de la Mision** is particularly lovely and the Juan O'Gorman mural alongside the pool is worth a visit in itself.   Cerro de Mision 32.  Telephone (762) 2-00-63.

Once I drove to Taxco from Cuernavaca for lunch and discovered the **Hotel Santa Prisca** quite by chance.  Lunch was so delicious that I ended up spending the night.  The next morning we made reservations to return four months later for Holy Week. The Santa Prisca, an old fashioned  inn that manages to maintain its dignity and tranquility

*The gardens of the Santa Prisca Hotel.* Photo by Vern Appleby.

in the very center of town, has that kind of charm.   On both visits I met people who came back year after year. It's easy to understand why.  There are two leafy courtyards with splashing fountains and a pretty pool.  The food is excellent — wonderful soups.  The hotel also offers a vantage point from which to view the Holy Week parades.   Be sure to request a room with a view and check on the bed situation as some of them are twins.  Plazuela San Juan.Telephone (762) 2-00-80.

In the 1940s everybody who was anybody stayed at the **Rancho Taxco Victoria**. Photos of the celluloid luminaries who once strolled the same lush gardens are prominently displayed at the reception desk.   A bit like a faded movie star herself, the hotel is still lovely and manages a frayed elegance.   Rooms are ample and picturesquely decorated, views are breathtaking.  Soto la Marina 14.  (762) 2-02-10.

## RESTAURANTS

A *Bon Appetite Magazine* award winner, **La Ventana de Taxco** is a culinary delight and also offers a spectacular "cinemascope" view of all of Taxco. The name means "window of Taxco". Five minutes out of town on the Acapulco highway in the Hacienda del Solar.

On the hill just opposite the center of town one finds **La Pagaduria del Rey** serving outstanding continental specialties prepared by its French chef. Once again the views are spectacular.

A personal favorite is **Restaurant Arnoldo** which not only has excellent Mexican food but also chicken, chops and even hamburgers. Plazuala de los Gallas 2, across the zocalo from the Santa Prisca Church.

Two good ones on the zocalo are **Cielito Lindo** (intimate and romantic) and **Sr. Costilla's** — the name means "Mr. Rib" — (lively and casual). The latter also has a balcony that's great for people watching. Another that overlooks the square is **Paco's Bar**, a traditional place to drink and snack.

Don't forget the restaurant at the **Hotel Santa Prisca**, a block off the zocalo at Plazuela San Juan. You'll understand why many people stay at the hotel on the American plan and never eat anywhere else.

## SIGHTSEEING

Life in colonial Taxco revolved around the town plaza dominated by the **Cathedral of Santa Prisca**. Looking down as it does on a colorful mosaic of peddlers, camera-toting tourists and lovers oblivious to everything but each other, the cathedral still dominates the plaza and remains a focal point for the lives of townspeople and visitors alike. Santa Prisca, the church that Borda built, was begun in 1751 and took seven years and eight million pesos to complete. It has been hailed as the most perfect example of ecclesiastical art produced on this hemisphere. Pink in color and baroque in style, the cathedral is the work of architects Juan Caballero and Diego Duran, who'd been commissioned to build the finest church in Spanish America. The twin, 130 foot baroque towers and richly carved stone facade are impressive in their own right, but the blue-tiled dome and pink exterior walls of the church are spectacular. Inside, there are twelve altars, gold altarpieces and original paintings by Miguel Cabrera, one of the most highly regarded of the colonial artists. These include two of his finest works, *The Nativity* and the *Ascension of the Virgin.* On the zocalo.

**Casa Borda**, the house that Borda built in 1759, looks relatively modest in front — only two stories — but actually rises to five stories in the back.  It's built on a hillside. Originally Jose de la Borda lived in only half the house. The other half was donated to the priests of the local church.  Open daily.  On the zocalo.

The American who gave so much to Taxco, William Spratling, was a great collector of pre-Columbian artifacts, many of them on display at **Meseo Guillermo Spratling.**  The downstairs is devoted to the life of the New York-born Spratling and to silver mining.  There are also fascinating exhibits on local history, pictures of the Holy Week festivities and samples of silver ore.  The three story museum was originally funded by Spratling himself before his death in 1967.  Appropriately, one whole section is given over to displays of silver.  Open daily.  Behind the Santa Prisca Cathedral.

*Holy Week is a spectacle that involves the whole town.*
Photo by Vern Appleby.

On the western end of the zocalo is the **Casa Figueroa** which originally belonged to Borda's friend, Count Cadena.  Cadena means "chain" in Spanish, an appropriate name because the house was built by forced labor gangs comprised mostly of Indians. According to the story, the count, who was also a local magistrate, made the Indians who couldn't pay their fines work for him.  Not too surprisingly,  the building is also known as the "House of Tears."  In 1943, it was bought and restored by Fidel Figueroa, a  Mexican artist.  Today it's a private museum where you can see a variety of tunnels and a room where women hid during the 1910 revolution. On the zocalo, open Monday through Saturday.

Notice the fine details on the doors and windows at the **Casa Humboldt,** one of Taxco's oldest and most beautiful mansions.  The Moorish style villa was built by Juan de Villanueva in the 18th century but was named for Baron Alexander von

Humboldt, who was a guest on the night of April 5, 1803, during the period of his extensive explorations in Latin America.  The building is currently being renovated and will open as the Museum of Colonial Art.  Juan Ruiz Alarcon 6.

## SHOPPING

Naturally, silver is *the* thing to buy in Taxco.  You'll find opportunities everywhere, but are best off sticking with the reputable shops.  Begin at **Los Castillo**, one store that visitors should never miss whether they intend to buy or not.  The store's workshops are open to the public, allowing an opportunity to watch while designs are being hand-crafted. Antonio Castillo was one of Spratling's first apprentices and learned his trade well.  Before long Tony had persuaded his three brothers to join him in opening their own silver shop.  Today there are branches in Mexico City, Acapulco, Puerto Vallarta, Cancun and Dallas, Texas.  On the zocalo.

Also in the zocalo area is **Pineda's Taxco**, an exquisite shop with fine stone and clay figures and gorgeous silver reproductions from Monte Alban.  Just down the street, **Plateria Linda** has a wide variety of exclusive silver, gold and silver plated items.  Two others to watch for are **Elena Los Ballesteros** at Celso Munoz 4 and **Talleres de los Ballesteros** at Florida 14, both with traditions going back to Spratling.

Though Taxco is known for its silver, the town has something else to offer as well. **Arnoldo Jacobos**, one of Mexico's foremost mask collector/dealers, has a treasure of a shop next door to his restaurant at Plazuela de los Gallas, across and up

the hill from the zocalo.  Jacobos, who ships masks to collectors all over the world, not only has a fascinating selection in his store, but will — with a little coaxing — take you out into the countryside on a buying trip. I spent one of the most pleasant and rewarding Sundays ever with this delightful and knowledgeable expert.

*Masks from this shop are sent to collectors all over the world.*
Photo by Vern Appleby.

*Views of the Cathedral of Santa Prisca dominate the town.* Photo by Vern Appleby.

## TIDBITS

Taxco is located three to four hours from Mexico City or Acapulco, depending upon your direction.  It's a fantastic place to break a trip between the two, but remains a worthy destination in itself.

Though one may easily book a one-day tour to Taxco from Mexico City, it's both exhausting, frustrating and expensive.    By far the better plan is to take the first-class bus which leaves Mexico City several times daily from the Estrella de Oro terminal.   By all means, plan to spend at least one night.

Taxco's weather is in the 60s and 70s year round.  The rainy season is between June and October, but showers fall briefly, usually in the late afternoon.

The Taxco telephone area code is 762.

# OAXACA
## FETING THE LIVELY DEAD & OTHER MACABRE ADVENTURES

It was nearly midnight and I was on my way to the graveyard. The streets of Oaxaca were nearly deserted, a stark contrast to the raucous excitement of previous days and nights when troops of mariachis and hordes of vendors jammed the roads and sidewalks, and fireworks lit up the sky.

It wasn't quite what I had expected, but then nothing about the *Fiesta de los Muertos* (Festival of the Dead) was.

If one can envision Halloween, Independence Day, Thanksgiving and Memorial Day all rolled into one—with a few ethnic touches added—that's an

*Candy skulls are a Day of the Dead staple.* Photo by C.J. Marrow.

Inside *Paneton General*, the largest cemetery in the city, flickering candles cast weird shadows across the cool, gray tombstones where small groups of mourners kept watch. Silently I walked among them, fearful of intruding. Most of the people sat quietly, some of them rocking sleeping babies, but others chatted amiably, sipping freely from bottles of Carta Blanca.

approximation of this annual event which begins on October 31. Each year, as October draws to a close, tension in Oaxaca mounts. Shopkeepers sell macabre trinkets — plaster or terra-cotta skulls, key rings with handles made of bone and etched in the likeness of demons, tiny plaster witch dolls clad in wisps of black.

More bizarre are the foodstuffs: licorice witches, bread baked in the shape of skulls with grimacing faces made of raisins and candy coating, candy skulls inscribed in colored sugar with names — Maria, Pedro, Jose, Felipe. Does the name imply the eater or the eater's dead sister or brother? I wondered, watching children reach eagerly for the skulls.

"Either way," a shop proprietor finally explained. "Candy is candy." And death is death and life life. Never was I more aware of the difference between the living and the dead.

By the 31st, Festival of the Dead trappings dominated the market place. Loaves of skull bread were stacked in pyramids and display cases were covered with parades of candy or ceramic witches, devils and tarantulas, seemingly frozen in a ghoulish march.

The plaza, too, was given over to these colorful improvised altars, which, as darkness fell, the whole town turned out to admire. Not one band but several convened. The candy skulls were hawked along with balloons in the shape of tarantulas and skulls. In near-by hotels local señoritas performed ritual Indian dances and political speeches were made. For the dead, there was tribute, for the living, promises.

*Oxacans bake special "skull" bread in preparation for Day of the Dead.* Photo by C.J. Marrow

In private homes and public buildings *ofrendas* or altars were erected against white, shroudlike backdrops. Over these altars flowered trellises arose bearing candles, skulls, witches, photographs of the departed and, surprisingly, fruits, candies and bottles of whiskey or beer. Apparently, whatever the deceased enjoyed in life is remembered and offered in death. Before these makeshift shrines, incense burns.

The following night, the conclusion of All Saints' Day, was even more colorful. The crowds had grown. New al-tars had risen, and there were additional breads and candies, more bands and mariachi singers. As a grand finale, a stream of fireworks rained down from the rooftops, surrounding the plaza — a shower of jewels, in some places a block wide, eerily illuminating both the altars and the political banners strung on  clotheslines that crisscrossed overhead.

*The ceremony culminates in the cemetery.* Photo by C.J. Marrow

The next day, All Souls' Day, bands continued to march through the city, wading through drifts of confetti and wilting chrysanthemums. But the main activity was in the graveyards, where families gathered, their arms filled with flowers, and vendors wheeled in an ample supply of tortillas, tamales, beer, soft drinks and the inevitable candy skulls.   Gay laughter, happy smiles and friendly waves abounded.

The same party atmosphere prevailed at the cemetery that night.  Returning at the witching hour for a final farewell, we found many families continuing the vigil.  Some would remain all night, but others were beginning to straggle home, whistling or humming softly, their sleeping children cradled in *rebozos.*

The Fiesta de los Muertos was coming to a close. The living had paid loving homage to the dead while also demonstrating a joyous awareness of the good things of *this* world — gaiety, friend-ship, food, color, beauty. What greater tribute to death than the celebrations of life?

*Altars in memory of dead loved ones are part of the tradition.* Photo by C.J. Marrow

*A stream of fireworks.* Photo by C.J. Marrow.

Oaxaca is a city, a valley, a state, a homeland of the gods, a birthplace of statesmen and rogues, a refuge for artists and intellectuals.

Located on the vast plateau of the Oaxaca Valley some 250 miles south of Mexico City and 100 miles east (but a world away!) from Acapulco, Oaxaca is both an Indian and a colonial city surrounded, like all of the valley, by the Sierra Madre del Sur.

And that is Oaxaca — a very lively city whose two main attractions are ruins — cities of the dead, quite literally ghost towns. The Fiesta de los Muertos is symbolic, representing as it does something primal and atavistic using the excuse of All Souls' Day to reveal itself.  It is as though the Catholic holiday has been grafted onto, or fused with a set of rituals and images.

There are more than 150 cathedrals in the city, the result of a colonial building boom undertaken by Dominican friars intent on one uping the Franciscans who'd beaten them to Mexico City.

It was an impressive effort, but it never quite worked.  Though the Dominicans succeeded in dominating the city landscape, they never quite managed to dominate the Indians.  It is this very blending of baroque architecture and ancient Indian culture that makes Oaxaca so totally unique.  In all of North America, you'll not find a more surreal, otherworldly city.

Within the high, protective wall of the Sierra Madre is the plateau world — 5000 feet above sea level at the city and rising to 9000 feet in the encircling mountains.  The city, with a population of 200,000, is the capital of a state which remains a cultural mosaic. Thousands of tiny villages dot the valleys, mountainsides and coastal lowlands. Two out of every three "Oaxaquenos" come from one of seventeen distinct groups within the Mixtecs and Zapotecs cultures — founders of one of this hemisphere's greatest pre-Columbian civilizations.  More than 200 dialects have survived and most of the state's three million inhabitants don't speak Spanish as a first language.

As part of their legacy, the Mixtec and Zapotec cultures, which flourished centuries before Christ, have left the magnificent ruins of Monte Alban and Mitla. All within a 25-mile radius of Oaxaca City, these rich archaeological zones bear witness to an elaborate and highly religious civilization that was versed in astronomy and had a system of writing that may be the oldest in the western hemisphere.

Unfortunately, intellectual prowess proved no match for the fierce Aztec legions and by the late 15th century, they were conquered. When the Spaniards arrived in 1521, they found the area under the control of Montezuma.

Replacing the Aztec's fort with their own, the Spaniards founded a city in 1529 which they named Oaxaca meaning "place covered with trees." An enchanted Cortes claimed most of the land for himself, took the title Marques del Valle de Oaxaca and established his own little fiefdom there. His descendants managed to hang onto the property until the 1910 revolution.

History — or would you say trouble? — passed Oaxaca by for more than three centuries. The city slumbered languorously through the colonial era awakening at last in the wars of independence and ensuing civil strife.

Then two Indian mothers gave birth to a pair of movers and shakers destined to change forever the course of Mexican history. Oaxaca was home town to both. Each man came from simple peasant stock, each rose to the presidency. There the similarity ended.

The first, Benito Juarez, has been called the Abraham Lincoln of Mexico. Born in 1806, Juarez, a Zapotec Indian, might have lived out his life as a simple shepherd if one of his sheep hadn't run away. Fearful of the consequences, Juarez ran away too. A kindly priest befriended the boy and sponsored his studies for the clergy. Not only did the religious doctrine not take — it appears to have alienated Juarez.

Another mentor — this one a lawyer — took an interest in the seminary dropout and sent him to law school. Within a very short time, Juarez became a lawyer, the state governor, chief justice of the Supreme Court and finally president. An amazing ascent for a boy who couldn't speak Spanish — let alone read it, until he was twelve.

Juarez had scarcely taken office before he locked horns with the Catholic Church, a most formidable opponent. Not only was the church the ultimate moral authority but the country's most powerful temporal one. For centuries, it had been the practice among the wealthy to leave part of their property to the church when they died. As a result, by the mid-1850s, the church was the largest landowner in Mexico with total control of both the country's educational system and its civil affairs such as marriage and the registration of births and deaths.

Juarez's move to permit civil marriages, open secular schools and force the church to sell its property touched off a civil conflict. His opponents — the church and wealthy conservatives backed the Austrian Archduke Maximilian as emperor. Juarez was chased to the border city on the Rio Grande that today bears his name.

In the end he triumphed. The Civil War that had kept the United States from defending the Monroe Doctrine ended. When General Philip Sheridan was sent with 50,000 troops to the Mexican border, Louis Napoleon of France decided to bring his soldiers home. Maximilian was abandoned to his fate.

The second Oaxacan to emerge onto the national scene was Porfirio Diaz, Juarez's gutsiest general. Though contemporaries with similar economic backgrounds, their allegiances were 180 degrees apart as was their approach to government. Many thought Juarez obsessed with the law, Diaz simply made his own. Failing to win the election, he took the presidency by force. Reelection was prohibited by law — until Diaz changed that law.

Like Queen Victoria of England, Porfirio Diaz placed his very personal stamp on the era in which he lived. In his case it was an opulent, grandeloquent stamp. Today the ornate architectural design and lavish lifestyle of his 35-year dictatorship is known as the Porfiriate. North Americans came to drill for oil, the British came to build railroads, the French became merchant princes and the great haciendas flourished as they never had before.

But the price was high. The haciendas were manned by serfs kept in line by a police force notorious for its brutality. In the cities, workers forbidden to join unions became second class citizens in their own country. The pressure mounted until it exploded into a full blown revolution in 1910. What followed was anarchy as revolutionary hero fought revolutionary hero. Today even the most brutal of them — acknowledged bandits — are honored. Diaz, the man who stayed too long at the party, alone remains the villain although it was he who brought Mexico into the family of nations and created the infrastructure upon which the modern nation rests.

Today Oaxaca is very proud of Juarez. Statues of him abound. Streets, museums, monuments and schools bear his name. No one speaks of Diaz.

*Oaxacan village home.*
Drawing by
Nancy Brannigan

## HOTELS

As far as I'm concerned, *the* place to stay in Oaxaca is the **Camino Real** *(ex-Convento de Santa Catalina)* otherwise known as the **El Presidente,** an exqui-sitely re-stored con-vent built in 1576. The charming, two-story structure with balconies overlooking a leafy courtyard and pool, has been desig-nated a National Archaeological Treas-ure of Mexico. A true treasure indeed, the hotel, in-sulated by thick adobe walls is a quiet oasis close to everything in town. Cinco de Mayo 300. Phone: 6-0611

A room with a view is what you get at **Hotel Victoria,** long a favor-ite with those who enjoy tranquil luxury. Surrounded by ter-raced grounds and well-kept gardens, the hotel is perched on a hill overlooking the city. At Km. 545 Rt. 190. Phone: 6-2633.

*The Camino Real is a former convent.* Photo by Vern Appleby.

The centrally located **Hotel Plaza** is charming and reasonable. Many "insiders" return here year after year, considering it the best buy in town. Trujano 112. Phone: 6-2200.

## RESTAURANTS

One of the highlights of visiting Oaxaca is the opportunity to enjoy its traditional cuisine, among the finest and most elaborate in all of Mexico.   The area is especially famous for its many mole sauces.   The nickname of the state is, in fact, the "Land of the Seven Moles."

Black mole — the king among moles — is traditionally used in making enmoladas, two fried tortillas that are folded into a triangle and soaked in the sauce, then garnished with onion rings and fresh Oaxaca cheese. Look for them in any Oaxaca restaurant.

---

Patricia Quintana, Mexico's foremost cooking authority, food columnist for the Mexican *Vogue*, restaurant consultant, and author of numerous cookbooks, including *The Taste of Mexico*, has shared with us her own recipe for **Mole Negro Oaxaqueno:**

*Patricia Quintana.* Photo by Jorge Conlieur.

2 cups vegetable oil
1 small sweet roll or croissant
3 ounces raw almonds, skinned
3 ounces raw peanuts or walnuts
4 ounces sesame seeds
1 medium plantain, sliced in 1/2 inch slices
1 1/2 white onions,
10 cloves garlic
10 chiles pasillas, preferably black pasillas, seeded, deveined and  soaked in water
2 chiles chipotles, roasted, seeded, deveined, and soaked in water
2 to 3 tablespoons mixed seeds from above chiles, roasted
1/4 teaspoon dried anise
1 tablespoon allspice
1/2 teaspoon black peppercorns
4 large plum tomatoes
4 tortillas, charred
1 1/2 to 2 quarts chicken skimmed of fat
4 onion slices
Salt to taste
3 to 4 ounces Mexican chocolate tablets, containing cinnamon, in pieces

Heat a little oil in a skillet.  Fry sweet roll until brown and remove.  Drain on a paper towel.  Add almonds, peanuts and sesame seeds and fry.  Remove and drain.  Add a little more oil and fry the plantain. Remove and drain.

*Chicken mole.* Photo by Jorge Conlieur.

In a blender or food processor, blend onions, garlic and chiles, chihuacles, pasillas and chipotles. Add enough water in which chiles were soaked to facilitate blending. Set chile mixture aside. In a blender or food processor, blend roll, almonds, peanuts, sesame seeds, plantain, chile seeds, avocado leaves, allspice, peppercorns, tomatoes and tortillas with enough broth (about 1 to 2 cups) to blend smoothly. Blend in batches, if necessary.) Strain and reserve.

Put remaining oil in a heavy saucepan. Saute onion slices until brown, and remove. Pour in nut-spice mixture, and fry over low heat until fat begins to rise to the surface. Add chile mixture. Continue cooking over low heat until fat rises to the surface. Salt to taste. Add chocolate and as much of the remaining broth as necessary to make a mole the consistency of thick cream.

Serve mole sauce with tortilla or with turkey, chicken, or pork that has been stewed and then cooked in the mole to flavor. The mole also makes an excellent sauce for squab.

Makes 8 servings.

---

One of the most delightful places to sample mole is the courtyard of the **El Presidente Hotel,** considered one of the best restaurants in town. If you don't stay there, be certain to schedule a lunch or dinner. Cinco de Mayo 300.

**Mi Casita** is another pleasant place to enjoy Oaxacan cuisine. Try to get a window table — Mi Casita is one flight up. A favorite choice is chicken enchiladas with spicy mole sauce. On the south side of the zocalo at Hidalgo 616.

Although the name means garlic and onions, **Ajos & Cebollas** is better known for its veal parmesan. Their intimate bar features a peppery house cocktail made with mescal, the regional liquor of Oaxaca. Everyone loves this lively restaurant located at Avenue Juarez 605.

Not to be missed is **Catedral** which has earned the nickname the "House of Filets" because of their menu which lists eleven tenderloin cuts from which to choose. There are also wonderful mole dishes and a variety of delicious soups. A block from the zocalo at the corner of Garcia Vigil and Avenue Morelos.

# SIGHTSEEING

Oaxaca has one of the liveliest zocalos or squares in all of Mexico. **Plaza de Armas** has a gazebo bandstand (in use nearly every night and on Sunday afternoons), outdoor cafes in all directions, many tree-shaded benches, vendors selling any number of strikingly beautiful items, and numerous strolling street musicians.

**Basilica of Solitude** (Basilica de la Soledad) is best known as the home of the Virgin of Solitude, a statue thought to have healing powers. Glass panels in the religious museum at the rear of the church depict the legend of her miraculous appearance. It seems that in 1682 a packtrain arrived in town with one more mule than the muleteer could account for. At the site of the present-day church, the extra mule suddenly collapsed and died. Upon examination, the poor animal was found to be carrying a stone statue of the Virgin. The church was built to commemorate this mysterious event. You'll probably see the statue robed in a black velvet cloak heavily encrusted with jewels, although the Virgin gets a costume change for various religious occasions. Calle Independencia on the Plaza de Baile.

**The Church of Santo Domingo** built in 1570 is the most spectacular to emerge from the Dominican building spree. The interior is covered in gold scroll and polychrome reliefs set against a white background with paved tile floors, and massive gold chandeliers. Eleven chapels are integrated into the church including the lovely Chapel of the Virgin of Rosario (off to the right as you enter). The Church of Santo Domingo is magnificent — one of a kind — and shouldn't be missed by any visitor to Oaxaca. Gurrion and M. Alcala.

The **Regional Museum of Oaxaca** is housed in the converted convent attached to the Church of Santo Domingo. This lovely museum is actually a series of rooms arranged around an open courtyard. Each has a theme which includes regional arts and crafts, costumes and archaeological artifacts. On the second floor, behind a heavily vaulted door are the incredible jewels excavated from the archaeological site of Monte Alban in 1932. These priceless objects dating back to AD 500 display a high degree of technical sophistication and include ornate filigree work and alabaster vessels. There are also jade and bone carvings from an earlier Indian culture. Closed Mondays. Calle M. Alcala.

The **Rufino Tamayo Museum of Pre-Hispanic Art** is an exquisite gem of a museum, among the loveliest to be found anywhere in the world. The 2,000 art objects that comprise the collection trace the development of art in Mexico from 1250 BC to AD 1500. They were donated to the city by the native Oaxaqueno muralist and painter Rufino Tamayo and his wife, Olga.

The museum itself is a beautifully restored colonial mansion redesigned by Tamayo himself.    Each gallery is arranged to represent a specific culture: Olmec, Totonac, Zapotec, Mixtec, Maya, Nayarit and Teotihuacan.    Morelos 503. Closed Tuesdays.

# MONTE ALBAN

Once a holy city to 40,000 Zapotecs, Monte Alban covers some 25 square miles and is considered one of the most magnificent archaeological ruins in Mexico. Monte Alban overlooks the Oaxacan valley from a flattened mountaintop leveled by the Zapotecs in about 600 BC. Buildings  were carefully arranged on a perfect north-south axis with the exception of one structure believed to have been an observatory, which is more closely aligned with the stars than the poles.

The oldest of Monte Alban's monuments is the **Temple of the Dancers,** so named because of the elaborately carved stone figures that once covered the building.  Actually, these naked figures, distorted as they are in strange positions, really don't look much like dancers.  A newer theory seems much more plausible. The figures may represent patients in what was once a hospital or medical school.

Another major point of interest is the **ball court**, where a complicated game — part basketball, part soccer — was played by the young men of the community. The players' object was to propel the ball using only their hips and elbows into the opponents' court. Tradition has it that the captain of the losing team was sacrificed to the gods as part of a fertility rite.

It's forever fascinating to speculate on what led to the abandonment of Monte Alban.  The period between A.D. 650 and 1000 was one of strife and upheaval for all of Mexico's major cultures.  A popular theory among archaeologists is the too many chiefs (priests, aristocrats), too few Indians (peasants) one.   In other words, too many idle mouths to feed.  Whatever the cause, by A.D. 900, most of Monte Alban was falling into ruin.

Some time in the next hundred years the Mixtecs marched in and took over. These new inhabitants never lived in Monte Alban, using it instead as a city of the dead, a massive cemetery of lavish tombs.  More than 160 of them have been discovered; and, in 1932, Tomb 7 yielded *a treasure unequaled in this hemisphere.*  Inside were more than 500 priceless Mixtec objects, including gold breastplates, jewelry made of jade, pearls, and gold, as well as fans, masks and belt buckles of precious stones and metals.  All are now on view at the Regional Museum of Oaxaca.

Buses are available to Monte Alban from Oaxaca.  Schedules and departure points can be obtained at your hotel or from the tourist office.  Arrive early and try to get a seat on the right-hand side for the best views. The ruins are open daily until 6 p.m.

# MITLA

Monte Alban ended up a city of the dead, Mitla started out that way.  This second Zapotec city holds many fascinations that stand in contrast to Monte Alban. Regal cemetery that it was, Mitla is one of the few ancient sites that is actually *alive.*  The pyramids of Teotihuacan near Mexico City were abandoned long before the arrival of the Aztecs, the jungle vines had strangled the palaces of Yucatan before Cortes's birth and the temples of Monte Alban had already fallen into decay when the Spanish arrived.  Not so Mitla. Today the temples and tombs, the cells of the holy men, stand as they did when the Conquistadors arrived.  A village of thatched huts huddles near the ruins, much as it must have 1,000 years ago. Its residents, busy making and selling "ancient" relics, are descended from the same people who made the originals.

Mitla is another complex of ceremonial structures begun by the Zapotecs but taken over and heavily influenced by the Mixtecs.  Its name,  derived from an Aztec word, means "Place of the Dead." The architecture  here is totally different from that of any other ruins in the area.  The walls of stone and mud are inlaid with small stones cut into geometric patterns forming a mosaic that resembles the style of ancient Greece.  And, unlike other ancient buildings in North America, there are no human figures or mythological events depicted — only elaborate geometric designs.

A trip to Mitla can easily be combined with a stop at the famous **Tule Tree** which somehow pulls everything into perspective.   The tree, 135 feet tall and with branches spreading at least that wide, is thought to be the oldest living thing in Mexico. It was a sapling 3,000 years ago and was of fair size when the Zapotecs were playing their bloody ball games.  It is said that Cortes stopped to picnic here on his way to conquer Central America.

Another attraction near the site itself is the **Frissel Museum of Art,** just off the plaza in the village of Mitla.  This museum, also then regional research center of the University of the Americas, is housed in an 18th century hacienda.  It contains a fine collection of Zapotec artifacts labeled in English as well as Spanish which clearly traces the development of the Zapotec/Mixtec empire.

The building also encompasses the charming **Restaurant La Sorpresa,** a welcome oasis after exploring the ruins.  A specialty drink here is a tangy blend of mescal and pineapple juice. The food and service are good.  La Sorpresa is open daily from 8:30 to 10:30 a.m. and from 1 to 4 p.m.

The museum opens daily from 9 a.m. to 6 p.m.    Buses leave every half hour from the terminal across from the Central Market in Oaxaca.  The ride takes one hour to reach Mitla,  24 miles southeast of Oaxaca on Rt. 190.

*Oaxacan scene* by Nancy Brannigan.

## SHOPPING ___________________________________________

Some time after burritos and before *la bamba,* Mexican folk art became a U.S. fad that shows no sign of abating.

Ritual masks, Zapotec rugs, black burnished pottery have had their fans for decades, but suddenly they've become so trendy that prices tripled within a year. The hottest sellers are relative newcomers:  wooden animals in bizarre shapes and fantastic colors — like chartreuse dinosaurs, indigo lions or magenta coyotes.  Now art dealers in Tokyo or Manhattan bandy the names of barefoot neo-celebrities, many of whom still subsidize their new professions by planting *frijoles* and corn.

Maybe it's too late to be the first kids on the block to display a wolf-headed mermaid, but it's still possible to go to the source and select treasures first hand. The state of Oaxaca is where it's happening.  Its capital, Oaxaca City, is ground zero.

Sunday is the big market day in town and artists from the surrounding countryside flock to the **Juarez Market,** many wearing their native costumes and all speaking their various dialects of Zapotec.   Considered one of the best and most colorful markets in Mexico, this one shouldn't be missed.

All the small villages surrounding Oaxaca have their own market days as well, and a quick check with the tourist office should provide you with a list that could keep a shop-a-holic busy for weeks. Of the three principal carving villages, **Arrazola** is the most expensive — but also the most accessible.   It's also the home of Manuel Jimenez, the carver who started it all.  His pieces are generally the priciest but may be collectors items. The oldest village, **San Martin Tilcajete,** is the richest in tradition and has the greatest variety.   **La Union Tejalapan,** the most remote (45 minutes by taxi), is the least geared to tourists and subsequently less expensive.

Prices begin at $10 and go up and up and up depending upon the carver and the size of the piece.  Prices are often negotiable, depending on the carver and the time of year — they rise in winter with the tourist season and drop in the summer months.

The easiest way to get to the villages from Oaxaca City is to hire a taxi for about $10 or try a less expensive *collectivo*  at the stand near the city's main outdoor market. Carvings are sold at any number of shops in Oaxaca City.  The best place to begin is the Alcala arcade near the zocalo.

> Once you get home, put your carvings in the freezer for ten days to two weeks to kill any bugs.  If the pieces are painted with aniline dyes (as opposed to the more common acrylic house paints), freeze them in plastic bags so the colors won't run.  If the carving is too big to fit into the freezer and powder begins to collect beneath it, bathe it with gasoline.

Also among the most uniquely Oaxacan items are the *calaveras*  or skeletons. Often these are done in miniature and posed on tiny stages in emulation and mockery of daily life.  They combine slapstick and satire, reverence and awe as they create a world of the dead with disconcerting similarities to the one inhabited by the living.

Many consider them Mexico's most beguiling folk art.  Grinning brides and grooms, dressed in their formal best, kiss with the blessing of an equally skeletal priest.  Musicians keep the beat with bony drumsticks.  Patients shrink from the questionable ministrations of knife-wielding surgeons.  Skeletal inebriates sleep it off under the watchful eye sockets of sepulchral jailors.

Calaveras celebrate the Mexican way of greeting death with laughter as much as with dread, with joy as well as sorrow.  As one Oaxacan storekeeper explained, gesturing at his collection of sugar skulls, "If you can eat death, how scary can it be?"

But wood carvings and calaveras aren't the only treasures in town.  They're really only the frosting on a very rich cake.  Oaxaca is a shopper's heaven.  Expect to find marvelous masks, beautiful weavings, exquisite jewelry fashioned after the tomb treasures.  You don't even have to move, just settle into a sidewalk cafe or a tree shaded bench on the zocalo and let the sellers come to you.  But for more ambitious shoppers:

Watch weavers at work at **Mercado de Artesania**. Corner of Garcia and Zaragoza. **Alfareria Jimenez** carries pottery, brightly colored and handmade. There too you can see the artisans at work. Zaragoza 402.

At **Aripo** you'll find ten rooms filled with rugs, pottery, weavings and ornaments. Garcia Vigil 809.  **Lixhi-Tuu** has wonderful masks — some of them antiques — as well as clothing and rugs.  Ave. Independencia 601  Look for jewelry reproductions as well as native handicrafts at **Tianguis.**  Portal Marques del Valle on the zocalo.

# TIDBITS

Currently there's no direct international air service to Oaxaca City.  Visitors arrive via connections made in Mexico City.  From the airport, frequent van transfers are available at reasonable rates.

There's also an overnight train from Mexico City which leaves the capital at 7 p.m. and arrives at Oaxaca at 9:30 a.m.  Sleeping compartments are available.

To get around the area, taxis are plentiful and cheap.  Many visitors will hire a driver/guide for an entire day when exploring outside the city.

# VERACRUZ
## "ONLY VERACRUZ IS BEAUTIFUL"

Unlike most of Mexico, Veracruz doesn't look back. It marches, or rather dances — this is the home of *la bamba* — to a different beat.

Palm thatched huts are never far from palatial townhouses and everyone from laborer to company president gathers under the arcades.

Veracruz, vibrantly erotic, pulsating with tropical rhythms, seems to have been created for love and lovers. Considering its history of invasion and attack by foreigners, it's surprising that the people are so tolerant of visitors.

It began with Cortes who did a number on them. When the Indians of the area

*A Veracruz sunset. Cortes and Malinche enjoyed the same gorgeous sunsets.* Photo by the author.

More than in any other city in Mexico, the social life revolves around the cafes. Drinking *cafe con leche* (a strong black coffee mixed with hot milk poured by the waiters to get just the right blend), gossiping and people watching are major events in Veracruz. Oysters on the half shell are a delicious between meal snack available everywhere, as are the plump, pink fresh gulf shrimp.

attacked the invaders who'd landed on their shores, they were routed by the Spanish artillery and cavalry. During peace negotiations with the defeated Indians, Cortes experimented with the shrewd, psychological techniques he would later use to even more devastating effect upon the Aztecs.

Playing on the Indians' fear of Spanish arms, he pretended that his artillery and horses had a life and will of their own.

After warning the natives that the cannon was still angry with them for their attack, he secretly signaled and a hidden artillery piece roared its displeasure, sending a cannon ball exploding into the nearby hills and causing the Indians to drop to their knees in terror.

*Street musicians add to Diamond Alley's charms.* Photo by the author.

Next Cortes ordered a stallion to be brought forth while a mare in heat was placed behind the chieftains, out of their view. Catching her scent, the stallion reared and neighed his excitement. Terrified, the natives now capitulated unconditionally, abandoning their gods and embracing the image of the Virgin Mary and a wooden cross placed on an improvised altar in their midst. In desperation, they offered the Spaniards food and gold and presented them with twenty women. One of these turned out to be the greatest gift of all.

Malinche had been born into an Aztec vassal nation, and in her childhood sold as a slave to the coastal Indians. Accordingly, she spoke both the Nahua language of the Aztecs and the Maya dialect of her masters. A communication link was quickly forged. Malinche translated Nahua into the Maya understood by Jeronimo de Aguilar, a shipwrecked Spanish sailor who'd been captured by Mayas and then freed by Cortes when he conquered the off shore island of Cozumel. Aguilar then translated the words spoken in Maya by Malinche into Spanish for Cortes.

Well, that's how it began. Before long, Aguilar was out of the loop entirely. Malinche quickly mastered Spanish and soon was doing all the talking. Cortes was listening very carefully. Today the name Malinche is synonymous to many Mexicans with treachery while others perceive her as a romantic figure, a naive girl willing to do anything to please the man she loved. Perhaps she was simply a realist and a survivor, a strong, adaptable woman who recognized that the war was over before it had even begun.

Whatever the case, Malinche became not only Cortes's mistress but his most trusted confidant. Through her, he discovered far more about his Indian adversaries than they could ever imagine about him or his men. Very soon Malinche acquainted Cortes with the existence and importance of the Aztec empire, its capital, Tenochtilan, and its system of subject provinces. What happened next was history.

Love him or hate him, Hernan Cortes was a remarkably durable fellow and as courageous as any swashbuckler who ever cut and slashed for king and country. Proclaiming his new city La Villa Rica de la Vera Cruz (the Rich Village of the True Cross), Cortes burned his boats to prevent fainthearted crew members from defecting, then marched on.

And as for the city that became Veracruz, Mexico's oldest colonial city? For nearly 500 years it has been Mexico's door to the world. From the arrival of Cortes to the expulsion of the final Spanish in 1825, through three foreign invasions (one French, and two American) and numerous pirate attacks, Veracruz has been the stage upon which many of the most pivotal events of post conquest Mexican history have been played.

At the end of the Mexican War of Independence from Spain, Spanish troops stationed in their last stronghold (the Castle of San Juan de Ulua) severely bombarded the town. Seventeen years later, the French again attacked the town. During the Mexican-American War in 1847, Veracruz played "host" to General Winfield Scott, who landed there, subdued the resistance he encountered and then, like Cortes, marched westward to Mexico City. In 1860, the French entered the city once more to prepare the way for Maximilian and Carlota; and then again, in 1914, the U.S. bombarded the port.

So much for the guts and glory, macho

stuff. Don't dismiss Veracruz as merely a doormat for invasion. This is Caribbean-a-la-Mexico, a balance of Afro-Cuban temperament and Spanish tradition with a Mexican spin. It began in 1598 when Veracruz was decreed the only port in Spain's American empire allowed to trade with the mother country. Tons of Mexican silver, slaves, and settlers (as well as invaders, pirates and rulers) came through the city. Exotic imports from the Far East (arriving from the Philippines via Acapulco and transported the width of the country on muleback to Veracruz) flowed to Europe through Veracruz.

Today a stroll through this historic city reveals the traditional Spanish style stucco buildings, but painted mellow Caribbean colors: pale pink, ocher, salmon and sky blue. Mariachi music, so popular in other parts of Mexico, is seldom heard in Veracruz. Here they dig the *marimba* and dance the *bamba*, both of Afro-Carib origin. As Veracruz's refreshing — and flamboyant — distinctions from the rest of Mexico reveal themselves it's easy to understand the city's slogan: *Solo Veracruz Es Bello* (Only Veracruz is Beautiful).

Outrageously chauvinistic perhaps, in a country known for its many beauty spots, but *bello* Veracruz certainly is.

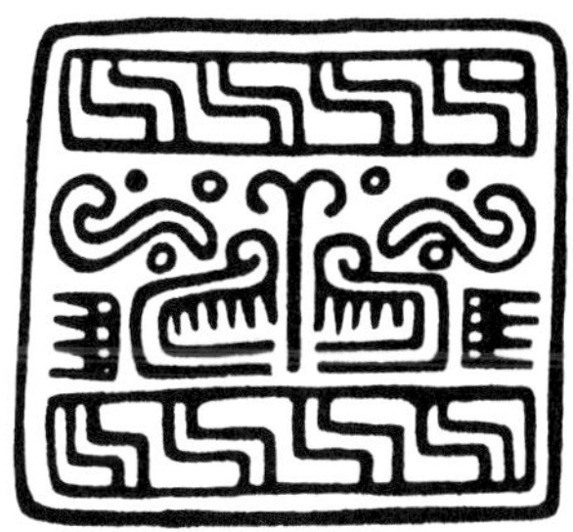

## HOTELS

Veracruz is an "action" city where people literally dance in the streets.  There couldn't be a better place to enjoy the action than the **Hotel Veracruz** which faces right on the city's lively main plaza.  Av. Independencia Esq. Miguel Lerdo.  Phone: (29) 31l-590.

**Hotel Emporio Veracruz** is the city's Grande Dame.  It, too, has a good location facing the Malecon and Carranza Lighthouse Museum.  The harbor views are lovely  and the hotel is just four blocks east of the plaza at Malecon and Xicotencatl. (29) 320-020.

Another grand old lady who has recently received a nip and tuck is the **Hotel Mocambo,** an art deco wonder, with attractive sprawling grounds and the best beach in town.  There's a lot of ambience here.  Shades of the silver screen add mystique to the lively bar.  Five miles south of town along the beach.  Phone: (29) 371-531.

## RESTAURANTS

Early in your stay be certain to stop at **Cafe de la Parroquia** for a meal, a nightcap or just a breather.   Once having found this place, you'll find yourself returning again and again.  The Cafe de la Parroquia serves wonderful breakfasts and is famous for its *media noches* (midnights) — turkey, ham and cheese sandwiches spiced with tomato sauce Cuban style.  They're very good as is the coffee, considered the best in town.  When diners tap their glasses, they aren't making a toast, they're hailing the waiters bearing kettles of hot milk to complete their *cafe con leche.*  On the Plaza de Armas.  You'll love this place!

Also on the Plaza de Armas, at Miguel Lerdo and Independencia, is the popular **Prendes** where you can enjoy lively regional music along with your fresh seafood. *Carne Asada,*  Mexican-style steak prepared with sauted vegetables is also popular here.

Another favorite for classic *Veracruzana* cuisine is **La Casona,** one of the prettiest (and priciest) restaurants in town.  Set in a two-story gray house dating from 1919 with balconies, shuttered windows and wood-beamed ceilings, the restaurant serves delicious red snapper broiled and bathed in a lush sauce of tomatoes, garlic, green olives, chilies, capers, and sweet yellow peppers. *Sopa de mariscos,* a fish stew brimming with the catch of the day is another excellent choice.  482 Xicotencatl at Rayon.

Naturally, at **La Paella**, you'll want to try the famous *paella* — shellfish, chicken and sausage served over rice. On the plaza at Zamora 138.

Tamales and tacos are considered breakfast fare in Veracruz. At least one day rise early and feast on tasty tacos, *picadas* (tiny tortillas filled with beans, cheese and a thick chili sauce) and *gorditos* (puffed tortillas spread with a thin bean sauce) at **La Fogata.** Diaz Miron 660.

---

The food of Veracruz is distinctive and delicious, a regional delicacy that's become world famous. One of the foremost authorities on this cuisine is Patricia Quintana, another "national treasure" of Mexico. Quintana, author of numerous cookbooks including *The Taste of Mexico,* represents the Mexican Ministry of Tourism as its official chef. Here are two of her favorites recipes from Veracruz:

### PESCADO Á LA VERACRUZANA
### (Fish, Veracruz Style)

A wonderful dish with a sauce that combines Spanish olives and capers with the unmistakable flavor of Mexican chiles.

**For the Tomato Sauce**
1 1/2 cups olive oil
6 cloves garlic, whole, plus 8 cloves garlic, minced
4 cups white onion, finely chopped
4 1/2 pounds tomatoes, finely chopped
1 1/2 cups pimento-stuffed green olives, finely chopped
1/2 cup capers
12 fresh bay leaves or 6 dried bay leaves
1 tablespoon oregano, dried and crushed
3 sprigs thyme or 1 teaspoon dried thyme
3 sprigs marjoram or 1 teaspoon dried marjoram
Salt to taste
1 teaspoon freshly ground pepper

**For the Chiltomate Sauce:**
8 tomatoes
1 1/2 white onions, halved
6 cloves garlic, whole
3 cups olive oil
4 bay leaves
3 sprigs thyme or 1/2 teaspoon dried thyme
3 sprigs marjoram or 1/2 teaspoon dried majoram
Salt to taste

1 8-ounce can chiles gueros
1 8-ounce can pickled chiles jalapeños with juice

**For the Red Snapper:**
one 6 1/2 pound red snapper, very fresh
6 tablespoons lime juice
6 cloves garlic, pureed
4 bay leaves
1 teaspoon dried oregano
1  1/2 cups olive oil
Salt and pepper to taste

**For the Garnish:**
4 fresh bay leaves
6 sprigs thyme
6 sprigs marjoram
1/3 cup chopped parsley

**To prepare the tomato sauce:**  Heat oil in a saucepan or frying pan. Brown 6 garlic cloves and discard.  Add minced garlic and onion and brown.  Add tomato, olives, capers, bay spring, oregano, thyme, marjoram, salt and pepper.  Simmer for 2 1/2 hours, stirring occasionally. Sauce will be thick.  Remove from heat.  Set aside.

**To prepare the chiltomate sauce:**   In a blender or food processor, blend tomatoes, onion, garlic, and fish stock.  Strain mixture.  Heat oil in a frying pan and add blended tomato mixture.  Season with bay leaves, thyme, marjoram, and salt.  Add half the chiles gueros and picked jalapeños and 1 cup pickling juices.  Simmer for 1 hour.

**To prepare the red snapper:**  Put fish in a baking dish.  In a blender or food processor, blend lime juice, garlic, bay leaves, oregano, oil, salt and pepper.  Pour mixture over fish and marinate for 2 hour in the refrigerator.

Preheat oven to 350 degrees.
Stir tomato and chiltomate sauces together, and cook for 25 minutes. Remove fish from marinade.  Place in another large baking dish.  Baste with some sauce. Bake for 35 minutes, basting every 15 minutes, with more sauce.  Then bake for 1 1/4 hours or until fish is done.

To serve, place fish on a platter, and cover with remaining sauce, warmed.  Garnish with remaining chiles gueros, pickled jalapeños, bay leaves, thyme, majoram, and parsley.  Serve any remaining sauce on the side. Accompany with white rice.   **Makes 8 servings.**

## FRIJOLES NEGROS ESTILO VERACRUZ
## (Refried Black Beans, Veracruz Style)

**For the Beans:**

    4 1/2 quarts water
    1 1/3 pounds dried black beans, washed and soaked overnight
    2 white onions, halved
    10 cloves garlic, whole
    Salt to taste
    30 cilantro leaves
    3/4 cup vegetable oil
    2 large white onion, finely chopped

**For the Garnish**

    2 to 3 quarts water
    1 pound bacon
    1 1/2 cups feta cheese, crumbled
    2 chiles jalapeños, chopped
    Crisply fried tortilla wedges

Bring water to boil in a large saucepan or clay pot.

Add beans, onion and garlic.  Cook at a slow boil for 1 1/2 hours or until beans are done.  Add salt after 1 hour of cooking.

Blend 1 cup beans in a blender or food processor with a little cooking water.  Add bean mixture to remaining beans.  Stir in cilantro leaves.

Heat  in a heavy frying pan.  Add onion and saute until dark brown.  Add beans little by little and fry.  Correct salt to taste.  Cool, and refrigerate for one day.

**Before serving prepare the garnish:**  Bring water to boil in a saucepan. Add bacon, and cook for 10 minutes.  Drain.  Fry bacon in a frying pan. Reserve fat.  Drain bacon on paper towels, and crumble.  Set bacon aside.

Heat bacon fat in a frying pan.  Add beans little by little, and mash, using the back of a spoon, until a thick puree is obtained.  Tilt frying pan, and using a spatula, shape puree into an oblong roll.

To serve, place beans on a plate.  Sprinkle roll with crumbled bacon, cheese and chiles.  Garnish with tortilla wedges.  Serve with eggs or roasted meat.  **Makes 8 servings.**

## SIGHTSEEING

Veracruz is Mexico's oldest colonial city, its largest port, and a thriving industrial center.   Few of its residents depend on tourism for their livelihood,  which means that the state-of-the-art infrastructure of a Cancun or Acapulco is missing.  Many will consider this a plus.  Any true traveler will be fascinated by a thriving ambience that's both lively and *real.*

Now a city of nearly 300,000, Veracruz remains much as the Spanish laid it out nearly 500 years ago.   The design features the ubiquitous main plaza, **Plaza de Armas** also known as **Plaza de la Constitucion**, thought to be the oldest in Mexico. Attractively landscaped with tall palms and tropical flowers, the plaza is flanked by a cathedral on one side and government buildings on the other with sidewalk cafes lining the two remaining sides.

Thousands of refugees from Republican Spain settled in Veracruz after the Spanish Civil War.  Possibly that's why the city goes in for European-style cafe life more than any other community in Mexico.  It's not exaggerating to say that life revolves around the cafes.   Stay here awhile and you may find yourself gravitating to a favorite two or three times a day.  Street musicians stroll through in the evenings and, since the area has been closed to traffic, you can enjoy your shrimp, beer or coffee without gagging on exhaust fumes.

The plaza itself is pretty and well cared for.  In the center of the park is not one fountain but five.  Lights in the main fountain are a brilliant pink, making for a stunning display at night when flanked by the red and green of the four smaller ones. It's a delightful spot from which to listen to the band concerts that take place nearly every night.

From the plaza it's just a few blocks to the dock and **Malecon**.  If shells are your thing, this is heaven.  You'll find them from everywhere.  And that's about all you'll find in the way of souvenirs.  Veracruz is not a shopping town.

To the right is the **Museo Historico de la Revolucion Venustiano Carranza**, a lighthouse museum that pays homage to the life and times of the city's native son, Venustiano Carranza, a revolutionary general who became president of the republic in 1915.  Closed Mondays.

Before you is the **Castillo de San Juan de Ulua**, once an island, now connected to the mainland by a causeway and open to the public.  Noted for its massive walls and ramparts, the castillo was built at a cost of 40 million gold pesos by Charles V. Originally a fortification to protect the city from buccaneers, the castle looks like the set from an old pirate movie.  Actually it did provide the background for a more recent film.  Remember *Romancing the Stone?*  Kathleen Turner, Michael Douglas and all those crocodiles?

The real story of the Castillo de San Juan de Ulua isn't nearly so amusing. Following Mexico's independence from Spain, the fort became a prison used as frequently for those with undesirable political leanings as for criminals. Some were thrust into dungeons half-flooded with water at high tide. Benito Juarez and Porfirio Diaz were among the former "guests." Some say that modern politicians campaigned to have the castle converted to a museum to insure that *they'd* never have to face incarceration in those miserable cells.

# AN EXCURSION TO JALAPA

Some more traditional locals prefer to spell their lovely town — the capital of the state of Veracruz — Xalapa, but no matter how you spell it, it's pronounced Halapa. Like Rome, Jalapa is built on seven hills. The townspeople claim that climbing them makes girls legs particularly pretty. Perhaps they're right. There is a saying, *Las Jalapenas son halaguenas* or Jalapa girls are enchanting.

Along with being the state capital, Jalapa is very much an intellectual center, a kind of tropical Guanajuato. There's very little of a cultural nature that doesn't exist in this small, but sophisticated city. Apart from the University, Jalapa supports a state theater, a symphony orchestra, a ballet group and an opera company.

The city is justly proud of its **Archaeological Museum.** Wandering in the lush gardens you may encounter the Olmec corn god, Tlaloc; the Aztec rain god and his wife, the water goddess; and the Huastecan god of love.

The indoor exhibits are located in two dome-shaped structures to the left of the lawn as you face the museum. Here also are figures from several archaeological zones. One of the most interesting is a large Olmec head. Another is the beguiling, bare breasted Tlasolteotl, the Huastecan goddess of love, childbirth, the moon and the harvest.

You won't find the usual "DO NOT TOUCH" sign at the state-of-the-art **Science and Technology Museum** where hands on contact is the whole idea. Here one can enjoy a fascinating display of cars and other machinery while acquiring painless lessons in biology, physics and astronomy. This new museum is fascinating and quite unique. Don't miss it.

One of the city's delightful streets may be haunted. Today **Callejon del Diamante** (or **Diamond Alley**) has a charmingly bohemian feel to it with its sidewalk cafes, streets artists and strolling musicians.

But of course there's a story attached to it, one that could be replayed today on *A Current Affair.* It seems that once a seemingly happy couple dwelt there. The enamored husband gifted his pretty wife with a beautiful diamond ring.    As he slipped it on her slender finger, she promised undying love.

Eventually the young husband was called out of town for a few days on a business trip.  Returning to Jalapa late in the evening, he decided to visit his best friend, hoping to discuss some of the events of the trip which had not gone well.  Entering the house unannounced, he found his friend sound asleep.  Beside him on the bedside table was the diamond ring.

Quietly the man picked up the ring and returned home to confront his wife. Nothing she could say could dissuade him.  In a jealous rage he killed her. Placing the ring back on her finger, he left the house — and the town — forever.

Today, it's said that the ghost of the faithless wife still walks the streets, her diamond flashing.  Who knows, anything's possible; but, today the street is so full of activity that she could easily float by unnoticed.  Don't miss this winding hillside street which boasts two extremely popular restaurants, **La Fonda** and **La Sopa.**  The food at both is excellent. Diamond Alley has some interesting shops as well.

*A ghost is said to haunt this street.* Photo by the author.

You can literally walk in the footsteps of the conquistadors at **El Lencero Museum,** a synthesis of nearly 500 years of history.  This magnificent hacienda was originally the property of Juan Lencero, one of Cortes's lieutenants who received a grant from the King of Spain to establish one of ten lodging houses between Veracruz and Mexico City.

Lencero chose his site well.  Situated on a gentle, sloping hill it overlooks a tranquil lake.  Beautiful gardens surround the mansion.  One very large fig tree may have been planted by Lencero himself.

In 1842 the deposed Antonio Lopez de Santa Anna, one of the most colorful and controversial presidents of Mexico, bought the house and land for 45,000 pesos. He lived there for fourteen years building the place into one of the most successful sugar haciendas in the state.  Among the many lovely antiques you'll see there is

Santa Anna's brass bed.  El Lencero Museum is located five miles from Jalapa on the Veracruz road.

Four miles beyond Jalapa is the charming village of **Coatepec**, which means "Mount of Fertility."  This is one of those totally unspoiled pueblos that looks like a movie set and this time it's true.   Much of *Romancing the Stone* was filmed here. Among other things,  you'll see the spectacular waterfall that brought the protagonists together (more or less).   Unlike so many of the colonial towns that revolve around tourism, Coatepec is truly the real thing — unspoiled for centuries.

A visit there would be incomplete without a stay at **Posada Coatepec**, one of the most romantic hotels in Mexico.   One of the seven prestigious Small Grand Hotels of Mexico, Posada Coatepec is a hidden treasure, the intimate getaway everyone dreams of finding.   The 18th century colonial mansion has just 20 rooms each a repository of priceless antiques.

The hotel's prize winning **Maria Enriqueta Restaurant** offers both traditional and international cuisine.   Everything is good, but don't miss the *omelette con huitlacoche* for a dream breakfast.

Those traveling between Veracruz and Mexico City by bus or car will find Coatepec and Jalapa on the way.  For those beginning and ending their holiday in Veracruz, arrangements can be made with the Posada Coatepec for a pick up in Veracruz.  The Posada Coatepec staff can also arrange any number of interesting excursions into the surrounding jungle or to the nearby ruins of El Tajin. Hidalgo 9. Telephone: (281) 6-0544.

*Posada Coatepec was once an 18th century colonial mansion*. Photo by the author.

*Posada Coatepec is the intimate get away everyone dreams of finding*. Photo by the author.

## TIDBITS

Continental now flies directly into Veracruz from its Houston hub.  Mexicana offers connecting flights from Mexico City.  From the airport, frequent van transfers are readily available and reasonably priced.  Around town, taxis are plentiful and inexpensive or you can take the old wooden trolley cars now on wheels (known as **Tranvias** ) which operate around town as part of the city's public transportation system.

Veracruz is hot all year and humid in the summer during the rainy season.  Starting in August and lasting for about three months, storms blow down from the north bringing high winds and more rain.  The best weather is from November through March.

Carnival here is fantastic — a true blowout, like New Orleans or Rio.  If you're interested, book reservations well in advance.

**Watch for** upcoming excursions to the "lost city" of El Pital, some eighty miles north of Veracruz.  A team of Mexican and U.S. archaeologists have so far located more than 100 earth and stone structures, including pyramids over 100 feet high.  Researchers believe the city was a major political, commercial and agricultural center that flourished from 100 to 600 A.D.

Covering some 40 square miles, the site includes suburbs and a highly sophisticated irrigation and agricultural system.  Archaeologists also think that the city may have been an important seaport that spread the use of corn and other technologies as far as the Mississippi Valley in North America.

# PALENQUE
## ROMANCING THE RUINS

*The Count's house is to the right.* Photo by Vern Appleby.

Many might have thought the 64-year-old Jean-Frederic, Count de Waldeck a bit old for a jungle expedition, but surely not de Walbeck himself — a man who would, in his nineties, turn down a handsome cash settlement in favor of an annuity. This is a man who, at 102, decided he was finally ready for marriage and then died five years later in Paris, struck by a passing carriage as he paused to admire a pretty young woman.

In the early 19th century, de Waldeck heard tales of an abandoned city deep in the Chiapas jungle and determined to explore the remote site. Eventually reaching Palenque, he selected the prettiest ruin and the most nubile of the village women and set up housekeeping.

Today it's fun to sit on the front steps of what is now known as the **Count's Temple** and speculate about the daily life of that amazing gentleman and his lady. Perhaps this is where they sat at day's end watching the sun turn the old stones to burnished gold. Maybe he sketched while she regaled him with local legends. It's possible that he offered her cognac; more likely, she introduced him to *balche*.

One thing is certain, the ruins of Palenque are far and away the most beautiful in Mexico. Today, only partially redeemed from the jungle, they remain a magnificent site rivaling the sanctuary of Apollo at Delphi. Gleaming like alabaster, Palenque lies upon the dark flanks of the Tumbala Mountains in the midst of the rainforest.

Though Cortes passed within a few miles of Palenque, the conquistadors somehow missed it completely. Ironically, this time, their brutal intrusion wouldn't have mattered. The original Mayan inhabitants had mysteriously abandoned their splendid stronghold centuries before. The city was left to slumber undisturbed for another 250 years.

It wasn't until 1773 that an Indian's tale of stumbling upon a city "far different, grander, more beautiful" than anything he'd ever seen or heard about piqued the imagination of Father Ramon de Ordonez y Aguilar, canon of Cuidad Real (now San Cristobal de las Casas). Father Ordonez literally mounted an exploratory expedition — his parishioners carried him sixty miles in a sedan chair — to investigate. What awaited them was a masterwork of Mayan art and architecture so impressive that the dazzled priest wrote to Spain.

His curiosity piqued by the story, King Charles III of Spain ordered a systematic exploration of the ruins. The assignment fell to an unlikely candidate, Don Antonio del Rio. A true dandy of his time, del Rio refused to forsake his foppish finery and tramped the jungles in an ensemble that included a three cornered hat, high heeled boots and a powdered wig.

Despite his dress sense, del Rio was a man of action. Too much action. At his bidding 200 Indians hacked away at the ruins with axes and machetes. Imagine the reaction of today's painstaking archaeologists. Nevertheless, del Rio's account was the first published book on Mayan archaeology.

His romantic conclusion that Palenque was probably a lost Roman colony — though del Rio didn't totally rule out a Phoenician connection — were what attracted Count de Waldeck to the site. A student of the artist Jacques Louis David, the amazing count had been the friend of Lord Byron, Beau Brummel and Marie Antoinette (whom he'd visited in prison shortly before her execution), had campaigned with Napoleon in Egypt, then become a pirate preying on British shipping in the Indian Ocean.

Today it's easy to understand how and why de Waldeck selected his "house" in Palenque, angled as the temple is in a manner that provides both natural air conditioning and a breathtaking view of the entire site. A fresh mountain stream flows close by; beyond it, ruins glisten like jewels against emerald velvet. From this vantage point he produced ninety extraordinary drawings.

John Stephens, the next adventurer on the scene, happened upon de Waldeck's name scribbled on the wall beside the drawing of a woman (probably his Indian mistress) with the date 1832. De Waldeck's drawings were incorporated into a book in which he concluded that the Chaldeans and Hindus were responsible for the construction of Palenque. The book was eventually published in 1866 when the incomperable count was 100 years old.

So many theories, so much conjecture, this much is known today: Palenque, uninhabited since the ninth century, but still pulsating with curious vitality, dates from the Classic period (300 to 900 A.D.) Its rise from minor ceremonial center to metropolitan city came rela-

*The ruins of Palenque are far and away the most beautiful in Mexico.* Photo by Vern Appleby.

tively late and owes much to one remarkable ruler, Pacal (A.D. 603-83), and his successors, Bahlum and Kuk. These three men seem to have formulated the official Palenque mythology based on a divine origin for the royal dynasty and on the supernatural passage of power from one ruler to the next.

Today the precision and order of the pyramids stand in sharp contrast to their lush jungle surroundings. From the top of any of the elaborate structures, one can enjoy a sweeping view of the Tabasco lowlands, a seemingly endless stretch of forest and savanna. The ruins themselves are not only exquisitely beautiful but continue to stimulate the imagination, for many of the motifs are strikingly similar to those found in Buddhist countries.

The Buddha's third week of meditation was said to have been spent under a sacred tree. It was during this time that a serpent spread his hood to shield the divine meditator from the sun's rays. Because of this tradition, the sun, the tree, and the serpent are three of the most sacred Buddhist symbols. They are equally sacred to the Mayas.

The similarities don't end here: both Buddhists and Mayas believe that the world has been destroyed four times with a fifth destruction yet to come.

You approach the ruins from the west. The **Palace** first comes into view and then to the right is the **Temple of the Inscriptions.** Smaller temples lie to the east including the **Temples of the Sun,** the **Cross** and the **Foliated Cross.** The **North Group,** a series of buildings (to the north of the Palace) includes the **Temple of the Count.** A pre-Columbian aqueduct directs the waters of the Otulun, a stream to the center of the city, the only example of this kind of construction yet known in Mayan civilization.

The **Palace** is a rectangular complex of broad stairways and numerous rooms, long corridors and a three-story tower, grouped around four large inner court-yards. This stunning building with its pagoda-like feeling contains 176 separate items of painting, stone carvings and stucco sculpture that have been called the finest examples of this ancient art in the world. Themes of death, divinity and royalty are never out of view.

As is so often the case in Mayan architecture, the building is a sort of time machine. When the great Pacal died, it was arranged in such a way that from any vantage point in the Palace Complex the sun at winter solstice appears to set into the earth at what was later discovered to be his tomb and the great temple constructed above it. Not only art and architecture, but the whole order of the universe were called forth to reinforce the ruler's religious and political ideology.

Scholars once agreed that Mayan pyramids were just that — pyramids — and not tombs such as those found in Egypt. But that was pre-Alberto Ruz Lhuiller. One day in 1948 the Mexican archaeologist was staring at the floor of Palenque's lofty pyramid, known as the **Temple of the Inscriptions.** The floor differed from the others by reason of its flagstones which were beautifully worked and fitted together almost perfectly. Some were particularly large. One slab had a double row of holes bored into it, so that the heavy stone could be lifted.

When Lhuiller investigated, he found that the floor appeared higher in places than the bottom of the walls.

Realizing that another hidden room must lie below, he had the heavy flagstone lifted. Below was a passage blocked by sand and rocks. It took four field seasons before the archaeologists reached the foot of the stairs. The concealed staircase led down into the interior of the pyramid. At the foot of the stairs they found sacrificial offerings consisting of jade earplugs and beads, red shells and a perfect tear shaped pearl. Another wall was removed to reveal the skeletons of six young men. Eighty-two feet below the floor of the temple and six and a half feet below the base of the pyramid the passage ended. Or did it?

Closer scrutiny revealed that a triangular stone stab blocked the way. On June 15, 1952 Lhuiller and his patient, hard working crew were rewarded when the last obstacle was removed. Before them was the first tomb ever found of a Mayan king — with all its priceless array of funerary gifts completely intact. It was, they soon realized, the tomb of Pacal himself. The great ruler and the attendants who'd accompanied him on his journey into the after-life were buried with a splendor unique in the entire Mayan civilization.

The tomb chamber itself was a large vaulted room containing nine great figures in stucco relief, slightly larger than life-size, forming a procession around the walls. In the center lay a sarcophagus with a huge elaborately carved stone lid. The skeleton inside was lavishly arrayed with jade jewelry which included a headdress, a necklace of beads in many forms, and elaborate, delicately incised jade earplugs.

At the time of burial, Pacal had been wearing a jade mosaic mask with inlaid eyes of shell and obsidian. In his hands he held great jade beads; in his mouth was another. Even more jade objects were twined about his feet. Red cinnabar had been sprinkled over the body, the jade ornaments and the interior sides of the sarcophagus. Perhaps the color red, with its association with the east and the rising sun, was symbolic of rebirth.

Today the treasures repose in the National Museum of Archaeology in Mexico City, but one can still descend into the tomb. Many find the covering of the sarcophagus particularly interesting, seeing in the intricate design the image of a man at the controls of a space ship.

Behind the temple a narrow path leads off into the jungle. It's only a short walk to the **Temple of the Jaguar**, but once away from the sight and sound of the main cluster of buildings one finds a lost world of contemplation. The wall carving inside the temple shows a man seated with one leg in a lotus position while the other dangles from a splendid throne which is supported by the legs of a jaguar. Jaguar heads protrude from either side of the throne. The over all effect is decidedly oriental.

One of the most distant temples is possibly the most architecturally intriguing. The relief work in the **Temple of the Foliated Cross** is identical to a temple found in Angkor Wat in Cambodia. Add to this the mysterious preponderance of

lotus flowers in the wall designs throughout Palenque — a flower that did not exist in Mexico at the time the city was constructed. Puzzles and more puzzles. Latter day skeptics call Count de Waldeck's conclusions "fanciful," yet the striking similarities between two far distant cultures are difficult to explain away.

*From Palenque, the lid of a sarcophagus depicting the venerated ceiba tree, and other objects, such as the two headed sky dragon and celestial birds.*

*Frederick Catherwood's drawing of Palenque, published in Antiquités Méxicaines, 1834.*

## HOTELS

"We have lived in the palaces of their kings, " the indefagitable American explorer John L. Stephens wrote in 1884.   "We went up to their temples and fallen altars and wherever we moved we saw evidences of their taste, their skill. . .their wealth and their power."

Though Stephens and his artist companion, Frederick Catherwood, were awed by the opportunity to camp among the ruins, they weren't too enchanted by the jungle insects.  Today accommodations are vastly improved — though Palenque could hardly be called hotel heaven.

Two favorites — because of their sensational locations — are the **Suites Chan Kah** and the **Motel Nutuntun**.

**Suites Chan Kah** — *not* to be mistaken for the Hotel Chan Kah Centro downtown — comes closest to elegant.  These attractive, well furnished bungalows look out at exotic gardens only inches from the jungle — expect to see brightly plumaged birds and forest creatures from your front porch.  Shallow, stone-lined pools in a large garden offer cooling relaxation and reading areas.   An attractive palapa-roofed building covered with exotic vines houses the pleasant dining room and lounge area.  The food here is good, so are the margaritas.   The hotel is located on the road to the Palenque ruins, about three miles to the east.  Transportation is provided.  For reservations, write to Suites Chan Kah, Apto. Postal 26, Palenque, Chiapas, Mexico.  Local phone: 5-03-18.

I love the atmosphere of **Motel Nututum.** Clean, comfortable cottages have thatched roofs and the riverside setting is lovely. Nothing seems quite as refreshing after a day of climbing up and down pyramids as a dip in the river. The palm thatched dining room serves excellent food and looks out over river and jungle. The hotel is located on the Palenque-Ocosingo Road about a mile from town. Local phone: 5-01-00.

*A sculpture in the Palace courtyard.*

The new kid on the block, **Hotel Mision Palenque**, is pretty country clubby — manicured lawns, air conditioning (the others have ceiling fans), all the "amenities." Not quite the Palenque of *my* dreams, but the hotel does have some advantages. The Mision provides transportation to and from the Villahermosa airport and the Palenque archaeological zone. *It also has an almost secret attraction — at least few seem to know about it. Follow the path into the jungle to the natural mud baths for an earthy soak complete with free beer or soft drinks.* For reservations, write Hotel Mision, Rancho San Martin, Palenque. Local phone: 5-02-41.

**Hotel La Canada** comes well recommended. Situated in a woodsy, forest-fringed area within walking distance of town, the place looks highly inviting. The food is good and the co-owner, Moises Morales, has lectured on Palenque at top U.S. and European universities. Calle Canada 14. Phone: 5-01-02.

**Hotel Chan Kah Centro** (same owners as Suites Chan Kah) has a convenient downtown location, is clean, modern and reasonable. For reservations, write Apto. Postal 26, Palenque, Chiapas, Mexico. Local phone: 5-02-06.

## RESTAURANTS

**La Selva**, on Calle Merle Green close by the Hotel La Canada, is probably the town's best restaurant.  The tropical palapa atmosphere is pleasant and excellent live music is a frequent dividend.   The **Mayan Restaurant** on the main plaza serves good regional food.  The dining rooms at the **Nutuntum** and **Suites Chan Kah** serve excellent meals in a lovely atmosphere.

*The sparkling beauty of Agua Azul is not to be missed.* Photo by the author.

## TIDBITS

The easiest way to reach Palenque is to fly into Villahermosa (a lively boomtown with a fabulous museum park filled with Olmec treasures).  From here you can catch a bus or rent a car.   First class buses (ADO)  leave Villahermosa twice daily and take about 2 1/2 hours.   The 2nd class bus leaves more frequently but takes much longer — just how much longer varies.   If you're planning to stay in town, getting to and from the ruins is simply a matter of catching one of the frequent collectivos.  The cost is nominal.   Taxis are also inexpensive.

If you choose to rent a car, you'll find   road conditions excellent.  It takes about two hours to cover the 89 miles.  Though not essential, a car unquestionably makes the stay more pleasant.  The independence and opportunity to explore are definite pluses.   One of the places you definitely won't want to miss is **Agua Azul**, an incredibly beautiful water fall with more than 500 cascades crashing onto a limestone bed.   The brilliant blue water ebbs and flows, boils and whirls, but there are calm pools for swimming as well.

The ruins are open from 8 to 5 daily, the price nominal.  If possible, go first thing in the morning, then return toward late afternoon.  Or go for the whole day and take your bathing suit.  There's a hidden pool near the tiny museum.

There's one question that everyone asks sooner or later in Palenque (better sooner!)  It concerns the safety of the water (which comes from a spring behind the Temple of the Inscriptions at the ruins).  The owner of Suites Chan Kah,  Roberto Romano, answers by passing out a card which says:  *"This water endowed the men who lived thousands of years ago on this site with the capability of a superior mind and who by drinking it brought to light the zero and discovered the infinite."*  Though Señor Romano speaks fluent English and is a font of knowledge about Palenque,   I still strongly recommend bottled water.

Baja California
Baja California Sur
Los Cabos

## BAJA CALIFORNIA
### CALAFIA'S LEGACY

She was created in the tenth year of the sixteenth century, A.D., a personification of all women.  She was a queen who led her triumphant band of amazons where no man dared to go.

and her subjects perpetuated themselves through breeding negotiations with the head-hunting Seris of Isla Tiburon.  Later, in the spring of each following year, sons were either killed or sold

*The arches that mark Los Cabos.*  Photo by Derro Evans

The creation of Garcia Ordonez de Montalvo, an obscure Spanish writer, who glorified her in a novel, *Las Sergas de Esplandian,* published in 1510, she captured the imagination of thousands. She was Calafia, reigning monarch of the fabled California, "the entrance to paradise on earth."

Calafia (the name, like czar, kaiser or caesar, designated supreme authority)

to their biological fathers while newborn daughters insured continuation of the Californians.

Montalvo's California was an island "on the right hand of the Indies" and "very near to the terrestrial paradise." Its beautiful queen wore an apron of precious black pearls, her warrior women carried weapons of gold for there was no other metal available on the island.

Small wonder Spaniards continued to search valiantly for this fabled island until they found it—or at least thought they'd found it. What they actually discovered was a peninsula protruding farther into the sea than any other. And what eventually resulted was not one California but two, Alta and Baja (upper and lower). Residents of the latter are certain that it is in their land of desert, mountain and sea that the spirit of Calafia still dwells, personified in the living, breathing beauty of Baja.

Some insist that the peninsula is different—friendlier, safer, slower, *mas tranquilo.* For years it was the forgotten piece of Mexico. Even today it's one of the last great frontiers for travelers, "a wonderful example" — as one affecionado has written "of how much bad roads can do for a country." The meager history of Baja is concerned primarily with treasure hunters, Christian zealots and a few seekers after geographical and scientific information. Most of the sporadic endeavors to colonize met with failure, leaving for the record a scattering of primitive artifacts, crumbling missions, and forgotten ranches.

The narrow land mass juts out for nearly l000 arid, sparsely settled miles, bathed by the crashing waves of the Pacific on the west and the crystalline Sea of Cortes (or Gulf of California) to the east. Overnight ferries connect southern Baja with mainland Mexico scarcely l00 miles — but seemingly worlds — away.

Nature bestowed upon Baja all the beauties of a dry, warm climate: towering snow capped mountains, flowery desert flats, blue water, bird-rich islands, and endless great, curving beaches—most of them deserted. Until recently, little of what we call "progress" had encroached upon it. Baja has never needed protection because the land protected itself.

Lured by the fanciful tales of gorgeous women, treasures and a mysterious island (probably in just that order) Diego de Becerra, one of Cortes's captains, landed near what would one day be the capital city of La Paz. It was a disastrous voyage. Bercerra was slaughtered by his crew, who in turn proved no match for the hardy resident Indians who'd reached the area centuries before by crossing the Bering Strait to Alaska and then moving southward down the Pacific Coast. Only a few sailors survived to tell the tale, but since that tale involved a vast quantity of priceless pearls, Cortes himself appeared on the scene in 1535.

Though no Calafia greeted him, Cortes was consoled by the pearls. Hoping to find more, he outfitted three ships under the command of Francisco de Ulloa who sailed north to the very mouth of the Colorado River discovering in the process that "California" was not an island at all. Ulloa named the waters El Mar de Cortez (The Sea of Cortez) in honor of his benefactor.

Pearls from the Sea's oysters and tales of Baja's precious metals drew adventurers from all over the world, among them British privateers —a euphemistic term for pirates. Many buccaneers sought protection in the Sea's sheltered harbors leaving their names on rocks that shielded beaches stashed with booty. Spanish treasure galleons were raided, coastal settlements pillaged and slave ships hijacked. Inevitably the pirates' greed took its toll on the native population. In some places, whole tribes disappeared, either killed by intruders or forced to flee.

Once discovered, Baja languished. Again and again the peninsula lured men only to defeat them. It was 150 years and many failures later before the first permanent mission settlement was founded in 1698. Others followed, slowly moving up the peninsula mile by painstaking mile. Of this daunting string of 18th century missions — thirty of them — only ruins remain. By 1854 even the padres had given up. The missions were abandoned. With the pearl beds fished out, there was nothing left that people wanted — nothing but wild beauty and far too much of that to be valued for its own sake.

"Everything concerning California is of such little importance that it is hardly worth the trouble to take pen and paper to write about it," one disgruntled missionary wrote. "Of poor shrubs, useless thorn bushes and bare rocks, of miles of sand without water or woods, of a handful of people, who beside their physical shape and ability to think, have nothing to distinguish them from animals, what shall I or what can I report?"

In 1848, Lady Luck (or was it the spirit of Calafia?) saved Baja California a second time, once more averting "progress." Following the Mexican War, when U.S. troops landed at Ensenada, La Paz and Mulege, negotiators whose job it was to hammer out a peace treaty with Mexico were instructed to ask for

Baja California, but not so insistently that it might have a bargaining power as an apparent concession. Mexico's tenacity served as a stay of execution that's lasted nearly 150 years. Unlike Alta California, Baja is not seamed with freeways or studded with shopping malls. Unfortunately some things are inevitable. Even as I write, roads are being improved, air strips widened. If desert wilderness is your thing, enjoy it *now.*

The peninsula is divided into northern and southern states, **Baja Norte** and **Baja Sur**, which share similar geography and climate. Baja's southernmost tip lying in the Tropic of Cancer, offers sultry temperatures in the summer. This area is also subject to *chubascos*, sudden tropical storms, striking from August to October when winds can get up to 150 miles per hour. More often, gentle sea breezes soften the dry desert heat and keep the nights balmy. Though winters can be cool in the north, rainfall on the peninsula is rare.

Empty, clean Baja is a moonscape— pale, flat expanses of sand, ridged with snow dusted mountain ranges 10,000 feet high, grand and solitary.

# BAJA NORTE
## BAJA NORTE'S BORDER TOWNS
## TIJUANA, ROSARITA BEACH, ENSENDA

Legend has it that Tijuana was named for Tia Juana or Aunt Jane, a lady famous for her excellent food and warm, *very* warm, hospitality. The border town has enjoyed a naughty reputation ever since.

*Tijuana's famous mecca, Fronto Palacio.*
Photo by Vern Appleby.

Conceded to be the busiest border city in the world with more than 56 million visitors crossing its two gates each year, people go to Tijuana for a close, convenient taste of Mexico.  One can drink margaritas, eat tacos, see bull fights, shop for arts and crafts. It's all there, easy and accessible, the whole — you'll pardon the expression— enchilada.

Officially founded in 1889, Tijuana moved onto the world stage on January 1, 1916, the day of its very first horse race. The population was under a thousand when James Wood Coffroth, said to be the notorious "Spider Kelly" who inspired the Clark Gable role in the movie *San Francisco*, opened the Tijuana Racetrack just 60 feet from the San Ysidro border crossing.

The success of the operation was virtually guaranteed by laws that prohibited gambling on horse races in the United States.  A crowd of 10,000 — ten times the population — attended the event which would transform a sleepy village into the world's busiest border city.

Among the celebrities present that first season were Will Rogers, Charlie Chaplin, Harold Lloyd, Eddie Foy and producer Mack Sennett. Obviously the success of the venture was far reaching. The State of California, which forbade gambling, facilitated the crossing of horses freely into Tijuana. As many as fourteen railway cars filled with horses arrived in San Ysidro in a single day. The horses were then unloaded and walked across the border to the Tijuana track.

General Plutarco Elias Calles, then president of Mexico, declared Baja

California a free commercial zone and General Abelardo L. Rodriguez, Governor of the Territory of Baja California and later president of the country, became a member of Coffroth's business group. Before long they'd purchased Spanish land grant property from the Arguello family who literally owned Tijuana and began construction of a luxury hotel above the nearby Agua Caliente hot springs.

The opening on June 23, 1928 was a landmark day for Tijuana. By the end of the year actress Norma Talmadge presided at the opening of the Agua Caliente Airport. A red, revolving light was installed atop the 85-foot-high bell tower as a beacon to the Ford trimotor air taxis that shuttled in racing fans every half hour from San Diego and Los Angeles.

The **Caliente Race Track** at Hiprodromo de Agua Caliente, Agua Caliente Boulevard 3737 officially opened December 28, 1929 on the grounds of the Agua Calienta spa, hotel and casino. The total cost was estimated at $3 million, $200,000 of which was spent on green areas. Grass for the lawns was imported from Europe and then unrolled like a giant green carpet. Hundreds of adult palm trees were brought in for planting. Curtains for the Jockey Club cost $64 a yard. Ceilings were intricately carved and painted and champagne was served in cut crystal stemware.

Racing enthusiasts, Baron Rothchild and the Sultan of Jahore among them, dressed in the latest fashions. Van & Schenk, the highest paid comedians in show business, entertained, perform-

ing afternoons in the Race-track's patio-dining room and evenings in the casino cafe. Al Jolson, who made famous the song, "Mammy," and starred in the first talking picture, was master of ceremonies for the Main Handicap; and, with his wife, tap-dancer Ruby Keeler, awarded the prize to the winning horse, Scot's Grey, while Paramount News filmed the ceremony.

With the repeal of Prohibition in the United States, Tijuana's "playground of the rich and famous" aura diminished, yet the Caliente Race Track continued to make news, acquiring the reputation of being one of the most innovative courses in the world by introducing the first electronic starting gate, the photo finish, the first regularly scheduled $100,000 race, the pick six wager and the jockey helmet.

Today the track is devoted to world-class greyhound racing. There are twelve races nightly with first post at 7:35 p.m. Matinee racing is conducted each Saturday and Sunday, first post time of ten races at 2. p.m.

## HOTEL TIDBIT

As a wide open town, Tijuana was once the playground of Hollywood stars and Spanish bullfighters.  Whispers of that ambience still remain. One  hears them most keenly at the landmark **Hotel Caesar** (Avenida Revolucion and Calle 5a Phone: 85-16-66).  Expect gaudy, gilt mirrors and red velvet bedspreads.  Many rooms are named for the famous bullfighters who've stayed there such as Manolete and Manuee Captillo.

Clean, camp and lively, the moderately priced hotel is conveniently located in the center of everything.  One should at the very least drop in to sip a margarita and view the nostalgic array of photographs of bygone  matadors.  The hotel has a gastronomic history as well for the popular Caesar Salad was born here in 1925, created by an inventive young chef, Caesar Cardini.

Justifiably proud of the spur-of-the moment invention that became an international favorite, the present chef consented to share the recipe for the original Caesar Salad.

**The Original Caesar Salad**
Toss together:

Romaine lettuce, chill, dry, crisp
Dash Worcestershire sauce
6 tablespoons grated parmesan cheese
1 cup croutons
1/3 cup garlic flavored salad oil
2 tablespoons wine vinegar
Juice of 1  1/2 lemon
1 raw egg
 Freshly ground pepper
Salt to taste

## MORE FUN AND GAMES & SHOPPING

The Aztecs and Mayas of Mexico played a ritual game which required players to throw a ball through a stone hoop without using their hands.  Some believe that the early Spanish conquistadors took the idea back to Spain with them.  Eventually, through the alchemy of time, it may have reincarnated as Jai Alai, the world's fastest ball game.

The building in which Jai Alai is played is called a *fronton*  and since l930 the **Fronton Palacio**, between 7th and 8th avenues on Revolucion,  has been a mecca for aficianados.  Despite the frantic pace (the ball is propelled faster than 160 miles an hour) and skill required to play the game, Jai Alai is easy to follow and understand.  Games are held nightly except Wednesday — thirteen games each night beginning at 8.

Shopping too is a kind of game.  Tijuana is a true *tianguis*, the ancient word for market place.  Avenue Revolucion is a veritable shopping mall with merchandise brought in from every corner of Mexico.  Prices are for the most part reasonable and bargaining is expected.  Vendors are warmly welcoming,  enthusiastic. ("Come in, I love redheads! Blonds! Brown hair.  Ah, black hair.  *La favorita!)*

There are buys to be found in Tijuana—provided you bargain and follow a couple of other rules.  Stores with doors tend to be more expensive than stalls.  Head for the door when you want to find out the shopkeeper's absolute bottom price for an item — he or she will call it out as you leave.

Two to definitely check out are **Bernardo Pieles** and **Tolon.**  Bernardo Pieles, at two locations, Avenue Revolucion 6l0 and 72l, offers outstanding buys in leather. Probably the best, not necessarily the cheapest, but far less expensive than in the U.S.

Tolon, across from the Fronton Palacio,  at 1111 Revolucion, specializes in folk art, hand carved colonial-style furniture, "Tiffany" glass, the best of everything brought from all parts of Mexico.  Wonderful for browsing, but if you fail to find your heart's desire, original ideas may be custom made to your taste.

# RESTAURANTS

Next to gambling and shopping, Tijuana's favorite tourist sport is eating.  You could hardly miss **Tia Juana Tilly's** (Avenida Revolucion 701 next to the Fronton Palacio) where the intriguing and provocative menu compares women to tacos and men to cucumbers.  There's an awning covered outdoor cafe and a carpeted dining room with assorted paraphernalia crowding the ceiling, a trademark of Carlos Anderson restaurants throughout Mexico.  A similar establishment is the **Guadalajara Grill** at Diego Rivera No. 19.  Expect good food, lots of noise and a lively ambience.

**Carintas Uruapan** on Blvd. Diaz Ordaz No. 550 has good food and soulful mariachis.  **Restaurant Boccaccio's** at Blvd. Agua Caliente y General Salina No. 2500 is justifiably proud of a gourmet menu and elegant ambience to rival any restaurant in Mexico.

The new restaurant row is **Pueblo Amigo,** also known as **Local 19 A Espaldas del Race Book**, a charming "colonial" village that's sprung up in the Tijuana river development area.   Some of the bars and restaurants have giant TV screens where games and races taking place all over the world can be  viewed and bet on. Several have color monitors showing up to nine sporting events simultaneously and as many as six racing signals assuring that every seat in the house is a good one.   There's a popular disco too and every type of restaurant.  My own favorite is **Restaurante Argentino de Tony,** intimate, elegant, and *quiet.*  This place is as romantic as it gets in Tijuana and the steaks are excellent.

One of the city's newest attractions is **Mexitlan**  (Ocampo Y 2a) a multi-million dollar cultural and tourist center which houses more than 200 scale model replicas of the more famous historic buildings and monuments in Mexico as well as several restaurants and a lively entertainment area.   This is the place to see it all:  Mexico literally at your feet, all the places you've loved and all the ones on your wish list to visit.

With more people from the United States visiting Tijuana than any other foreign city, Mexico's fourth largest city maintains an information service every day of the week from 9 a.m. to 7 p.m.   The Tijuana Tourism and Convention Bureau is located at Paseo de los Heroes #108.   There's also a tourism protection office headed by Jesus Montanez Roman. Telephone:  (66) 88-04-55.

## THE "GOLD COAST " FROM ROSARITO BEACH TO ENSENADA

There's a haunted hotel fifteen minutes or 27 kilometers south of Tijuana.  The ghosts—if you don't actually see them—will still make their presence felt. They're an interesting lot, some famous, some infamous.  That plump fellow in the corner, the one with the dark glasses, the fez, the cigarette holder......Isn't he King Farouk? There's Lana too, and Orson and Rita—one would recognize them anywhere.  But who's that elegant couple lounging in the corner?  He—olive skinned, charismatic, always an eye for the ladies despite the gorgeous brunette beside him.   She so lovely with her stunning clothes and sultry green eyes—ethereal looking, wouldn't you say? Well, of course you know them, it's Ali Khan and Gene Tierney.

What draws these restless shades?   Memories, what else!  The **Rosarita Beach Hotel** (1-800-343-8582)  fairly oozes yesterday's glamor.   Admittedly, it's a bit tired.   More than sixty years in the fast lane do take their toll.  A little nip and tuck might improve this faded  beauty but could also destroy  her time warp appeal.

The most colorful hotel in twentieth century Mexican history,  Rosarito Beach's famous inn is Baja's best known landmark.   It's story reaches back to the days of

*The Rosarita Beach Hotel, Baja's most famous landmark.* Photo by Vern Appleby.

the dons when, in 1827, Juan Machado received a land grant for 407,000 acres which included El Rosario — today's Playas de Rosarito.  During the 1920s the property passed into the hands of a promoter long on ideas, short on cash.  His luxurious "El Rosarito Resort and Country Club" advertised in San Diego newspapers was in reality a few rooms in a primitive coastal area with few amenities and no reliable road.

It took the imagination and drive of Manuel Barbachano, the entrepreneur credited with bringing electrical power and telephone service to Baja Norte, to turn a few tourist cabins into a world famous resort.  The timing was perfect.  Wide open gambling in Baja California combined with Prohibition in the United States added a forbidden fruit appeal to the ready made lure of a foreign country. Tales of celebrated guests proliferated — cigar-chomping race driver Barney Oldfield, author and sports columnist Damon Runyon and movie favorites, Mickey Rooney and Paulette Goddard.  The rich and famous list went on and on drawing everyone who wanted to see and be seen.

Then, with the repeal of Prohibition in 1933, the bubble burst.  A final  blow came two years later when the Mexican government outlawed gambling in the country. Of the three mega resorts, the Rosarita Beach Hotel, Tijuana's Agua Caliente and Ensenada's Riviera del Pacifico, only the  former survived.

Not only survived, but flourished.  In 1937 Barbachano consolidated his gains with an extensive remodeling project.  An internationally known  Belgian architect was hired to execute his grand designs which included a huge lobby and the bar still used today.  Massive arches provided the focal point for the construction of additional guest rooms and Mexican  artist, Matias Santovo, was retained to create the dramatic murals still admired in the imposing lobby.  The building was lavishly appointed with a colorful use of tile and  decorated ceiling rafters.

During this period of extensive construction, Barbachano also built an ornate and spacious mansion next door for his young bride, Maria Luisa Chabert—now an elegant restaurant which adjoins the hotel.

Throughout the years the hotel has maintained its glitzy, slightly naughty reputation, remaining as always a romantic trysting place.  Take a good look — there's really no telling who you might see.

The Rosarita Beach Hotel is reached by both the toll road and the free road.   Turn off at the third Rosarito Beach exit.  Drive under the arch and go two blocks west to the hotel's arched entrance.

Six miles south on the free road is **Las Rocas Hotels** (1-800-733- 6394) by far the most elegant of the inns which hug the coast line.  Each room in this slightly surreal white Moorish looking palace has an exquisite ocean front view from its private balcony.   Some have fireplaces as well, and, for real nesters, there are mini-kitchens.

My own favorite is **La Fonda** (Tijuana-Ensenada free road, 59 Km. south of Tijuana; or take the La Mision exit off the toll road. Reservation address: P.O. Box 430268, San Ysidro, CA 92143). Deceptively simple, the pink brick inn stands back from a cobblestone drive leading to an intimate compound of red tiled roofs and ba-nana palms. No two bedrooms are alike.   Some have romantic proverbs above

*Sunset view from La Fonda.* Photo by Vern Appleby.

the beds, fireplaces and pastel balconies facing the prettiest beach in Baja Norte. Newer rooms, reminiscent of caves, are reached by spiral staircases and have glass enclosed showers facing the sea.

La Fonda also has an excellent restaurant which overlooks the sea. Most afternoons there are mariachis and on weekends music for dancing.

And speaking of restaurants, 10 Kms. south of Rosarito Beach is its star attraction, **Puerto Nuevo** (Newport), a village where you can savor fresh lobster with rice, beans and tortillas. Puerto Nuevo began in the late '70s when a few enterprising families started opening up their homes to visitors who were eager to enjoy freshly caught lobster. Guests often sat around the kitchen table with the family. Soon dining rooms were added and eventually restaurants appeared. At last count there were ten, plus a hotel, the **New Port Baja**. The free road runs right by Puerto Nuevo; or from the toll road, take the Cantamar exit.

Of all the good restaurants in the area my own favorite is **Calafia,** just north of Puerto Nuevo. On August 19, 1773 Father Francisco Palou, president of the missions of California, placed a wooden cross on the site now occupied by the restaurant Calafia thus establishing the first division of the Californias. The spot defined the border between the Mexican states of Antigua (old) California and Nueva (new) California. Surveyors of the time had identified this as the farther

*Califia—where pool meets the sea.*
Photo by Vern Appleby.

most point of land before reaching the sea between the missions of Father Santo Domingo and Father San Francisco, making it the southernmost point of the San Diego Mission Parish.

*Mariachis are part of the ambience at Califia.*
Photo by Vern Appleby.

The cliffside setting above the shores of El Descanso Bay is breathtaking, the food and service unbeatable. Lobsters are divine, Mexican dishes and breakfasts delicious. I really can't say enough good things about the food or the friendly and *efficient* staff.

Cut off from mainland politics, Baja early on developed a hardy, roughneck style of its own, often attracting fugitives and shady opportunists. Despite its pious sounding bay, Bahia Todos Santos — All Saints Bay — **Ensenada** has had a typically rip roaring history. Settled in 1602, the port became an active trading and shipping center, a supply point for the early missions—and a magnet for pirates. Hardly had buccaneering gone out of fashion before gold was discovered in 1870. Suddenly it was "Oh! Susanna" with a salsa beat.

The mines eventually played out and with them the rootin' tootin' excitement—but not for long. The advent of Prohibition in the United States quickly livened the pace once again. Ghosts of the padre fathers who brought the first grape cuttings to what would become California might not have been too dismayed to see All Saints Bay turned into a safe harbor for rum runners. The film *Lucky Lady* celebrated such adventures but the true story was hardly less notorious.

Jet setters before there were jets flew down in biplanes to gamble at the **Riviera del Pacifico**, owned by Al Capone and managed by prize fighter Jack Dempsey. You can safely bet that spirits flowed freely in this beautiful seaside hotel-casino, a pearly white mini Monte Carlo on Boulevard Lazaro Cardenas at Avenida Riviera. Now a convention center, its shadowy old bar is open for drinks. Remembrance of things past is palpable.

Designed to resemble one of Baja California's lost missions, the **Mision Santa Isabel** is now the only colonial style hotel in Ensenada. Inside the arched entrance is a pretty courtyard, ample pool and parking. Colorful tile hallways connect two floors of attractive rooms with beamed ceilings,  mission style furniture and views of sea or hills. (Avenida Lopez Mateos and Avenida Castillo. Phone: (U.S.) 619 942-9108; (Mexico) 01-52- 667 8-36-16.)

Ensenada boasts a world class restaurant, pricey but worth it. **La Cueva de los Tigres** or Tigers' Cave. One entire wall is crammed with awards for the Cave's cuisine—most particularly its renowned abalone with crab sauce. Perched above the beach, the Cave boasts a smashing view of the sea. (Located one mile south of town on the Transpeninsula Highway at Play Hermosa—watch on your right for the tiger sign. Phone: 6-64-50).

The Tigers' Cave is romantic, but lively **Cafe Hussong**, the current "in" spot. Cruise passengers don't believe they've been to Ensenada if they haven't acquired a Hussong T-shirt. Besides delicious fresh seafood and Mexican specialties, the menu boasts BBQ Baby Ribs and Red Hot Chicken Wings. Founded in 1892 during Ensenada's gold rush days, the cantina continues to slake the thirst of countless rowdies and wannabes. Margaritas are lethal and too good; or for a variation, try Hussong's own bottled beer. (Located in Plaza Hussong, corner of Avenue Ruiz and Lopez Mateos.)

Ensenada is a "love boat" destination.  That means capital S shopping.  The best shops line **Avenida Lopez Mateos** between Avenida Alvarado and Avenida Riveroll.  Take your pick.

For a variation, consider a tour of the cavernous **Bodegas de Santo Tomas,** the oldest and biggest winery in Mexico. Guided tours lead into cool, heady-smelling cellars where some 500,000 cases of wine are produced each year.   Established in 1888, Bodegas de Santo Tomas draws from 25 varieties of grapes grown in the fertile valleys surrounding Ensenada.  (Avenida Miramar 666; 8-25-09).

# TIDBITS

**Long Distance Calling:**  To call Tijuana from the United States, dial (01152) (66) plus the local number.  To call Rosarito, it's (01152) (66l) plus the local number.  To Ensenada, (01152) (617) plus the local number.

**Within Mexico**, dial 91 plus the area code (Tijuana-66; Rosarito-66l; Ensenada, 617 and then local number.

Emergency calls to the police (134) and fire (136) require only 3-digit dialing and are operational in Tijuana, Rosarito and Ensenada. Emergency medical and mechanical aid are available on the road by using any of the  29 bright yellow roadside call boxes, complete with instructions and operated by bilingual personnel, which are located every 3 Km. on the Tijuana-Ensenada toll road.

The legendary Green Angels also patrol the highways with their radio controlled units to supply assistance and protection for any motorist in distress.  There's no charge for their time, but if your car trouble is due to a part which must be replaced, you will, of course, have to bear that expense.  If you meet with an accident or are otherwise unable to drive, the Green Angels will render aid and, if necessary, communicate by radio for you.

Mexican insurance isn't mandatory for a U.S. driver in Mexico, but it's certainly recommended.  If involved in an accident, you may not be able to establish proof of your ability to pay unless you have a valid Mexican policy.  Drivers may be detained until liability has been established.

# BAJA SUR
## DESERT BACKED BY MOUNTAINS, BORDERED BY WHITE SANDS AND AZURE WATERS

Like a slender arm, Baja stretches 800 miles from Tijuana to **Los Cabos**—the capes. Los Cabos is the name popularly applied to the region of Baja California Sur that lies on the very tip of the peninsula.  It comprises the towns of San Jose del Cabo (St. Joseph of the Cape); Cabo San Lucas (Cape of St.

waters. The area both relaxes and invigorates, inviting true romantics to share its timeless beauty.

To the west, waves of the Pacific spill on empty shores, carving dunes from which agaves sprout, strong, spiky, startlingly green.  To the east, the Sea

*The desert meets the sea at Twin Dolphins.* Photo by Vern Appleby.

Luke) and the super scenic 18 mile highway that links them.

Only 70 miles wide on average, Baja is twice as long and twice as narrow as Florida.  The peninsula is virtually all desert—but where else on the North American continent can one find desert surrounded by sea?  Los Cabos is the apex of Baja, the superprime A-plus desert backed by vermillion mountains and bordered by white sand and azure

of Cortes, glassy, becalmed, the gulf washing craggy coves patrolled by pelicans and cormorants. At the southernmost point, the terrain dwindles to a narrow promontory where a jagged rock arch marks the spot where the Sea of Cortes and the Pacific Ocean swirl together in a crescendo of frothing waves—the symbol of Cabo San Lucas and Cabo San Jose, twin towns that have become a magnet for lovers.

*A sheltered cove along the Los Cabos corridor.* Photo by Derro Evans.

One glimpse of the sandy beaches at the end of the Baja Peninsula explains why. They're broad, bright, expansive. No matter how many people are there, it's always possible to find a private retreat. Though no longer the forgotten peninsula once described by naturalist Joseph Wood Krutch as "a ragged and meaningless appendage precariously attached at the point where California ought to end," Baja remains a place of silence and solitude with the same sharp, clean air breathed by the Spanish conquistadors in the 16th century.

Once the two sleepy villages of Cabo San Lucas and San Jose del Cabo were known only to a few dedicated adventurers who dubbed the area "Marlin Alley." Hemingway was among them, coming often to fish and hunt doves. Then the area was discovered.

Today the eighteen mile stretch—lined by desert on one side, sea on the other—linking the towns is known as "the corridor"—an increasingly well traveled corridor. Though for convenience sake, the two are frequently lumped together as "Los Cabos," each has a distinctly different atmosphere.

**CABO SAN LUCAS** is a town in transition, a place where family-run, white stucco grocery stores co-exist with luxury condos. Despite the lovely new marina which curves around the bay serving as a departure point for fishing boats and a port of call for cruise ships, the place has a pioneer last-stop-at Land's End mentality. Canned opera music booms from a pizza parlor. Rock music explodes from a Chinese disco. Welcome to the end of the world!

## HINTS & TIPS_______________________________________________

TOURIST ALERT: Time share sales people are relentless, indefatigable. Unless you're seriously interested in buying into one of these arrangements, be very careful what you say yes to.  There are *no* free lunches, rides or breakfasts!, and once you've obligated yourself, you've lost precious holiday time to sales presentations that literally go on for hours.

Once you've learned to run the sales gauntlet, Cabo San Lucas has a rambunctious liveliness that charms many. The population last estimated at 25,000 is growing daily.  Despite its boomtown persona, this is a clean town.  The public restroom (next door to the police station) is the cleanest I've seen anywhere in the world.

Prices are higher in Baja Sur because nearly everything must be flown, ferried or trucked in.  Neither Cabo San Lucas or San Jose del Cabo are true shopping towns, yet there are lovely things to see and buy at each.

**Rostros de Mexico** (Faces of Mexico) on Calle Cabo San Lucas offers museum quality masks, some of them more than 200 years old.  **Vida Y Olas** on Blvd. Marina has lovely painted T-shirts and **Piel** down the street has luxurious leatherware.  Also on Blvd. Marina, **Necri** offers distinctive resort clothes.  **Cabo Museum & Galeria** on Avenida Hidalgo at Pericu Plaza #l is an elegant store with particularly attractive handpainted china.

For "bargains," try the open air market on the marina—a block of covered stalls stacked with handicrafts, bangles, baubles, beads and shells.  But the best buys in town are found at the **Glass Factory**, (2 blocks west of Hwy 1, off the Cabos San Lucas bypass road to Todos Santos) where genuine handblown glass is created by Mexican artisans.  The store is open from 8 a.m. to 5 p.m.  Demonstrations of the ancient tradition  are available from 6 a.m. to 2 p.m.

But surely the most romantic excursion will be a boat trip to Land's End.  In addition to cruising past El Arco, you'll stop for a swim and snorkel at secluded Lover's Beach.

## HOTELS _______________________________________________

The most appealing hotel in Cabo San Lucas is on the outskirts of town, along the corridor.  Located on a bluff overlooking its own protected cove, the sumptuous **Hotel Twin Dolphin** (1-800-421-8925) isn't just out of town—it's out of this world. As much a sanctuary as a resort, once you get there you won't want to go anywhere else.   Small wonder Raquel Welch chose it for her wedding!

*Twin Dolpin's signature pool.* Photo by T. Pappas

Built in a kind of power spot where the spectacular coastline of the Sea of Cortes meets the foothills of the Sierra de la Laguna Mountains, the site was revered by ancient man as a place of meditation, a site where miracles were wrought by forceful elements and clear heavens.

Hotel owner David Halliburton has done his thing with style. Without a doubt, Twin Dolphin is the slickest hotel along the entire Baja coast.  Though the flamboyant oilman controls 155 acres of ocean front property, his hotel occupies only a fraction of the land.  Upon acquiring that land in 1977, Halliburton surveyed the bone dry desert, the craggy coastline, thick with cacti and thorn trees, and saw beauty where others might perceive only heat, sand and scrub.

Combining the inspired architecture of Guy Moore with the desert- sensitive landscape design of Chuck Ito, he constructed a white-washed village of 56 single storied rooms and suites that combine total elegance with the serene simplicity of a zen monastery.

Many of Baja's famous cave paintings—the renowned art that makes up a beautiful and mysterious part of the peninsula's history—have been recreated on the walls, a subtle reminder of the desert's timeless beauty, its eternal mystery and its peace.  In his book, *The Cave Paintings of Baja California* , Richard F. Poraude perhaps said it best:  "These paintings reach back beyond the natives who were there when the first Europeans arrived to a people with surprising artistic ability who painted great murals on rock walls that match and often excel those found in

Pre-historic European caves.   Where they came from and what happened to them is lost in antiquity but these paintings are proof of a prolific existence and are becoming a treasure of Mexico."

*The murals at Twin Dolphin are replicas of Baja cave paintings.*
Photo by Vern Appleby.

Arriving guests are greeted with complimentary margaritas—some of the best in Mexico.  They come by chartered plane, private yacht, commercial plane—at least half of them from Europe.  Welcome to a hidden oasis designed to soothe the soul while awakening the senses.

In rooms joyfully devoid of TVs and telephones, they watch a continuous show staged by the myriad sea fowls that thrive on the Sea of Cortes:   A gull swipes a fish from a pelican only to be struck on the back by a frigate bird, who will nab the dropped fish in mid-air.  A flock of pelicans repeatedly circles a school of fish, then peels off in dive-bombing formation hitting the water in perfect unison.

Flanked on one side by beautiful Santa Maria Beach and on the other  by the sculptured coastline of Shipwreck Bay, the hotel grounds comprise a botanical garden of cactus.  Besides jackrabbits, ground squirrels and lizards, guests

*Santa Maria Beach.* Photo by Vern Appleby.

not only hear coyotes but sometimes see them in the early morning or at twilight. Foxes, audacious and cunning, not at all afraid to draw close to the kitchen door are more frequent visitors; and, occasionally at night, someone catches a glimpse of a bobcat, twice the size of its domestic cousin, with a short tail, chunky body and mottled brown coat, a predator among predators.

Twin Dolphin has a world class restaurant.  Everything's good, but a particular favorite was the gazpacho soup. Carl Marts, the handsome chef, whose recent bride is a guest who came for a weekend and never left, agreed to share the recipe.

> **Soccoro's Gazpacho**
> Serves 8
> > 5 tomatoes
> > 2 celery stalks
> > 1/3 white onion
> > 3 cloves of garlic
> > 1/2 green pepper
> > 1 cucumber
> > 1 liter tomato juice
>
> Salt, black pepper, Tabasco and Worcestershire sauce to taste.  Blend all ingredients together, season and chill.  Garnish with diced cucumber, toast and parsley.

*The spectacular Finisterra Hotel.* Photo by Derro Evans.

Another long time favorite is **Hotel Finisterra** (land's end), an enchanted citadel anchored to craggy cliffs overlooking both the Pacific and the Sea of Cortes.  The setting is so captivating that it's easy to understand why Rolling Stones guitarist Keith Richards and model Patty Hansen chose it as the site of their wedding, and countless other newlyweds have spent their honeymoons there.

Engineers and workmen blasted away for two years to build Finisterra, perched like a fortress of wrought iron and rock high above the Pacific. Today the hotel commands a breathtaking view in all directions save the north, where an even higher peak blocks the view.  Think of it as a new spin on Wuthering Heights. Finisterra has a comfortable, lodgelike feel to it and a laid-back sense of style. Guests at the hotel's **Whale Watcher Bar**, the most popular in town, can watch the sea below explode like champagne against the rocks.   (1-800-347-2252)

**Hotel Cabo San Lucas** looks a bit like a Castillian castle.  The atmosphere is romantic with lovely views; the dining room and bar are massively impressive, made of rock and wood with large windows facing the water and a huge fireplace for chilly evenings.

One of first hotels in the area, Hotel Cabo San Lucas is possibly the most legendary.  This is where those macho, die-hard fishermen return for their yearly hunt. Though the rooms could do with a little refurbishing, the warm, clubby ambience is appealing and the grounds have grown more and more spectacular over the years. Add to this:  it's hard not to have a romantic evening at a hotel with the best mariachi group in Baja. (1-800-282-4809.

*The Hotel Solmar enjoys one of the most striking settings.*  Photo by Vern Appleby.

Some people find the **Hotel Solmar** reminiscent of a Moorish facade, others see the low, white-stucco buildings as resembling space colony pods. Everyone seems to agree that this pleasant hotel positioned against the granite foothills of the Sierra Gigante is situated in the most striking location of all.  The rocky ridge extends into the sea at the peninsula's tip, cupping the hotel in stark seclusion. The Pacific pounds onto a dramatic stretch of pristine beach.  Does it look familiar?

Possibly.  This surreal beach was the setting for the more memorable scenes in *Planet of the Apes.*  (I-800-344-3349.)

*The Westin Regina Resort, Los Cabos.*

Newly opened and drawing raves is the **Westin Regina Resort, Los Cabos.** The architect responsible for the extraordinary design is Javier Sordo Madaleno. He incorporated Baja's unique landscape, using the desert and rocks to inspire a structure curved into the hillside to create indelible sea views. Each of the 242 guest rooms features a private balcony overlooking the Sea of Cortez. The beachside hotel also has two swimming pools, two tennis courts, a fully-equipped fitness center and a variety of water sports ranging from scuba diving to wind-surfing. The hotel's de-luxe restaurant, **Arricefes** has acquired a reputation for its excellent seafood and innovative Mexican delicacies. (1-800-228-3000)

# RESTAURANTS & NIGHTLIFE

In the late afternoon the **Giggling Marlin** (Marina Boulevard) turns into margaritaville. It's a favorite for swapping fish stories and downing seafood and Mexican dishes.  More party pandemonium can be experienced at **Squid Roe,** the "cerveza central" on Blvd. Marina.

Where do the real insiders go?  **El Faro Viejo** (The Old Lighthouse).  Don't let the location — a trailor park just outside town — fool you.  Town officials go there to drink brandy and make major noise while downing barbecued ribs or large grilled lobsters. (Located on Abasolo and Morelos, north of town, but it's easier to just take a taxi.)

For a more romantic ambience, try  **Las Palmas**, a palapa on Medano Beach overlooking El Arco, a view *Modern Bride* editors rank among the best in the universe.  Seafood favorites include Pacific shrimp, lobster and abalone.  Or if you're finally weary of both sea food and Mexican fare, and lust after something Italian, say homemade pasta or pizza—wonder down Blvd. Marina.  Could anything be more romantic than **Romeo y Julieta?**

The Cabo San Lucas area code is 684.  From the U.S./Canada, dial 011-52-684 and the local five-digit number.

# SAN JOSE DEL CABO
## ONE FOOT IN THE PAST AND THE OTHER IN 21ST CENTURY

San Jose Del Cabo has been said to have one foot in the past and the other in the twenty-first century.  Maybe it's only a toe in the past; but in Baja, that's something.   Here one sees mellowed stone archways and white-washed cottages that have been used and mis-used by famous and infamous characters since 1709 when the Scot, Alexander Selkirk, thought to be DeFoe's real life Robinson Crusoe stopped there after being rescued from Juan Fernandez Island.

You'll enjoy visiting San Jose Church, rebuilt in 1940 from ruins of the original Jesuit mission founded there in 1730 and later sacked by rebellious Indians. A curious mosaic over the church entrance depicts irate Indians dragging a bound priest toward a fire to burn him— retribution for his presumptuous attempt to halt their polygamy.

*Palmilla, a desert oasis.*

## HOTELS

Today's traditional romantics will find a hospitable welcome at **Hotel Palmilla** (1-800-637-2226) where the owner has even built a small mission style wedding chapel.

From the very beginning the place has been special.  Built in 1956 by Abelard

Rodrigez, son of the former President of Mexico, Abelardo Luis Rodrigez, Palmilla was originally an intimate and let's say it—elitist—club, a get away for such celebrity sports enthusiasts as President Dwight D. Eisenhower, John Wayne, Bing Crosby and Desi Arnaz who arrived by private plane and yacht.

Then, as years passed, the graceful and charming colonial style enclave evolved into one of Mexico's most prestigious hotels while still retaining its secret hideaway image. Today, with 72 rooms, suites and villas and 2.5 employees for each guest, the Palmilla is one of a select number of hotels to receive the Mexican Government's highest rating, "Gran Turismo/ Clase Especial."    Recently, Andrew Harper's *Hideaway Report* rated it as the "Best of the Best" of beachfront hotels in Latin America.

*The Pamilla, A Baja tradition.*

Beautifully landscaped — a veritable desert oasis — with a forest of swaying palms, this villa-style hotel on Punta Palmilla has a nostalgic Old Mexico flavor. Colorful handcrafts, bright painted tiles and hand-carved furniture liven the large rooms over looking the sea. Fountains sing softly and amber lanterns glow in the haunting darkness of Land's End. What with red tile paths leading to blue tile loveseats only a whisper from the sea, the Palmilla seems tailormade for lovers.

> **For golf enthusiasts,** Palmilla has yet another plus—one of the few courses in the world with ocean, desert and mountain scenery.   So impressed was the 29-year touring golf pro and world famous course designer Jack Nicklaus that he chose this sight for his first signature course in Latin America.   Sweeping ocean views, impressive rock outcroppings, desert arroyos and lush coastal areas with abundant palms are all a part of the dramatic scene. Each of the 27 holes is dramatically different to provide golfers with a wide selection of environments from which to play.

*Palmilla golf course.*

The **Tropicana Inn,** clean, reasonable and charming, is a welcome addition to San Jose. In the center of town, but built around a colonial style courtyard, the new, forty-room inn has a quiet oasis feeling. A tiled reproduction of a Diego Rivera calla lily painting accents the reception area wall, and the theme is continued throughout the complex. Spacious showers are a riot of handpainted flowers.

All of San Jose's attractions are within walking distance of the Tropicana which provides shuttle service to the beach eight blocks away.

Don't be put off by the football games, blaring from the TV in the front bar. Beyond the cheering fans, the scene in the **Tropicana Bar and Grill,** is tranquil and charming. This courtyard restaurant is a gathering spot for locals and visitors alike; and, at night, the romantic ambience of alfresco candlelight dining is a decided plus. (1-800-794-6335)

The **Stouffer Presidente Los Cabos** rests on a solitary piece of land between the crashing sea and a lush, junglelike estuary. The best rooms are on the first floor facing toward the beach, with shaded patios near the sand. Mornings, when the estuary's birds are in full chorus, are especially lovely here. (2-02-11)

## RESTAURANTS

**Damiana** ( Blvd. Mijara 8)  The magic aphrodisiac plant of Baja has  given its name to this charming 18th century hacienda incarnated into an excellent restaurant. Open from 10:30 a.m. to midnight — Damiana's huevos rancheros are a delightful beginning to the day, their garlic abalone a delicious ending.   Damiana's gracious sitting room has plush couches and chairs that provide a comfortable setting for a drink — possibly a margarita laced with Damiana.  The inside dining rooms are filled with folk art and antiques, the outside is a courtyard ablaze with bouganvillea.

**Ivan's** (on Blvd. Mijares, upstairs across from City Hall)  Very, very good food, a perfect place for people watching and classical background music is a pleasant and unexpected touch.

**Le Bistrot** is a French country cafe transplanted to Baja.  You'll find their delightful buffet featuring fruit crepes a piquant change from huevos rancheros.  Dinners often include imported pates and cheeses. The ubiquitous fresh fish gets a provencale touch.  This tiny restaurant is tough to find but worth the effort.  Open daily from 8:30 to 10 p.m., Morelos 4, behind the Telemex office.

Scottish expatriate Tracy Dunlop has created a surprisingly urbane establishment. His **Cafe Europa** offers imported wines and cheeses.  His stereo plays everything from old Beatles tunes to New Age no-tunes.  And his blackboard menu displays rare for Baja offerings such as scrambled eggs with smoked salmon or salad nicoise. Blvd. Mijares.

**La Paloma** (Hotel Palmilla)   High backed chairs and Spanish tile floors lend a Spanish castle feeling to the excellent restaurant known for its Mexican and Continental dishes as well as for hosting the best and most colorful Mexico fiesta night (Friday) in Los Cabos.

## SHOPPING

**La Casa Vieja** and **Antigua Los Cabos**, both on Blvd. Mijares,  have  excellent selections of decorative items, folk art, resortwear and accessories. For fresh fruits, vegetables and local color, shop the village's **Mercado Municipal**, off Calle Doblado behind the bus station.

**TELEPHONE:** The San Jose del Cabo area code is 684.  From the U.S./Canada, dial 011-52-684 and the local five-digit number.

# LOS CABOS
## BY THE SEA, BY THE SEA ... BY THE BEAUTIFUL SEA

Los Cabos is one of the world's premier sports fishing destinations.  Marlin, sailfish, tuna, dorado, wahoo and roosterfish are among the prize catches.  There are more than 850 species to try for in these fertile waters, where a 50 lb. fish is considered small!

Not just fishermen, but all sports lovers will find absolute bliss in Los Cabos. Windsurfing and surfing conditions rank among the best in the world.  Nature has

*A sheltered cove along the Los Cabos corridor.* Photo by Derro Evans.

carved numerous safe bays and coves where swimming  and snorkeling can be enjoyed.   Divers will find that this area, where visibility often reaches 120 feet, teams with undersea life.  Several wreck, cave and canyon dives are popular and Cabo's unique undersea sand falls just off the tip of Land's End are not to be missed.

**Thar she blows!**

From November through April, Baja's most popular water sport is a spectator one. Thousands of gray whales migrate from Alaska to the Sea of Cortes to mate and bear calves in the warm, shallow lagoons of Baja California.  These California gray whales, nearly hunted to extinction by greedy whalers as recently as 1940, have made a remarkable comeback and can be easily observed breeching, spouting and cavorting with their young.

Whether one perceives them as indomitable Moby Dicks or gentle giants, the opportunity to watch them at play is an unforgettable experience.

# NITTY GRITTY______________

Los Cabos is 1000 miles (805 air miles) south of San Diego/Tijuana on Transpeninsular Highway #1. It lies just below the Tropic of Cancer and is in the Mountain Standard Time Zone.

The average annual temperature is 75 degrees Fahrenheit, the weather generally warm and dry. This semi-tropical desert oasis boasts an average temperature of 72 degrees in the winter months (November-May) and 78 in the summer

*Los Cabos is a haven for sports fishing.*

(June-October). The desert climate is usually warm in the daytime and cool at night. Evenings between November and April can be cool enough for sweaters and jackets after the sun goes down. Though the dress is casual, shirts, cover-ups and shoes are required in all establishments. Men never need ties.

Aero California, Alaska, United and Mexicana Airlines operate direct service from Los Angeles, San Diego, San Francisco, Seattle, Denver and Phoenix. Aero California and Mexicana link Los Cabos with Mexico City. Drivers can follow Transpeninsular Highway #1 all the way from the San Diego border to Los Cabos.

Because of its geographic separation and isolation from mainland Mexico, Los Cabos differs in many respects from its Mexican Riviera counterparts. Probably the least "Mexican" resort in the country, Los Cabos has a cultural duality that may appeal to first timers south of the border. U.S. dollars are accepted everywhere and English generally understood.

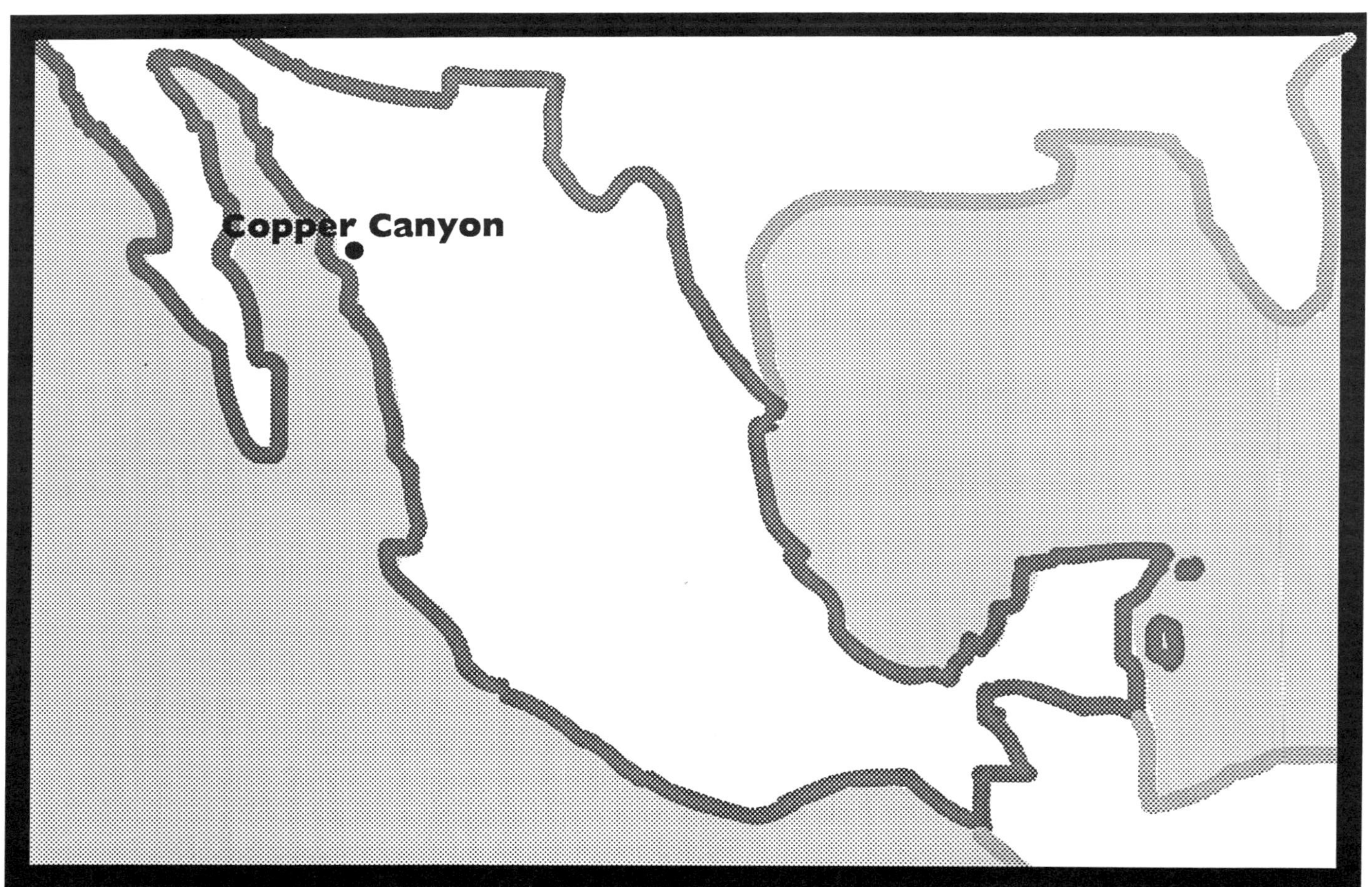
Copper Canyon

## COPPER CANYON
### RAIL ADVENTURE AND A VISIT TO PANCHO VILLA

The ghost of Pancho Villa haunts the Copper Canyon.  His restless shade lurks forever behind giant boulders and crumbling adobes.  Sometimes you're certain that his living clone rides the rails beside you for this is a wild place, an awesome place, a last frontier where anything might happen.

The Chihuahua Choo-choo — otherwise known as Ferrocarril de Chihuahua al Pacifico — chugs through 86 tunnels, bounces over 37 bridges and puffs its way through some of the most rugged and remote reaches of the Sierra Madre Mountains.  It offers an outdoor experience so shockingly pure and majestic that visitors feel as if they've entered into a yet undiscovered civilization.

The railroad snakes 415 miles from Las Mochis, near the Sea of Cortez, to the inland desert city of Chihuahua, climbing from desert scrub to alpine forest, winding from sea level to nearly 8000 feet, maneuvering along narrow ledges and criss-crossing the Continental divide three times.  Along the way, adventurous travelers not only see some of the most spectacular scenery anywhere in the world but also have an opportunity to spend nights in true frontier towns — the haunt of Pancho Villa and the  home of the Tarahumara Indians. The Tarahumara cling to their ancient ways, many living in caves, the men wearing only loincloths.

Once in Chihuahua City, the excitement accelerates for this was Pancho Villa's fiefdom.  At his home, now a museum, a wide variety of

*The legendary Pancho Villa.*

memorabilia can be viewed — including the bullet riddled car where the bandit met death while returning home from an afternoon's dalliance with one of his mistresses.

Except for missionaries seeking souls to save and prospectors searching for lost gold and silver mines, the Copper Canyon area remained  largely unexplored through the mid-l9th century. Then, in 1872, Albert Kinsey Owen, an American visionary, conceived the idea of building a railroad linking Kansas City, Kansas, with Topolobampo Bay on the Sea of Cortes.  His grand design was to be a short cut for freight traveling by ship from Asia to East Coast ports in the United States, a means of  avoiding the lengthy, arduous and sometimes dangerous trip around South America.

Construction began in 1885, the first rail laid in 1902.  Ten years later they were still at it, inch by painful inch.  The spectacular scenery that thrills visitors today — canyons carved thousands of years ago when volcanoes lifted the land and rivers cut deep fissures into the earth, towering walls of sheered stone, dense forests, and monstrous boulders scattered randomly like marbles — are merely a series of seemingly insurmountable obstacles.

Pancho Villa called an abrupt halt to the painstaking project.  The Mexican bandit turned revolutionary had gained control of the area and wanted no possible interference.  His "army" cut the line in numerous places, effectively stopping all work.  It would be many bloody years before the political situation stabilized, but by that time the Panama Canal had opened putting an end to Owen's dream.  Periodically others would pursue the vision but the task was always too great, the mountains too steep, the cost too high.

After some of the world's top engineering brains and pocketbooks foundered and went under, it remained for Mexican engineers to conquer their own defiant land.  In 1940 the Mexican government bought the Kansas City,

Mexico and Orient Railroad and began construction of the final phase — the 161 mile gap that crosses the high, wild Tarahumara Indian country winding through some mountains and plunging right through others.  It would be more than twenty years before the last stubborn section of track — a drop

*A journey through one of the last frontiers.*
Photo by Vern Appleby.

of 7000 feet in 122 miles — was finished.  Almost 90 years after Owen's original venture, the engineering feat that "couldn't be done" was complete.  The year was 1961, the cost $90 million.

Today more than 500,000 passengers a year ride what is popularly known as the "Copper Canyon Railroad" — something of a misnomer because the train doesn't actually go through Copper Canyon itself, but rather passes along its rim. *And* although this area is most commonly referred to as Copper Canyon, it is, in fact, a maze of more than 200 smaller canyons which combine to form a series of five interconnecting canyons or *barrancas*. These five — the others are Barranca de Sinforosa, Barranca Batopilas, Barranca Urique and Barranca de Guaynopa — are 1.5 times assuming it's on time — but no one would want to do such a breathtaking journey all in one day, for the Copper Canyon is not a single place or a solitary destination. Rather, it's a collection of sights and sounds, from the tropical vegetation to the incredible vistas. Overnight stops along the route enhance the trip and permit leisurely exploration of the vast and fascinating country.

An expansive maze encompassing 900 square miles of rugged mountains and lush canyons. Photo by Vern Appleby.

deeper than the Grand Canyon and cover four times its area. The canyons link three main rivers flowing the length of the Sierra Madre Occidental Mountains to Los Mochis and the Bay of California.

The expansive maze of lush canyons, tropical vegetation and alpine forest encompasses more than 900 squar miles. The train trip takes 14 hours —

Though the trip may be started from either end of the line, west to east is far and away the most desirable. No matter what time of year you travel, the last part of the trip will be in darkness. It would be unfortunate to miss the spectacularly beautiful western scenery.

The most frequent starting point is from **Los Mochis,** the spawn of yet

*A Tarahumara Indian home.* Photo by Vern Appleby.

another American entrepreneur. The now thriving city was just a scattered collection of huts when Benjamin Johnston arrived on the scene in 1903 and began to grow sugarcane. Johnston was luckier than Owens. His sugar mill became one of the biggest in Mexico, the village he laid out prospered, his home evolved into the Sinaloa Botanical Gardens.

Today's city is literally wrapped in gold, for marigold fields surround the town. They're worth their weight too — a cash crop. The petals when added to chicken feed, enhance the deep yellow of egg yolks. Nearby Topolobampo Bay, where wilderness glides down to the water's edge and fish glide up to the beach, is the third deepest natural bay in the world.

*El Fuerte, once an outpost against Yaqui Indians.* Photo by Vern Appleby.

## STOPS ALONG THE WAY

In Los Mochis, **Hotel Santa Anita** (Avenida Leyva and Calle Hidalgo. Phone: (681) 5-70-46) is clean, comfortable, well located and serves a great margarita. Boat trips to Topolobampo Bay arranged from its travel office are a memorable experience. The train departs Los Mochis at 7:30 a.m.

An alternative is to spend the night in **El Fuerte**, a picture postcard hill town fifty miles to the east. Founded in 1564 by Spanish silver dons as an outpost against the Yaqui Indians and still a village largely undiscovered by tourists, El Fuerte (the fort) has charming old buildings, cobblestone streets, and a 300-year-old church with cactus growing on its steeple. Once the last frontier be-fore venturing north into Indian territory, this is really "Old Mexico."

second floor courtyard with its fountains and lush plantings. Twenty foot ceilings, antique furniture and Spanish armor lend a sense of romantic—and dramatic —yesterdays. Revolutionary leader and later president, Venustiano Carranza, the ally/rival of Pancho Villa, was a guest here in 1913 during the height of the fighting.

A colorful collection of folk art enlivens the delightful dining room. Food is excellent and the menu extensive.

*La Posada del Hidalgo was once the governor's mansion.* Photo by Vern Appleby.

The **Posada del Hidalgo**, formerly a mansion, now a small first class resort with 17 rooms, was built nearly 130 years ago for the territorial governor. A beautiful building restored to its original elegance — with modern bathrooms added along with a swimming pool — the Posada Del Hidalgo has a carriage way entrance where the gentry rode, not walked, up to the

Among the highlights: fresh water lobster and large mouth black bass, also Tortilla Anahuacalli soup. Don't leave without sampling Mas Bonita, a delicious punch made from local fruit and tequila. This place is a hidden treasure, and highly recommended. Since the Posada del Hildalgo is the only hotel in El Fuerte, travelers should call (681) 3-02-42 well in advance to book a room.

The Chihuahua choo choo departs El Fuerte at 8:30 a.m., heading into the high, cool Sierra Madre on a track that winds through breathtaking gorges, river valleys and mountain villages.

*The charming Mision Hotel de Cerocahui is the departure point for adventure.* Photo by Vern Appleby.

The engineering masterpiece includes sections of railroad that twist and weave around, creating circles of tracks along the way. To enjoy the roller coaster ride, position yourselves between cars so that you and — hopefully — your cameras will capture the thrill of the track dropping away to the shimmering Rio Fuerte and the train inching across the dizzying 335-foot-high Chiapas Bridge. Sometimes cliffsides are so close you can easily prick a finger on a cactus sprouting from the rocks.

The tiny whistle stop, **Bahuichivo**, three hours into the mountains, is a perfect place to break the trip. A courtesy bus from the **Mision Hotel de Cerocahui** meets the train and will take you to **Cerocahui**, considered one of the most beautiful mountain towns in Mexico. Set on the rim of Urique Canyon, Cerocahui was founded in 1680 by Jesuits who still maintain the mission there. The tiny pueblo of some 600 inhabitants is a throwback to another time, perfect for exploring. Hotel guests also enjoy horseback riding through pine and oak forests to a beautiful Cerocahui waterfall. The Mision has 32 clean, comfortably furnished rooms and the food is excellent. Reservations may be made by calling (681) 5-70-46.

A trip by bus down a winding one-lane road to Urique, an historic gold and silver mining town on the canyon floor, is an adventure, but the excursion's main attraction is a visit to the caves where a number of Tarahumara Indians live.

The Tarahumaras probably migrated from Asia by way of the Bering Strait some twenty thousand years ago. Unlike the Aztecs who drifted south, they continued a hunting and gathering lifestyle in the northern mountains. To this day the Tarahumaras, little touched by modern civilization, remain the most pure and primitive of the Mexican Indians. They may also be the most remarkable.

When the Spaniards arrived on the scene and attempted to establish their preach and plunder agenda, the Tarahumaras — which means "foot runner" — literally ran for their lives retreating deeper and deeper into the Sierra Madres.  Nobody runs like a Tarahumara and today there are some 50,000 of them inhabiting caves and rude cabins throughout the mountains and canyons.

Though roads and pickup trucks have made inroads into the canyons in the past twenty years, many Tarahumaras still live in isolated areas where running remains a way of life. They continue to travel tremendous distances both for fun and necessity, easily running in one day terrain that would kill a horse.  Tarahumara foot races, sometimes lasting as long as 72 hours, are a tradition passed down for countless centuries. These competitions have two components — the physical and the magical.  Runners and their village shaman spend as much time preparing defenses against witching by their opponents as they do in actually training. The practice apparently serves them well.  Tarahumaras have been known to run down wild deer and turkeys on foot and a 26 mile marathon seems to them "just too short."

The Tarahumaras are also known for their beer parties or *tesquinadas* where a heady corn brew is served. Most adults attend two a month and anthropologists estimate that each Tarahumara spends an average of 100 days a year directly involved with preparing, consuming and recovering from the effects of these corn beer binges.

*Tarahumara Indians.* Photo by Vern Appleby.

Travelers are urged to respect the customs and traditions of the Tarahumaras. Friendliness and sensitivity is often rewarded by a handshake, a smile and possibly an invitation into a private home — maybe even a glass of Tesguino, the heady fermented mixture of corn combined  with leaves, roots and grass seeds.   It's good and strong!

Reboarding the train at Bahuichivo, you continue to climb. Look out the window and then down and you'll see the end of the train entering a tunnel going the other way!  Look out both windows and you may see nothing — you're on a bridge hundreds of feet above a river. Then suddenly  darkness blots out everything as you rumble through a tunnel.  As the ascent continues, the evergreens thicken and sting  your  nose  with  minty  pine mingled with the fragrance of burning wood. Stoic Indian faces peer up from station platforms.

At the longest stop of the ride — the **Divisidero Barranca del Cobre** — everybody pours off the train for 45 minutes. This is the Copper Canyon's highest reachable point, rising more than 7,700 feet from the canyon floor. The air is pure and crisp, the view, extending more than 100 miles across the Copper Canyon, breathtaking: shining citadels of rock bathed in coppery iridescence reaching into blue sky.

The town is also a shopper's delight. As the whistle sounds Tarahumara Indians swoop down to set up their stands in time for the scheduled stop. Sale items in-clude handcarved wooden violins which the Tarahumara men make and play, green grass baskets and hats, wood dolls, masks and jewelry. *Regateando* , or bargaining, is the order of the day.

Forty-five minutes really isn't long enough in Divisidero. It's simply too beautiful to leave. Consider a "plush rendezvous in the wilds." That's how the **Posada Barrancas** describes itself. And the first class hotel more than lives up to its promise. Without getting out of bed, you can view the light and shadow play across rippling slopes and bleached pinnacles in a multi-hued, mile-deep gorge. Built right on the canyon rim, each room has a wide balcony and fireplace. Outside, in the shade of the pine trees, Tarahumara women weave and sell baskets. Reservations may be made by calling (681) 57-046 in Los Mochis.

A pleasant alternative is the nearby **Cabanas Divisadero Barrancas**, a

*Perched on the canyon's edge, Posada Barrancas has incomparable views.* Photo by Vern Appleby

*Posada Barrancas has rustic elegance.* Photo by Vern Appleby

picturesque stone lodge with 55 well appointed rooms. Regional meals such as carne machacada (sun-dried beef) and soups of Chihuahua-grown beans, are served family style in the large dining room. Call (14) 15-11-99 in Chihuahua City for reservations.

Another is **El Mansion Tarahumara** which looks like a medieval castle. Delicately balanced atop a hill, this picturesque hotel also offers individual cottages, large rustic rooms with fireplaces. Call (14) 15-47-21 for reservations.

The last major stop on the journey is **Creel**, named for Enrique C. Creel, the former governor of Chihuahua and one-time nemesis of Pancho Villa. Surrounded by pine forest, mountain meadows and Tarahumara villages, the logging town has a strong frontier feeling. A main attraction is the Mission Store where Tarahumara crafts are sold to benefit the Children's Hospital. **Motel Parador de la Montana** is clean, comfortable, moderate. (145) 6-00-75.

As the train descends from Creel, the scenery changes from alpine forests to plains and finally desert. Night closes in and in the distance lights glitter against a blackened sky. This is Chihuahua City, the home of Pancho Villa.

## MUCHO MACHO

Sprawling inside an immense desert crater formed by the rugged mountains surrounding it, Chihuahua City lies almost directly in the center of the state for which it was named. Those mountains so rich in ore, so bare and ugly to a stranger's eye, were perfectly fashioned for the *guerrillero's* purpose — for Pancho Villa's purpose.

Individualistic, buckling to no man or nation, desirous of finding a niche where deeds rather than status would earn recognition, Villa exemplified the *norteno* spirit. His adventures, romanticized by folk songs and novels, resulted in a myth, an image, a stereotype. In the popular mind, the revolution was Pancho Villa.

A bandit turned folk hero, Villa's impact on the imagination evolved not only from his own exaggerated masculinity, but from the whole Mexican idealization of *machismo*. Sexual prowess is, of course, the universally recognized component, but is not the totality. The underlying concept behind the macho ideal also encompasses courage, steadfastness in the face of adversity, assertiveness and total conviction. A man who — even as death engulfed him — had time to draw his gun and, relying on his legendary marksmanship, drop one of his assassins, Pancho Villa was its personification.

Born Doroteo Arango on October 4, 1877, he grew up a sharecropper living quietly until 1894 when his sister was raped by the patron. It was an insult to the family honor that could not be ignored. Arango shot and killed the man. One month short of his seventeenth birthday, he was a fugitive — a condition that would continue until the revolution lent him a modicum of legitimacy in 1910.

Hoping to elude pursuit, the youth

attempted to change identities, finally striking upon Francisco Villa, a name that twenty years later would reverberate throughout Mexico as a symbol of violence, unbridled brigandage and vigilante justice for Mexico's *compesinos.*

Villa roamed through the mountains becoming increasingly more feral as his reputation as a bandit, train robber, and cattle rustler grew. In the one recorded attempt at an honest living, Villa's former occupation proved an asset when he established a butcher shop in Chihuahua City. Whatever cattle were needed, he rustled and when the animals were unbranded, he sold the hides as well. Unfortunately, the powerful Creel family who ran most of the state also controlled the public slaughterhouse in Chihuahua City. Feeling oppressed and squeezed by their domination, Villa returned to full time rustling.

By now a barrel-chested 180-pound man standing five feet, ten inches tall, Francisco "Pancho" Villa had came to dominate Northern Mexico. His auburn hair was almost curly, his broad moustache reddish; deep etched lines on the round burnished copper face indicated that this was a man who laughed often. The hint of a belly under his belt was surprising considering the hard life he'd led and the fact that he never drank and was said to eat less than an average child.

Harried law enforcement agencies placed a reward on the head of the man who struck everywhere and anywhere seemingly at once:    dead or alive. The threat of betrayal did nothing

to curtail his activities. Soon Villa was the most wanted man in Chihuahua, continuing to steal cattle, rob trains, and leave now frantic law officers wondering just where he would appear next. By the fall of 1910 his notoriety had spread across the country.    A society based on position rather than talent had created Pancho Villa, the bandit. Now the disintegration of that tired hierarchy would transform the bandit into a revolutionary.

In Mexico City, Porfirio Diaz, after a forty year dictatorship, was re-elected "by an overwhelming majority" (tabulated by his adherents). His announcement to an "ecstatic public" that despite his "ardent" desire to return to private life he would "humbly submit" to his people's demands and again take the office of *presidente* resulted in anarchy.

Insurrectionists in the south searched hungrily for potential allies. Who was this unconquerable horseman whom the newspapers had dubbed "The Centaur of the North"?    Men were tough in the north, they reasoned, the environment demanded fortitude  — and    Villa personified that northern temperament, a place where practical application triumphed over ideology. What did it matter that he was mercurial? Perhaps he was impossible, unmanageable as some claimed:  a savage. But he was also a living legend in those mountains, the man who'd killed more soldiers than the plague.

Pancho Villa had never been a solider, and had never trained as one, "but," he boasted to potential allies, "I've been chased by more uniforms than the

*Pancho Villa with the first of his twenty-five known wives, Luz Corral.*

half fortress. A massive structure with fifty rooms embracing an interior courtyard, it afforded Villa the opportunity to enjoy domesticity without sacrificing the comraderie and protection of his bodyguards — men he euphemistically called *dorados* or "golden ones."

town whore — and it's easier to know an enemy than a friend." Life became much simpler for Villa once *he* was doing the chasing. Mexico's revolution became a private vendetta for him as he parlayed eight men into an army that seemed to rise out of the earth, born out of the seed of his own determination.

It was at this time that Villa met his future wife, Maria Luz Corral, the daughter of a poor but respected widow. Luz first encountered the fabled outlaw in her mother's store where she was helping to hand out merchandise to the revolutionaries. It must have been love at first sight for Villa who—according to Luz's autobiography —"frankly confessed his love for me and told me of his lonely and errant life." Villa's shared dream was a quick end to the Revolution after which he would settle down and establish a home. Deciding not to wait, the couple was married May 29, 1911.

Both as luxury and necessity, Villa built a home for his bride in Chihuahua City. "Quinta Luz" was half mansion and

Luz was his first wife, but by no means the last. How many women were there in his life? Surely not enough. There could never be enough for a man who felt about them as he apparently did. And no need to bother with such matters such as bigamy. Villa simply took his ladies to bed and then to the preacher because he felt "women like to get married." Because merely taking a mistress seemed to somehow upset his sense of propriety, Villa chose instead to marry the ones who appealed to him. The Museum de la Revolucion in Chihuahua City estimates a total of twenty-five wives; and, at the time of his death, five "legal" widows appeared on the scene to claim his estate.

Selectively moral, Villa admonished his men against rape though he himself abducted a Frenchwoman in Mexico City when he took the town in December 1914 — sweeping her up and carrying her before him on his horse right into the hotel. Villa claimed

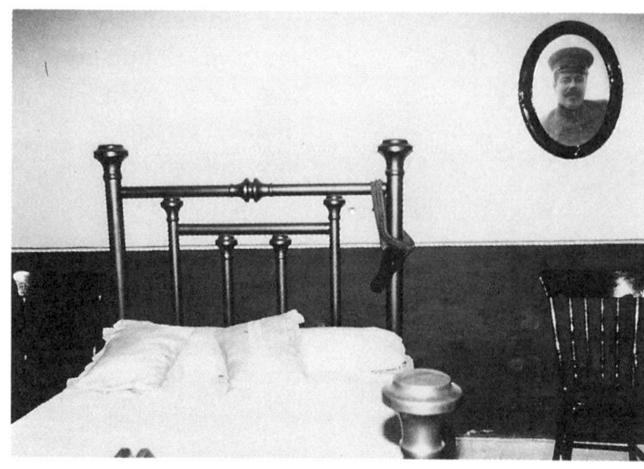

*Pancho's bed. Note gun and holster at the ready.*
Photo by Vern appleby.

Corral's dressmaker, the first Mrs. Villa was forced to serve the nuptial couple breakfast in bed. Not surprisingly, a fierce animosity existed between Austreberta and Luz that ended only with Luz's death in 1981.

No doubt ever existed that Villa possessed *cojones*. Moody and unpredictable, a bull, a tiger, a savage soul who could fight like twenty devils when the chips were down, Villa remained a peasant pure and simple. Initially he had been viewed as a potential Robin Hood. People formed long queues to receive money and food from his very hands, but later others were not so fortunate. In one tiny town, the bandit massacred seventy-two young boys and old men, and, because he was short of ammunition, he stood them domino fashion so that one bullet might do the job of two.

that she was merely being shy, she called it abduction. "Who is to stop you from getting married?" he challenged his compadres. "When a wedding is needed, it will be arranged. There is no judge nor priest who can resist the reason of a carbine."

As for the women, what did *they* think? It's unlikely that the idea ever occurred to a man whose imagination rarely strayed beyond his own imme-

Then at last the war was over. Politically out-maneuvered by his allies Carranza and Obregon, Villa settled down on a twenty-six thousand acre ranch confiscated from a hated land owner of old. Living like a sultan with his Luz (and a few others), he was a law unto himself.

Three years passed in feudal splendor. Sometimes Villa wore plain, white cotton peon pants with a sombrero, sometimes the latest fashions with Panama hats. He rode, he practiced pistol shooting at paper targets and he put on weight. He raised fine horses and acquired two new automobiles, one a

*The car in which Pancho was riding when shot.*
Photo by Vern Appleby.

diate gratification. It's said that when Villa married Austreberta Renteria, Luz

grey Dodge touring car.   He played the guitar passably well and had a better than average voice that he happily exercised at the slightest provocation. Sometimes Villa did a little business in the surrounding cities mostly in Parral, where he owned a townhouse and a hotel.  And had a mistress.

Villa and his bodyguards were returning from Parral one afternoon when the gleaming grey Dodge was ambushed.  All were killed.  The man died in a blaze of glory and gunfire. His legend promises to go on forever.

## CHIHUAHUA CITY

Chihuahua City  still has something of a frontier feeling , partly from history and partly from its location.  Founded in 1709, a century before Mexico's War of Independence ended Spanish control, Chihuahua is the capitol of Mexico's largest state — also called Chihuahua.  It's a clean,  prosperous city with broad boulevards, a pleasant contrast to the arid, desolate plateau that surrounds it.

The magnificent, baroque cathedral in the center of town is an excellent example of colonial architecture. It also personifies some of the city's violent history.  Begun in 1724, incessant battles with Indians delayed completion for 102 years.   And not only was Chihuahua, Pancho Villa's headquarters, but it was also the scene of the imprisonment and execution of the father of Mexican independence, Padre Miguel Hildalgo.

A modern well appointed hotel in the center of town is the 5-star **Palacio del Sol** at Independencia No. 500, a high rise with spectacular views (1-800-852-4049). Also highly recommended,

*Murals by Piña Mora depict Chihauhua's history.* Photo by Vern Appleby.

the **Castel Sicomoro** at Blvd. Ortiz Meno 411.Reservations: (14) 13-5445

**Avenue Juarez** is restaurant row, **Galeon** at 3312-B, a highlight.    **La Calesa** on Avenue Juarez and Colon is also highly recommended. A personal favorite is **El Bandido Pub** — Mexico's Old West with a Texas touch. Good steaks.  Avenue de las Americas 1303.

Chihuahua City is a shoe town.  If you ever wanted a pair of boots, this is the place.  The variety is unbelievable and

try on September 15, Mexican Independence Day.    The priest, who launched Mexico's independence from Spain, was held prisoner in Chihuahua with another patriot, Ignacio Allende, and executed in what is now the state capitol (**Palacio de Gobierno**) in 1811.  A plaque commemorates the spot where they were killed and spectacular murals by Pina Mora depict the most famous episodes in the history of Chihuahua.

Construction of the grand mansion that would one day become the **Regional**

*The Regional Museum Quinta Gameros, once a grand mansion, contains an exquisite collection of art nouveau treasures.* Photo by Vern Appleby.

so are the low prices.  Take a stroll down the pedestrian plaza in the town center opposite the cathedral.

The cathedral's inner courtyard boasts a monument to Father Miguel Hidalgo, whose *grito,*  or cry for independence, is still heard in plazas across the coun-

**Museum Quinta Gameros** began in 1907.  It took Don Manuel Gameros four years to complete one of the finest examples of art nouveau architecture in the world.   The glasswork and antique French furniture is exquisite. Open 10 a.m. to 1 and 4 to 7 p.m. Bolivar 401.

But the real reason for visiting Chihuahua is the **Museum of the Revolution** — Pancho Villa's Villa. Quinta Luz — as it is still known locally — became a museum in 1981 following the death of the first Mrs. Villa, Dona Luz Corral.  Located on the north side of town at Calle 10 No. 3012, the mansion, once Revolution Central, contains Villa's firearms, cartridge belts and other personal effects.  Don't miss the brass bed — adorned with pistol and cartridge belt or the bullet-riddled car in which the revolutionary was assassinated.

## TIDBITS

A one way ticket on the Chihuahua-Pacifica train is approximately $33. Reservations  may be made by calling 1-800-228-3225.  Information on packages is available from 1-800-44- MEXICO, but do-it-yourselfers can fly into Los Mochis from Los Angeles via Aero California with a return flight from Chihuahua on Aeromexico. There are also connecting flights from Mexico City.  There are also connecting flights from Tijuana and Mexico City.  The train has dining car service. Dress is casual.  Jeans, a warm jacket for the crisp nights.

An elegant option is the **Sierra Madre Express**, a deluxe train (something like a frontier Orient Express) that originates and terminates in Tucson.  Everyone seems to love it.  (1-800-666-0346).

> *La Cucaracha* was originally a ballad of the revolution. Sung by followers of Pancho Villa, *La Cucaracha*, is said to refer to the nickname of Villa's rival Venustiano Carranza.  The chorus captures the mocking humor of most **corridos**, tropical ballads set to music: "*La cucaracha , la cucaracha* (the cockroach) *Ya no puede caminar* (doesn't want to travel on)/ *Porque no tiene, porque le falta* (because he hasn't, oh no, he hasn't) *Marijuana que fumar* (marijuana to smoke)."

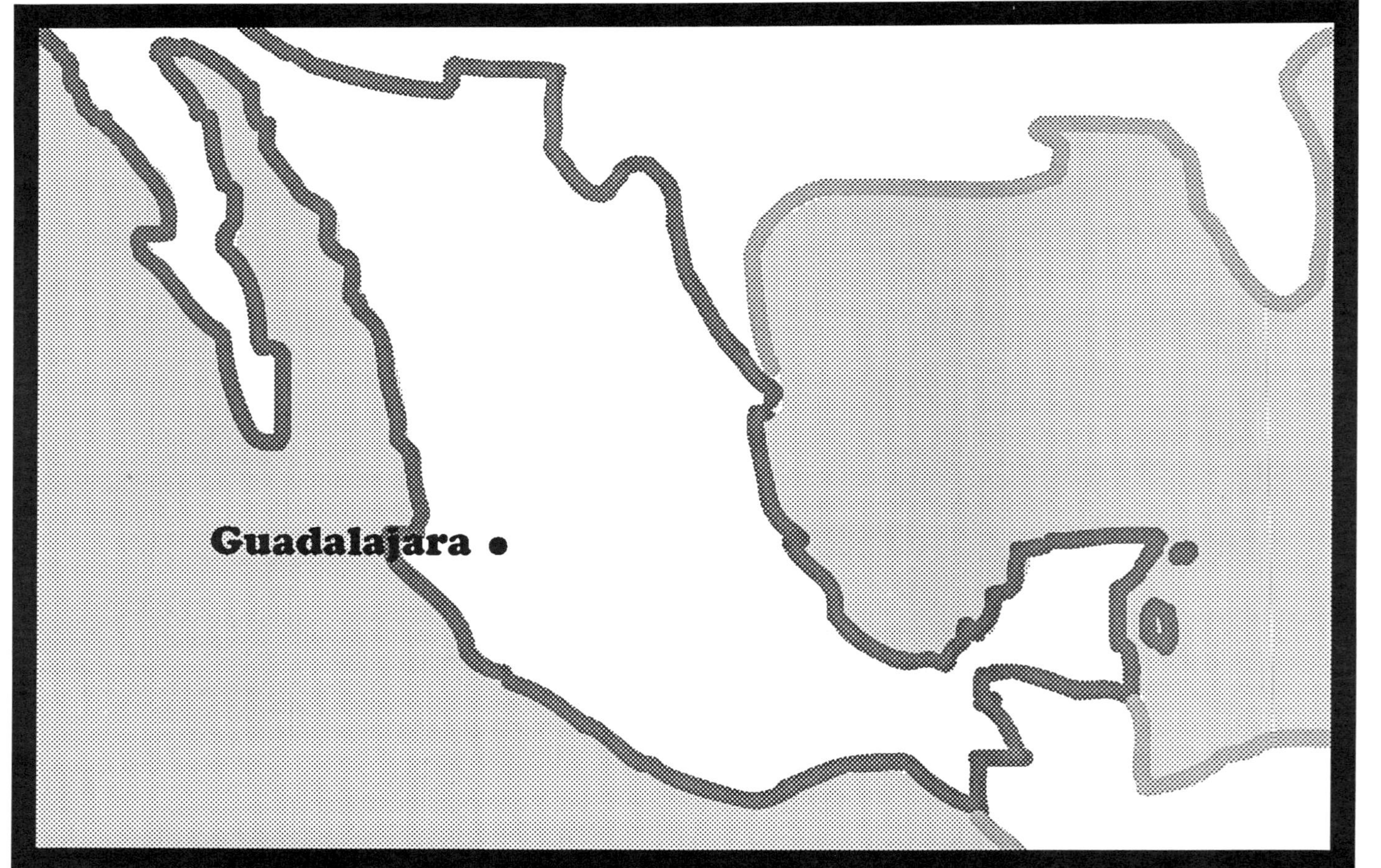

Guadalajara

# GUADALAJARA
## A DEIGHT ON EVERY LEVEL

"Guadalajara! Guadalajara! *Guadala-jaaaaaara!*" The lilting name so often celebrated in song, evokes sweeping images of colonial romance: splendid mansions, sweeping plazas, luxuriant flower gardens.

And the real city is no less alluring.

Appropriately, mariachi music was born near Guadalajara during the days of the grand ranchos. Some of the songs were blatantly macho, boasting of horsemanship and vendettas; but most were soulful, lamenting lost loves. Today a visit to Mariachi Plaza is a trip to a musical supermarket where hundreds of musicians wait to be hired, for just one song or for the evening.

Though Guadalajara is Mexico's second largest city, with some five million residents, it's still a place where horse-drawn carriages and caravans of laden burros share the right of way with late model cars. This is a sophisticated city known for its art and culture. It's also a shopper's paradise.

Founded in1542 under orders from Hernan Cortes, Guadalajara remains a romantic city aflame with roses, bou-

gainvilleas and jacaranda. Much of what is generally considered "Mexican" originated there—not only the mariachis whose irresistible melodies are known the world over, but the *charro*

*A leafy menagerie in Guadalajara's sculpture garden.* Photo by Vern Appleby.

costume originated by gentlemen cowboys, the *charreada* or rodeo, the famous Mexican Hat Dance, even the sombrero itself. It's also the tequila capital of the world.

Unlike the Mexico City area, where the Aztecs enjoyed a highly developed civilization, the Guadalajara region remained primitive. The Spaniards discovered the region in 1542 when Nuno Beltran de Guzman set forth to conquer the western lands. Conquer he did, in a most bloody fashion, but it wasn't easy. Not until 1551, was the province of New

Galicia finally established with Guadalajara as its capital.

The Spanish charter instructed builders to use the finest materials in constructing the new city intended as a showplace. Streets were to be wide with ample room allowed for parks. During the three centuries of colonial rule, these instructions served as a guide. Somewhat apart from the rest of the country, Guadalajara became "more Spanish than Spain." So much so that its residents came to be known as *Tapatios*, a name derived from the tasseled cape favored by Spanish gentlemen. Even today residents of the state of Jaslisco (of which Guadalajara is the capital) proudly refer to themselves in this way.

Guadalajara largely escaped the century of turmoil which followed Mexican independence. This was a city that kept to itself, clinging to traditions. Not until the late nineteenth century, when a new railroad linked Guadalajara to the capital, did the city become an integral part of Mexico. Even then the train service was so un-reliable that its effect seemed negligible. For years the standard joke was that newlyweds who took the train to Mexico City for their honeymoon would have their first child before they arrived.

Though today Guadalajara is the hub of a network of airline routes, railway lines and super highways, it still remains a city of parks and fountains, monuments and flower-lined boulevards. "Pearl of the West," the poets call her, boasting that Guadalajara has the soul of a provincial maiden.

## SIGHTSEEING

*La Catedral de Guadalajara dominates the main plaza.* Photo by the author.

Guadalajara is a great walking town, with several pedestrian plazas and more than its share of eye-catching architecture. From **La Catedral de Guadalajara** which dominates the main plaza at Hidalgo and Alcade streets, pedestrian plazas stretch out in four directions, forming a cross.

The cavernous Cathedral begun by Spanish missionaries in 1571 was fifty years in the building. Today it offers a study in contrasts both inside and out. Twin 200 foot towers contrast sharply with the mirrored glass highrises that surround them. But that's only the beginning. Step inside the Cathedral's massive doors and you've entered a time warp. The architecture is Early Everything: Gothic, Moorish, Byzantine, Tuscan, Mudejar, Baroque, Rococo, Doric and Corinthian.

Thirty handsome columns lead to an altar de-signed in Italy — but there are eleven other altars.  One of them, dedicated to Our Lady of Roses, is superb.  The Cathedral contains many art treasures donated by a grateful King Fernando VII of Spain in recognition of the city's support during the Napoleonic Wars.  Don't miss the Murillo painting *The Assumpton of the Virgin* in the sacristy.  Crane your neck and you'll see seventeen towering arches rising dramatically to a pinnacle in the vaulted ceiling.

Directly in front of the Cathedral, facing west, is **Plaza Laureles**, with a large fountain and attractive shops in shady arcades.   Behind it is the **Plaza de la Liberacion** and the **Park of Illustrious Men** where Grecian columns commemorate

regional heros—artists, poets, and leaders of the independence movement.  To the side is the town's main square, or **zocalo**.  You can hardly miss the zocalo's starring attraction: a kiosk with a difference.   When presented to the city by the French government in 1907, the fanciful, art nouveau bandstand created a scandal.  Fortunately, romantics prevailed and the kiosk with its lovely filigreed columns, supported by bare breasted women, was allowed to remain.  Today free band concerts are held there every Sunday at 6 p.m.

Another landmark on the square is the **Palacio de Gobierno**, built in 1643. Notice the hole in the town clock outside. In  1915, so the story goes, Pancho Villa rode up to the state building and shot a hole in the clock so that people would always know exactly what time he entered Guadalajara.

*When presented by France in 1907, this art nouveau bandstand created a scandal.* Photo by author.

Inside, the main attraction is the muralist Jose Clemente Orozco's passionate vision of Father Miguel Hidalgo — the parish priest who championed the cause of the Indians and led an 1810 uprising against Spanish rule.  Orozco handled a difficult architectural space brilliantly, enveloping the viewer in imagery.  His drama begins at the bottom of the staircase:   flames, knives and corpses piled beneath red banners confront the viewer.

On the ascent, the view is of a colossal Hidalgo holding the torch of rebellion— flames destined to bring both liberation and destruction.  At the top of the stairs the view is of two side panels expressing the artist's despair over the state of the world. The combination of the swastika with the hammer and sickle in his *Carnival of Ideologies* would prove prophetic.

The palace is open daily from 8 a.m. to 8 p.m.

The city's most famous son, Orozco, considered one of the monumental figures in modern Mexican art, did much of his work in Guadalajara. His paintings hang in the great museums of the world. In the United States, his murals may be seen at Dartmouth and Pomona colleges and at the New School of Social Research in New York.

Today Orozco is acknowledged everywhere as an artistic genius, yet he owes a great debt to an American woman, his close friend and confidant, Alma Reed, who introduced him to the New York art scene during the 1920s. It was only after the artist had achieved success in the United States that many Mexicans were willing to recognize his greatness.

More of Orozco's work may be seen at the **Instituto Cultural Cabanas** on Plaza Tapatio. Originally constructed in 1801 as an orphanage, this magnificent structure was reopened in the 1970s as a center for the arts and a museum for Orozco's works. In 1938 Orozco covered the Hospicio's vast chapel with his greatest mural cycle, once again expressing a horror of violence, ignorance, oppression, greed and dehumanization in a series of Mexican historical scenes.

It would take more than a day to view all the artist's work compiled here, but a must see is the world famous, *Man of Fire*, which is painted on the ceiling. It suggests both humanity's urge for renewal and its annihilating rage. Is the subject falling into hell or ascending into heaven? You decide. Many visitors bring mirrors to make viewing easier while others lie on large wooden tables provided for that purpose.

*Man of Fire by Jose Clemente Orozco, Guadalajara's most famous son.*

Lit by flashes of dark imagination, Orozco's work offers visions, not facts and it needs to be felt, not fathomed.  So awesome is his achievement, ranked among the world's greatest, that it's difficult to conceive that the artist was not only extremely near sighted but had only the use of one hand — the other lost in a boyhood science experiment that misfired.

The murals' fiery hues are a dramatic contrast to the stark chapel's  ancient gray stone walls.  The orphanage itself is a remarkable structure consisting of 26 flower-filled patios linked by tile passages.  Considered a perfect example of neoclassical architecture, the museum also houses a great deal of Jalisco's history. It was here, in  1810, that the independence leader, Hidalgo, signed an anti-slavery bill — forty years before Abraham Lincoln.

Orozco's former home has been turned into a museum, **El Museo Orozco.** Nearly one hundred paintings are on display in the workshop where many of them were painted.  It's fascinating to view the progression from youthful talent to artistic magnitude reflecting a driving, powerful, political voice.

Located on Avendia Aceves 27, near the arches that span the road from Guadalajara to Nogales.  Closed Mondays.

Frequently compared to La Scala in Milan, the **Degollado Theater** at Degollado and Morelos streets on Liberation Plaza is the home of Guadalajara's symphony orchestra and the city's major cultural center.  Operas and concerts are presented there and visiting musicians perform throughout the year.  More than a century old, the building is an exquisite example of Grecian architecture.

Unless it's in the United States or Europe for a command performance, the **Grupo Folkorico** of the University of Guadalajara is "command attendance" for visitors. This colorful and thrilling presentation of the nation's songs and dances dramatizes the history of the eight Mexican states from Aztec times up to the present.

The theater itself is a masterpiece, its entrance lighted by crystal chandeliers and the center dome, also lighted by crystal brilliance, a mural of the fourth part of Dante's *Inferno*.   The Degollado's five tiers are trimmed in rich red velvet and gold leaf.  The ballet is performed Sundays at 10 a.m. Telephone:  13-11-15.

**Plaza de los Mariachis**, at Calzada Independencia and Obregon, is one of those "love in the afternoon" places.  Relax, sip an aperitif (or maybe a Corona) while listening to a kind of "battle of the bands"—roving mariachi groups—guitar, violin and trumpet bands outfitted like *charros* — vying with one another to entertain those willing to pay while they wait to be contracted for a nighttime serenade.

## HOTELS

The **Quinta Real,** 2727 Avenida Mexico, is far and away the most romantic hotel in Guadalajara — who knows, maybe in all of Mexico.  The ambience is old world elegance combined with all the modern amenities.  Each room or suite is a gem filled with antique furniture and museum quality art work.  Stone and rick walls, exquisite tapestries, marble fireplaces and flowers everywhere make for a warm and romantic setting.  A fantasy come true, you really won't want to leave.  Reservations: 1-800-878-4484.

*Each room at the Quinta Real is a gem.* Photo by author.

Built in 1610, the **Frances,** at Maestranza 35, is said to be the oldest hotel in Guadalajara.  Benito Juarez (one of Mexico's most beloved presidents) stayed there and in 1981— following its renovation, the hotel was designated a national monument.  Conveniently located off the main plaza, the three story structure is entered through an atrium lobby with a skylight and marble fountain at its center.  Frosted glass, period paintings, and a bird cage elevator add to the charm. There's piano music in the lobby bar and live music for dancing in Maxims—an excellent restaurant. Reservations (36) 13-11-90.

Another favorite is the **De Mendoza**, opposite the Teatro Degollado at Venustiano Carranza l6. This colonial charmer is within easy walking distance to Guadalajara's historical buildings and museums. The public areas are newly remodeled with graceful arches, marble and tile work.  Some of the prettiest units are split level. The De Mendoza has an excellent restaurant as well as a rooftop cocktail lounge. Reservations: (36) 13-46-45.

Located in a quiet residential area, the **Camino Real** at Avenue Vallarta 5005, has a luxurious garden/country club feeling with five swimming pools, a lighted tennis court and golf service in the best clubs of the city.  Reservations: 1-800-722-6466.

The stunning **Hyatt Regency**, at Lopez Mateos and Montezuma, a fourteen-story glass pyramid, boasts many features, among them a lively atrium lobby with waterfalls, several excellent restaurants, a pool and—most spectacular—an ice rink surrounded by elegant shops.  Reservations: 1-800-228-9000.

## RESTAURANTS

**Place de la Concorde** in the Hotel Fiesta Americana, 225 Aurelio Aceves, is thought by many to be the city's best restaurant.  Both intimate and elegant, its many attractions include an enticing menu, marvelous piano music, flaming desserts, giant shrimp and a romantic view of the Minerva fountain.

**Aquellos Tiempos** in the Camino Real Hotel, at Avenue Vallarta 5005, offers gourmet Mexican and International favorites in an elegant turn of the century setting.  Also to be enjoyed is their Sunday brunch.  The sweet lime juice (and other delights) are not to be missed.

On weekdays the **Quinta Real** is *the* place to go to watch power breakfasts.  Something about the harp music in the background—*Don't Cry For Me, Argentina*, the most frequent selection—adds to the fascination.  Dinner there, either in the Cuatro Estaciones garden pavilion or the elegant Virreinal Room, is also highly recommended.

At **Rio Viejo** you can enjoy excellent paella and *chiles en nogada* in an intimate, antique filled town house (Las Americas 302).  **Oui el Cafe,** Francisco de Quivedo (between Vallarta and Lopez Cotilla) offers chili tamales and Mexican-style beef fillets with an Art Deco flair.  Try French-Creole cuisine at **La Vianda**, Chapalita 120; or charcoal-grilled and regional foods at **Restaurant Los Cazadores**, Golfo de Mexico 606.

## SHOPPING

Why not admit it?  Some of us were born to shop.  And you would almost imagine that Guadalajara was created to satisfy our fondest dreams and desires.  Temporary insanity strikes every time I visit this elegant city with its splashing fountains, gourmet restaurants and stunning galleries.

The sentence for my crimes of passion is being forced to carry home whatever I buy — brass and copper pots and parrots, hand-painted dishes, primitive paintings, papier-mache flamingos.  But since there *is* life after vacation, the effects of momentary madness are pleasant to live with.

The **Mercado Libertad**, in continual use since the 1500s, is said to be the largest public market in the Western Hemisphere.   Whether this is accurate or not, with l,000 colorful stands, you can expect to be kept busy for a long, long time.   Visitors should be ready to bargain in this see-it- to-believe it in mother of all malls.   Residents and tourists alike browse for crafts, live birds, love charms—everything and anything.  This is the place to buy *huaraches* — Mexican walking shoes — in every conceivable color.  It's also the place for exotic costume jewelry.

A large red-light district once centered about the Libertad area, but was closed down to avoid excessive proximity between the city's newest attraction, **Plaza Tapatia**, and the world's oldest profession.   The state- of-the-art Plaza Tapatia, located between the Degollado Theater and the Libertad Market, is an indoor-outdoor shopping center with about 200 shops offering everything from sombreros to sandals to stereos.

The tongue-twisting but decidedly trendy suburb of **Tlaquepaque** offers a very different approach.  Put on your walking shoes.   This colonial enclave still retains its

ancient cobblestones. Those huaraches will come in handy because strolling the picturesque streets *with their 300 boutiques* is the only way to see it, feel it, know it.

About one hundred years ago, Tlaquepaque, five miles east of Guadalajara, was a fashionable weekend getaway.  Today it's the largest producer of handcrafts in Mexico.  Many of the beautiful old mansions, with their high ceilings and flower-filled inner courtyards, now house boutiques, pottery shops and hand-blown glass factories.   A few of the many places where I left my heart and wallet are:

*Tlaquepaque has 300 boutiques to beguile you, and is the largest producer of handcrafts in Mexico.* Photo by Vern Appleby.

**El Porvenir**, Independencia 208, where the sunny showroom is lined with hundreds of terra-cotta nativity sets.  Some of the figurines are tiny; others almost life-size.  Many are painted with complex folkloric patterns; others shine with deep colors—emerald or ruby red—accented by gold leaf.  A business for more than forty years, the company employs thirty craftspeople, fourteen of which are related to one another. Among them are two brothers, Mario and Martin Orozco-Hernandez, grandchildren of the founder, who grew up watching their parents and grandparents working in the leafy courtyard. A decade ago they decided to follow suit.

**El Aguila Descalza,** Juarez 120. Art, handcraft and fashions by Josefa, an internationally known designer, are featured there. These range from one-third to one-half the price of similar costumes at home.

**Aresanza J.B. Marquin,** Avenue Independencia. Fanciful brass and papiermache figures and Mexican primitives are the speciality. For the person on your shopping list who has everything, what about a shiny copper jaguar or a lanquid pink flamingo? The only drawback is that once you've carried one of these cunning creatures home, you'll be so bonded, you'll never want to part with it.

*Mexico's magical realism is personified in the work of Segio Bustamante.* Photo by author.

**Artes de Mexico**, Independencia 155. This shop offers hand- embroidered clothing with Indian designs. Tablecloths or mats and napkins are a fantastic bargain.

**Mia & Reales Bazaar,** Independencia 172. Superbly crafted silver and gold jewelry, picture frames, handblown glassware, pewter and artifacts are the best buys at this store.

**Sergio Bustamante Gallery,** Indepencia 238. One of the loveliest stores featuring the work of Mexico's best known and possibly most popular sculptor. The showroom with its myriad fanciful creations is a veritable temple to the magical realism that personifies Mexico.

If you've never seen glass blowing demonstrated, be sure to stop at **La Rosa de Cristal**, Tlaquepaque's oldest glass factory right next to the Bustamante gallery on Indepencia. Typically, the shop's wares are displayed in a front showroom that seems to be a way station for a number of dogs and cats that roam at will.  Step over them through the narrow hallway to the rear and you'll find yourself face to face with the glowing red mouth of a glass furnace.  Around it, young men and boys—some as young as eight—shape molten glass into stunning or sometimes whimsical bowls, plates, etc.

They put on quite a show, dipping ten-foot-long tubes into the roaring furnace to pick up a red hot glob that's puffed into a bubble to be whirled and teased until it evolves into a tumbler, brandy snifter, beer mug or vase. Demonstrations take place Monday through Saturday until 3 p.m.

Tlaquepaque's plaza, **El Parian**, is lined with cafes and stores all facing a center courtyard with the traditional bandstand.  Mariachis stroll about playing guitars— it's a perfect place for cold beer and people watching.  Streets on two sides of the Parian have been converted into pedestrian malls and all six blocks of Avenida Independica are paved with red tile.  Another nearby square is lovely **Hidalgo Gardens** with brilliant flowers, splashing fountains and a bandstand where mariachi performances and folkloric events are presented on Sunday afternoons.

After a hard day's shopping one can scarcely leave Tlaquepaque without dinner at **Restaurante Sin Nombe** (or no name restaurant) located at Madero 80.  This renovated colonial mansion with no sign over the door features a truly spectacular dining place, art gallery and informal exotic bird sanctuary.  The menu features time-honored family specialties tailored to today's tastes.  Reservations are advised. 35-45-20

---

Tlaquepaque claims to be the original home of the mariachis.  Legend has it that these groups first became popular during the brief reign of Emperor Maximilian.   Having heard the machiachis in Tlaquepaque, he brought them to Chapultepec  Palace in Mexico City so that they could perform at wedding feasts — hence the name from the French word *mariage.*

# TONALA

Just four miles southeast of Tlaquepaque, Tonala is another suburb famous for its crafts. It's a little less expensive too. You can easily browse for hours in what seems like hundreds of little shops looking for that perfect Mexican work of art. If you don't have that kind of time, begin your safari at city hall, across from the *zocalo* or main square from the town market. Here you'll find displays of ceramics by the town's leading artisans along with addresses of their shops and studios.

Among the most acclaimed is the work of Daniel Bernabe dispayed at **Galeria Bernabe** at Hidalgo 83, one block off the zocalo. *But* shoppers, take note: these creme de la creme ceramics are pricey and the store doesn't accept credit cards. Take plenty of pesos—you'll be sorry if you don't.

If you associate papier-mache with elementary school, a visit to the **Sermel Gallery** next door will be a real eye-opener. Sermel's fanciful menagerie includes graceful unicorns, 8-foot giraffes, regal lions. Founded in 1968, the widely imitated company, ships its sleek coated creatures round the world to discriminating collectors who prize their fine detailing and rich colors.

Take time to visit the nearby studio where you'll first be confronted by a jumble of white molds piled on the dirt floor or stacked on floor-to- ceiling shelves, labeled with dusty signs—jaguars, toucans, flamingoes. Seated at a nearby workbench, artisans dip damp gray paper into a flour paste and smooth it over molds, pressing out wrinkles and seams with the heals of their hands.

Down a step into a wide, bright room, skilled finishers join the molded halves together, coat them with white paste and sand them smooth — suddenly what you see is an albino zoo. But look again, nearby are painters who brush on a white base coat and then shade it with bright color. The most highly skilled use needle pointed brushes to outline feathers and fur in black and to bring hollow eyes to life.

Finally, in a glassed-in cubicle, women apply the seven coats of varnish needed for the requisite shine. The painting alone takes more than a week to complete.

Prices for Sermel papier-mache animals start at around $25 and climb to $500 for the larger pieces.

Another place to keep in mind is **Ceramica El Palomar** a showroom and factory at 1905 Bulevar Tlaquepaque — the Tlaquepaque road. Though most of Palomar's designs are formatted and plentiful, a tour of the painstaking work going on in the factory leaves no doubt that these are hand-crafted items. Each artisan takes pride in his or her work which is signed with a name or personal trademark—a fish, a dove, a ladybug.

The showroom is divided into first-quality goods and seconds — all guaranteed lead-free. Dinnerware patterns range from the traditional royal blue flower set off by a glaze, named for the town, to a modern, asymmetrical, green-gray and white pattern high-lighted by a simple butterfly. Also on sale are mats and napkins to match the stoneware.

Salespeople will pack your purchases so they can be checked as luggage on your flight home or shipped. Be aware, though; shipping fees can equal the price of your buys.

Store hours are 9:30 a.m. to 7 p.m. Monday through Saturday; l0 a.m. to 2 p.m. Sunday.

The most interesting time to visit Tonala is on Thursday and Sunday mornings when the bi-weekly *tianguis*,

or market is held. The deeper you get into the market the better it gets. You'll see *everything*:: love charms, healing herbs, freshly butchered mystery meat as well as ceramics and straw work. Next to a table of exquisite embroidery, you'll find plaster statues of Mickey Mouse or a portrait of Jesus with an aging hippie spin.

# LAKE CHAPALA

Down the road from Tonala, 45 miles from Guadalajara, is Mexico's Inland Riviera, Lake Chapala, a mecca for North American writers, artists and retir-ees.   The largest lake in Mexico, Cha-pala is fifty miles long and ringed by charming little towns.  Two of the most interesting are **Chapala** and **Ajijic.**

The former was immortalized by D.H. Lawrence in his torrid novel, *The Plumed Serpent.*  Happily, Lawrence's residence has incarnated into an inn, the legendary, **Quinta Quetzalcoatl** (Keen-tah ket-zal-co-ah-tul) or "Inn of the Plumed Serpent," considered one of the ten best in Mexico.  Most cer-tainly it's one of the most evocative of romance.

How could it be otherwise when one considers the controversial Lawrence's much chronicled penchant for strong, lusty women — both as fictional hero-ines and personal companions?  Hid-den behind vine covered adobe walls, the inn contains eight suites opening onto riotous flower gardens.   Each guest room has as its theme a work by

*Legendary Quinta Quetzalcoatl.* Photo by author.

Lawrence. Yes, of course, there's a "Gamekeeper Room," right next door to "Secret Lane." And in the "Lady Chatterley's Room" two robes hang in the armoire: one pink satin, the other blue-striped seersucker. How many guests have slipped them on for a few hours of make believe?

Don't miss the photograph of Lawrence taken in 1923 while he was working on *The Plumed Serpent*. Dark, brooding, bearded, his eyes are thoughtful, their expression

*The residence where D.H. Lawrence wrote* **The Plumed Serpent.** Photo by author.

*The Gamekeeper's Room.* Photo by author.

surprisingly gentle. Rates are American plan and include bar, airport transportation and numerous excursions. Reservations: 1-800-523-1586.

It's pleasant to stroll down to the lakefront where one can enjoy an excellent meal at **Cazadores Restaurant**, a converted mansion, once the home of the Braniff family of aviation fame. Wrought-iron lamp posts line the streets leading to the lake where one can see boatmen with colorful launches for rent.

*Lady Chatterley's Room.* Photo by author.

Possibly the best known landmark along the lake is the **Beer Garden,** the area's largest restaurant, which celebrated its 65th anniversary in 1994. Next to the Beer Garden on Madero 200, is **Bing's Ice Cream Parlor,** one of a chain founded by a North American retiree. Each delicious flavor is made from natural ingredients. Also on

Madero is the **Nido,** Chapala's oldest and most central hotel.   The Nido serves good meals at reasonable prices, including a traditional four-course Mexican *comida* , or mid-day meal.

In the park across the street from the pier is the **Chapala Handicrafts Market.** You'll find an excellent assortment of well crafted items:   leather goods, hand-embroidered blouses, wonderful carved wooden items.  Some excellent buys here for good prices.

Nearby **AJIJIC** (pronounced ah-hee-HEEK—pretend you're clearing your throat) is a picturesque village with a population largely composed of writers and artists.   It seems to have been made for gallery and boutique prowling and people watching at numerous sidewalk cafes overlooking the lakefront.

The prettiest hotel in Ajijic is the **La Nueva Posada**. Though newly constructed, it has plenty of colonial ambience with lovely antiques and original watercolors. Surrounded on three sides by lush tropical gardens, the hotel faces directly on the lake. The food is excellent and all dining areas overlook the lake.  Add to this a fantastic gift shop. (Donato Guererra #9, Reservations: (376) 5-33-95.)

A pleasant alternative is the **Posada Ajijic** which also faces the lake.   A landmark for more than forty years, the inn and restaurant, owned by a North American expatriate, offers excellent and inexpensive meals.

Oh, yes, the shopping's great in Ajijic. You won't want to miss the **Casa de las Artesanias** on Carretera Jocotepec which offers a wide and distinctive variety of not only regional items but the best from all parts of the country.  Two other favorites are  **Los Helechos**, Blvd. Ajijic 62 B, for decorative gifts, household items, arts and crafts; and **Opus Boutique** for distinctive fashions, jewelry,   paintings   and   sculpture, Ocampo 30.

# TEQUILA

Thirty-five miles to the northwest of Guadalajara is Tequila — that Teguila.  Would a trip be complete without a stop there?   This tiny town, the birthplace of Mexico's best known export is still actively bottling its baby.

Mexicans generally prefer their tequila straight, usually after licking salt and sucking a wedge of lime held between the thumb and forefinger.  But most tourists prefer tequila in cocktails—like the popular margarita (with lime juice and triple sec or cointreau).  In either case it comes from  "mezcal" produced in the area around the town of Tequila — just as cognac is the regional name of a particular brandy.

It all begins with the maguey, or century plant, a spike-leaved cactus averaging three and a half feet high and used all over the central highlands as fencing.  When the plant reaches 10 to 12 years of age, its leaves are removed, revealing a pine-apple-shaped heart weighing about 80 pounds.  This is roasted and mashed, fermentation is induced, and most of the resulting product distilled into white tequila. The remainder is aged until  it takes on a yellowish hue—which some find smoother.  You can ask for this as tequila *anejo* (an-Yay-ho).

Some thirty distilleries can be toured in Teguila where they encourage you to sample their firewater.   Orendain, Cuervo, and Herradura are among the best known. The Orendain plant, though state-of-the-art, retains the wonderful old walls, gates and antiques of bygone days lending it a romantic movie set feeling.   It's true that the town itself doesn't have a great deal to recommend it, but the drive is pretty and the fields of blue maguey memorable.

Arrangements for the trip may be made through your hotel.

## TIDBITS

Aeromexico, Alaska, American, Continental, and United Airlines all fly into Guadalajara which is also serviced by Grayline Tours (1-800-321-8720) and Armadillo Tours International, 1-800-284-5678.

The city has an average daily temperature of 73 degrees.  Very much a city, the dress tends to be more sophisticated than in the beach resorts.

The telephone area code is (36) to be followed by a six digit number.

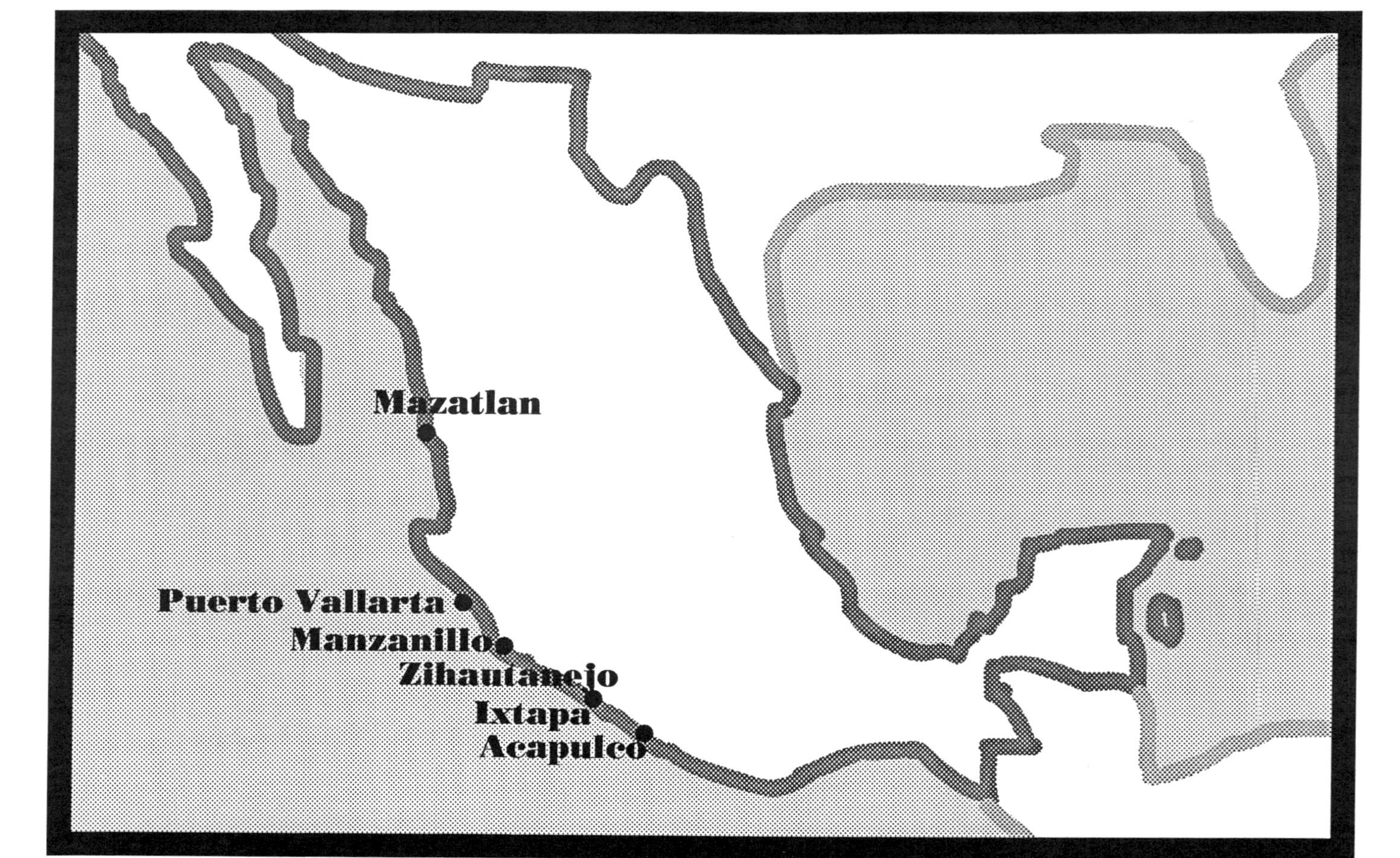

Mazatlan
Puerto Vallarta
Manzanillo
Zihautanejo
Ixtapa
Acapulco

## MAZATLAN
### "PEARL OF THE PACIFIC"

---

When the fiery Mexican revolutionary, Francisco "Pancho" Villa, first saw the Pacific ocean, he bragged, "It's not enough to quench my thirst!"

Pancho wasn't only fiery, he was greedy.

His ragtag army called him "General." Everyone else called him a bandit. For years Pancho made an excellent living holding up trains.

The pristine coastline that Villa saw is now dotted with luxury resorts. Fortunately, hotel operators have learned they don't have to hold up visitors to make a living. This is particularly true in Mazatlan, the least expensive of the four "Gold Coast" resorts.

Admittedly, Mazatlan is not as glitzy as Acapulco, as beautiful as Puerto Vallarta or as quaint as Zihautanjeo, yet it remains a perennial favorite and is known as the "Pearl of the Pacific".

What accounts for the resorts popularity? Maybe it's because Mazatlan is a party town plain and simple. What else could one expect from the home of Pacifico beer and Mexico's largest shrimp-fishing fleet? Yes, they *do* dance on the tables at Señor Frog's, the town's most popular dinner/disco spot. How else could they write graffiti on the ceiling?

But there's another side to Mazatlan as well, a gentle, serene side. Balmy breezes ruffle the palms, the sea is as warm as silk, the sand soft as face powder. Sunsets seem particularly spectacular there—streaks of crimson shimmering through the clouds like gilt threads spun into a tapestry. That side — the serene side— of Mazatlan appears unchanged since the early 1600s when the first Spaniards took it for one of the fabled seven cities of Cibola.

Growth was restricted by protective Indians, the Chibchas, and marauding pirates. Sir Francis Drake was one of the plunderers. Most likely the English privateer and the Mexican bandit would have understood one another very well.

Though a few Spaniards settled in Mazatlan the town wasn't incorporated until 1806 and had no municipal government until 1837. Nothing really happened until 1850 when a group of enterprising Germans established a permanent colony there. By the end of the century, Mazatlan was involved in international trade with countries as far away as the Orient. Today, the city is Mexico's largest Pacific Ocean port and supports the country's largest shrimp fleet. Tons of shrimp are frozen here every day and shipped off to the United States, Mexico's biggest customer.

Obviously, this is not one of those charming little towns that oozes history. On the other hand, no one is ever going to complain about being dragged from one historical monument to another. Mazatlan is a resort dedicated entirely to sun and fun. There's plenty of beach and sports activities during the day and a plentitude of party spots at night.

The food's outstanding here and, to no one's surprise, delicious shrimp and fresh fish are highlights on every Mazatlan menu. A sport fisherman's paradise, this is one of the few places in Mexico where marlin and sailfish bite year round. The result is a daily fresh catch of marlin and a multitude of scrumptious dishes. Each morning, restaurateurs visit the street markets to buy the freshest catch of the day. Then they return to their various establish-ments to prepare a variety of delicious dishes such as smoked marlin tacos, marlin empanadas or marlin tostados.

On-the-beach dancing, live music and nightclubs are plentiful, as are more romantic piano bars. Fiesta Nights are popular at most hotels. Competitions ranging from sports fishing to body building are held throughout the year.

Mazatlan's most famous party is a five-day one from Friday to Tuesday prior to Ash Wednesday. It's been a Mazatlan tradition since 1898 and is now the third largest Pre-Lenten Carnival in the world with music, dancing, exuberant parades, fireworks and extravagant galas.

## HOTELS

The surf sings love songs and then lullabies at the **Camino Real**, far and away the most romantic hotel in town. Overlooking the sea on a rugged cliff, the hotel offers exquisite views. Spacious accommodations are decorated in passionate pinks and purples; but, for a total treat, go one step beyond and request the **Royal Beach Club** where the views are the best of the best. The club has special concierge service, complimentary Continental breakfast as well as cocktails and hors d'oeuvres every afternoon in the club lounge. Sabalo Beach Road, Punta del Sabalo. Reservations recommended. Phone: 1-800-722-6466.

If you like pink, you'll love the dome-ceilinged rooms, king-sized beds and tile baths all designed with romance in mind at the **Pueblo Bonito.** An opulent chandelier crowns the beautiful lobby and antique art tastefully  accents the public rooms of this elegant hotel. 212 l Camaron Sabalo North. Local phone: 4-37-00.

John Wayne loved the **Hotel Playa Mazatlan** and so do I. Maybe it's the "old Mexico" feeling of the happy, carefree atmosphere. Be certain to request an ocean view and a balcony in advance. The tri-weekly Mexican fiestas with colorful dancers, tipico food and fireworks are the best in town. Camaron Sabalo (on Playa Las Gaviotas). Reservations recommended: 1-800-762-5816. Local phone: 3-44-55.

*Beaches are the top priority in Mazatlan.* Photo by Nick Wheeler.

# RESTAURANTS

At **El Shrimp Bucket** you can dine by candlelight to great food, singing waiters and outrageous conversation.  The house specialty is literally a bucket of shrimp, but aficionados can request their crustacean favorite cooked any way imaginable. This landmark restaurant — something of a national shrine — is where Carlos Anderson (Mexico's best known restaurateur) got his start in 1968.  Live music, great margaritas. Olas Atlas II.

**Señor  Frog's** was Anderson's second venture.  The noisy, crazy bar and grill (Anderson's touch) is open from noon to midnight.  The food's good, the disco light show spectacular; besides,  how will anyone know you went to Mazatlan if you don't come back with a Señor  Frog's T-shirt?  Avenue del Mar, next to the Sands Hotel.

Chef Cipriano Gonzalez at the **El Cid Resort Restaurant** prepares a scumptious coconut shrimp cnsisting of delicately battered jumbo shrimp coated in coconut and served with a spiced mango sauce.  His Lobster Tenochtitlan — broiled with blue cheese — is not to be missed either. Camaron Sabalo.

The splashing fountain at the entrance to **Casa de Tony** is the beginning of a romantic evening.  This century old hacienda transports guests back to the gracious days of yesterday.  No, this is one place you don't wear shorts!  The perfect combination of elegant ambience and  superb food attracts dignitaries and celebrities from Mexico City as well as foreign visitors.  Be certain to try the tequila shrimp, a tantalizing mixture of shrimp, onions, celery and tequila flamed at your table.  Mariano Escobedo III.  Reservations are suggested.  Phone: 5-12 -62.

Another charmingly converted old mansion is **Doneys** which consistently provides outstanding home-style Mexican cooking.  It's particualrly fun to go there on Sunday afternoon when the restaurant is filled with local families enjoying the traditional *comida da corrida.*  Those in the know order *asada al carbon* (Mexican-style barbecued meat), spicy sausage and fried platano or the fiery *mole.*  You'll be delighted too by the photos of old Mazatlan.  Don't miss them.  Mariano Escobedo 610 .

**Los Comales** is another fantastic *mole* oasis.  Mole, a multimix of some 25 ingredients, takes a day to prepare.  Even though chocolate is one of the components, the chile ingredients make it quite spicy.  If you want fancy, Los Comales is not the place; but for a mole connoisseur it really can't be beaten.  The restaurant offers other excellent Mexican dishes as well. Benito Juarez.

Don't allow the name **Chiquita Banana** fool you.  This elegant restaurant overlooking the sea and adjacent cliffs serves food to please the most serious bon vivant.  The chef is known for his shrimp á l'orange but everyone should taste the grilled lobster at least once in their lives. Located in the Camino Real Hotel.

Ask anyone in Mazatlan to recommend a quality steakhouse and you'll invariably find yourself at **Señor  Pepper's.**  Choose between rib eye, porterhouse or filet mignon barbecued over mesquite coals.  These are such enormous steaks, you may want to share.  If you ask the waiter, he'll bring them cut in half on two plates with all the trimmings.  The margaritas are divine as is the fried zucchini appetizer.  Of course since this is Mazatlan, you can also be certain that the jumbo shrimp and cajun blackened fish are too.  After your meal, you can order *brewed* defaffeniated coffee — one of the few places in Mexico that has it. The atmosphere at Señor Pepper's is intimate and romantic with a piano bar, excellent service to match the food, crystal and silver settings.  Camaron Sabalo (across from the Camino Real).

Mexican food with a nouvelle twist can be enjoyed in the candlelit **Las Palomas**, a very charming restaurant with live music and a lush garden setting.  For a special treat try medellions of abolone in *chipotle*  sauce (a very picante chile) with the chef's salad.  Located inside the Pueblo Bonito.

Two excellent restaurants are located in the El Cid Resort on Camaron Sabalo. **La Concha,** located on the beach in one of the largest palapa dining rooms in Mexico, features mushroom quesadillas and marlin tacos.  If Las Vegas-style shows are your thing, you can view something very similar here; otherwise, enjoy the sea outside on the deck. The whole town's talking about the new **La Cascada**.  Homemade tortillas hot off the *tomal* — you can't get much fresher than that! — are a treat but so are the *nopalios* (salad made from young cactus leaves) and *chiles con queso sopa* (a rich broth made of chiles and cheese).

A palapa shades the tables at the **Terraza Playa Restaurant**, the perfect place to check the beach action.   Strolling vendors on the other side of the rope barrier will beguile you with enticing possibilities:  straw hats and bags, silver jewelry, table-cloths.  If you're not in the mood, avoid eye contact, but you'll be missing some of the best buys in town.  Be prepared to bargain.  Located in the Hotel Playa Mazat-lan.

The most spectacular view in Mazatlan may be enjoyed at **Juan's El Mirador.** Though the restaurant is out of the way (on the southern cliff of Cerro del Viga) you won't want to miss the breathtaking view of harbor,  cliffs and sea.  You can always expect a cooling breeze and the shrimp *ceviche* (marinated in lime, cilantro, toma-toes, onions and peppers) are the best in town.

Don't leave Mazatlan without visiting its hidden treasure and "in" spot, **Mamucas.** Many argue that the inexpensive, unpretentious Mamucas serves the best sea-food in all of Mexico.  Could be.  Everybody raves about everything, but the house specialty, *parrillada de marisco* (seafood for two, grilled in an earthen pot), is not to be missed.  Downtown at Simon Bolivar 73.

## SIGHTSEEING

A charming way to enjoy the lovely ocean views for which Mazatlan is known is to take one of the horse-drawn carriages called *aranas*  along the sea boulevard. Late afternoon is the best time to go.  The air is cooler and  the sunsets are often spectacular.  For the best panoramic view, stop at **El Faro**, the massive lighthouse at the end of Centenario Drive.   Standing more than 500 feet above the water, El Faro is second only to Gibraltar in height.

**Mazatlan Arts & Crafts Center.**  Shoppers should allow plenty of time to explore the labyrinth of stores in this two-story, thatch-roofed arcade in which crafts from all over Mexico are sold.   Potters create original ceramics on the spot while carv-ers work wood into both traditional and modern creations.   Rug weavers, tin-smiths, jewelers and dressmakers will fullfil your dreams with their custom made designs.

Then, when your feet start to tire (or during the siesta time from I to 4 p.m.), enjoy the best guacamole in town along with a chilled glass of Mazatlan's homebrew, Pacifico, at **Tequila Charlie's** in the center's treeshaded courtyard.   Cameron Sabalo, north of the traffic circle.

**Mercado Central** (the old market) offers everything from fresh tortillas and tropical fruit to folk art and pottery.  This is the place to experience "real" Mexico away from the razza-ma-tazz of boutiques and discos.  Leather goods, straw hats, gold and silver are sold in the small shops surrounding the the market.  Corner of calles Juarez and Serdan. Close by is **Plaza Machado**, Mazatlan's oldest park and the center of the yearly Carnaval festivities.  A cool place to relax under tall, leafy trees.

Built in 1860 and declared a national monument in 1990, the **Angela Peralta Theater** has been restored to its original grandeur after years of neglect.  Once considered a gem of neo-classic architecture, the theater has survived a revolution, a hurricane and a ficus tree that grew through the middle of the stage.

Originally built by Santiago Leon Astengo, a nationally acclaimed architect, it was known as the Rubio Theater.  The name was changed in 1885 in honor of the famous opera diva, Angela Peralta.  Peralta, a musical prodigy who'd made her debut at the National Theatre in Mexico City at fifteen, was known as "The Mexican Nightingale."  After conquering Madrid, the rising star made her debut at La Scala when only seventeen — winning cheers and critical acclaim.  At thirty-eight, Peralta's brilliant career came to a tragic end in Mazatlan where she contracted yellow fever and perished with hundreds of others that unlucky year.  The National Theatre closed and performances were canelled everywhere in Mexico as the country mourned the loss of its first great diva.

During the Porfiate, famous performers played to packed audiences drawn from Mazatlan's upper classes.  Then, following the revolution,  the building fell into disuse and finally decay.  In 1975 Hurricane Olivia delivered the final insult.  The roof caved in, revealing a rotting interior behind the still beautiful facade.

In the 1980s, in an effort to raise funds for repairs, the townspeople hosted a series of benefits.  One of the performers was the popular Mexican opera star, Gilda Cruz Romo, who sang in front of a huge ficus tree that had thrust its way up from the center of the stage.  Because of the roof's collapse, the now open-air theater had to end performances each night at exactly 10   p.m. when the evening Mexicana flight passed over the theater.

In 1988, reconstruction finally began and, by a quirk of fate, Juan Jose Leon Loya, great grandson of the original architect, designed the new theater.  After a monumental face-lift, the pink palace with its graceful white columns, again echos to the sound of music. Osuna and Carnaval. Phone: 85-33-44.

The first bombing in the Americas and the second in the world occurred in Mazatlan when the city was under siege by Pancho Villa and his compadres in 1914 .  **Cerro de la Neveria,**  a munitions center, was the object of the bombing run, but the bi-plane lurched suddenly causing the hand-held bomb to be released accidentally.  It landed instead on Carnaval Street.

Cerro de la Neveria or **Ice Box Hill** got its name in the 1840s when tall masted ships from San Francisco sailed into Mazatlan's port carrying all manner of cargo. One of the most important items was ice.  A ship was  scarcely docked before the precious load was rushed up to Ice Box Hill and placed in tunnels and caves packed carefully with gunnysacks and sawdust.  This ice preserved fresh-caught shrimp for the fledgling industry and pampered those who could afford such a luxury.   Years later those caves were used to store munitions.  Take the coast highway (Paseo Claussen) south until you reach the turnoff.

A sinister-looking shark cruises nervously back and forth watching visitors to the **Mazatlan Aquarium** as they enter.  Dozens of smaller tanks are filled with some 250 species of day-glo tropical fish covered with striking patterns:   zigzags, silver streaks, polka dots, not to mention eels, lobsters, seahorses.  Four times a day sea lions perform and the facility also includes a lovely botanical garden and small zoo. Don't miss the crocodiles — cousins to many who live in nearby jungles.  Daily 9:30 a.m. to 6:30 p.m.  Sea lion show at ll a.m., l p.m, 3 p.m. and 5 p.m.  Deportes 111.

Visitors can watch a spectacle at the **Diver's Cliff** where daring Mazatlecos plunge 45 feet into turbulent water surrounded by rocks.  The dive requires expert timing because — without a high wave — the waters are only six feet deep.  Diver's Cliff is located on Claussen Boulevard near the **Monument to the Women of Mazatlan** — a unique tribute to the beauty of the local women.

## SOMETHING SPECIAL

Nearly five centuries have passed since the last loser was sacrificed to the gods, but the ancient game of **ulama**, dating back to the dawn of Mesoamerican civilization, continues as a popular cultural pastime — but only in Mazatlan.

The Maya Indians of Yucatan believed that a ritual death sacrifice at the game's conclusion brought good fortune to the village.   The more peaceful Mayos, who settled around Mazatlan, played the same game but omitted the sacrifice.  Perhaps that's why it is still played today.

Little has changed in the practice of ulama, from the simple leather uniforms worn by the players to the mysterious rubbery ball still used in the game and still fashioned by hand from ancient instructions. To preserve ulama, villagers have passed it down for centuries, encouraging successive generations to play in the age old manner.

The traditional game is typically played by teams of five players (*tahures*), a sixth player who only serves the ball, and officiated by two umpires (*veedores*). Players try to volley the ball (*hule* ) with their hips from one end of the court to the other.  If the ball is touched by another part of the body, the ball is considered burned and a point is lost.  To win the game, one team must score eight points by passing the ball beyond a designated line at the upper end of the court eight times.  If the sun sets before the game is finished, it's continued the next day.

The ball, which meets ancient specifications, is made by hand from a regional plant known as aguama and the milk of a second plant called machaguana.  The mixture is cooked until it thickens, resulting in a rubbery fluid called hule.  The ball, which weighs about nine pounds, is placed in a special wooden mold so it won't lose its form and texture.

The game is played on a sandy, rectangular court (tachtli), approximately fifty meters by four meters with a dividing line in the middle. Courts are traditionally placed north to south so the players won't have to face the sun. According to records kept by Fray Andres Perez de Ribas in 1604, the tribes that inhabited the area around Mazatlan had to establish where the ball game court would be located before the village could be settled.

The traditional attire for the game (*fajado* ) is still worn by the players.  This consists of cotton shorts, a deer skin loincloth tied with a cotton strip and covered by a leather belt. The players are barefoot.

Ulama has its roots in astrology and mirrors a conflict between the sun and the stars.  The game is played frequently in Mazatlan.  Ask the concierge at your hotel.

## SPORTS

With water that rarely gets colder than 68 in winter and warmer than 78 in summer, **beaches** are a top priority in Mazatlan.   The longest stretch of uninterrupted beach in Mexico extends north from the center of town for 12  miles and is open to the the public — there are no private beaches in Mexico.  **Sabalo,** the farthest, is sheltered, quiet and fashionable.   Remember, one need not be a guest at the Camino Real to swim there.  **Las Gaviotas**, closer to town, is a bit more crowded, but a pleasant place to swim.  **Playa Norte,** though less exclusive may be more fun.  You can rent lockers, beach chairs and umbrellas.  Mariachis play at the little restaurants that dot the beach and provide inexpensive places to lunch.   **Olas Alas** means high waves and that says it all.  This is a popular spot for surfing, but the tide can be tricky.

**Boating** — Motorboats, sailboats, water skiing and parasailing are available all along the northern beaches.  For parasailing, you wear a parachute and are pulled by a speedboat.  The speed and wind lift you up and you'll soar like a bird for about five glorious minutes.  When the boat stops, you'll float gently down onto the beach or into the sea below.

*A fisherperson's paradise.*

Known as the billfish capitol of the world, Mazatlan offers unsurpassed **deep-sea fishing**.  Red snapper, sea bass and dorado are caught along with the treasured trophies, sailfish and marlin.  A new practice of "catch and release" — a quick photo on board ship to preserve the excitement and then slash the line — is becoming increasingly popular. Several excellent outfitters located at the boat docks on the south side of Creston Hill offer day-long private charters.

At the mouth of the Sea of Cortez, Mazatlan has one of the world's great fish traps. Thousands of sailfish, blue marlin, black marlin, striped marlin, swordfish, dolphin and tuna are landed yearly.  A record black marlin weighing l,362 pounds was hooked in 1990.

**Tennis** — the **Resort Hotel el Cid** has eight clay courts that can be rented by the hour. and sponsors a "John Newcombe Tennis Ranch" program one week of every month.  Two other hotels with clay courts for rent are **Costa de Oro** ( 3) and **Hotel de Cima** (2).  **Club de Tenis en Espanol** has four clay and one hard court also rented by the hour at Playa Matzatlan, near the Arts and Crafts Center.

**Golf** — There's an 18-hole course at the **Resort Hotel El Cid**, five miles north on the Sabalo Beach Road, and a 9-hole course at **Club Campestre de Mazatlan**, at International Road.

## EXCURSIONS ______________________________________

Three islands that dot the Mazatlan horizon make delightful day excursions. **Isla de los Venados** can offer a peak experience to shell collectors and snorkelers. **Isla de los Pajaros** is a bird-watcher's paradise. **Isla de la Piedra** has a remote South Seas air to it. Boat rides can be arranged from the El Cid resort, get your hotel to pack a lunch for you.

**Concordia**, a charming craft center, is an hour's drive inland from Mazatlan, through low hills covered with lush, green mango groves. The pueblo founded in the late 1500s by Spanish settlers and Jesuit missionaries, is known for its hand-carved hardwood furniture and whimsical pottery. Most of the sixty resident cabinet-makers practice their craft in workshops attached to their homes. You'll also enjoy seeing the town's large *zocalo* (plaza), which dates back to the colonial era, and its charming church.

A few miles further is **Copala**, once a booming silver town and now a well-preserved Mexican pueblo of some 600 residents. The small zocalo is dominated by what must once have been a very elegant church. Donkeys are tied to its iron gate and in the early morning hours, pigs and roosters own the cobblestone streets. It's easy to see why the charming town of Copala is a haven for artists and writers from the U.S. Aged stucco homes with red tile roofs are postcard quaint on the outside, but many of the interiors have been totally modernized.

Opposite the plaza is the cozy **Hotel Posada San Jose**, totally delightful and reasonable too. One could stay here a long, long time. You can enjoy a memorable tamale lunch at the **Copala Butter Company**, an excellent restaurant named for an old mine. Don't leave town with out a slice of the best coconut-banana pie in Mexico at **Daniel's.** The shredded coconut is fresh, so are the bananas. The custard's homemade. Daniel is one of those North American expatriots — an Errol Flynn clone.

Another to check out is **Las Moras**, a new 3000-acre complex in the Sierra Madre foothills, with a dude ranch feel to it. Activities include overnight riding trilps, hiking, swimming and tennis.

*A resort dedicated to sun and fun.*

## TIDBITS

Mazatlan, a city of some 500,000 is located on the mainland opposite the tip of Baja California.  It's airport — a thirty minute drive from down —  is serviced by Aero California, Aeromexico, Alaska, Delta, Continental and Mexicana airlines. Look for the combi ticket counter at the airport to get a ticket for the colectivo van that provides inexpensive service to your hotel.

A daily ferry boat links Mazatlan to La Paz, Baja's second largest city.

Mazatlan's area code is 698.

# PUERTO VALLARTA
## AND THE POWER OF VIOLET EYES

If your boy friend's job took him to some godforsaken place that no one had ever heard of, would you follow him?

Perhaps not. But then suppose his co-workers included a gorgeous redhead, a sultry brunette and a blond nymphette?

Of course you'd go! So no one was the least surprised when Elizabeth Taylor made the same decision. And, because her boy friend was Richard Burton and his working associates were Deborah Kerr, Ava Gardner and Sue Lyon, the whole world took note. Burton's out of town assignment was the filming of *Night of the Iguana,* an event that turned the tiny fishing village of Puerto Vallarta into a household word.

*Ruins of the **Night of the Iguana** set. Photo by author.*

The situation was potentially explosive. Taylor's ex-husband, Michael Wilding, had been hired to publicize Burton. Peter Viertel, Deborah Kerr's husband, had once been involved with Ava Gard-ner. Gardner's "attendants" in the film were two local beach boys who fol-lowed her everywhere. Every other macho male in town was after Sue Lyon, the 17-year old who'd become an overnight star playing the nymphet in *Lolita..* She was closely guarded by both her mother and her fiance.

Add to this a cinematographer, Gabriel Figueroa, who burst into operatic song while drinking, and a director, Indio Fer-nandez, who had shot his last pro-ducer. Tennessee Williams was also there with both his lover.

Real life fantasy overshadowed the screen variety when Taylor arrived. She and Burton had begun their epic affair on the set of *Cleopatra* the previ-ous year, and when the fabulous Liz arrived — not only a mega star in the Hollywood gallaxy, but a woman in love protecting her turf — pandemonium ensued. Her presence — enriched by trunks and suitcases, an ex-fighter bodyguard, secretaries for her-self and Burton, a British cook, a chauffeur and three children by two ex-husbands — was a mon-ument to the grand old style.

What would happen next? To whom? How soon? The whole world seemed to be speculating. To heighten the excitement, John Huston, who was producing the film, presented Richard, Elizabeth, Ava, Deborah and Sue each with a velvet-lined box. Inside was gold-plated der-

John Huston, a patron saint of
Puerto Vallarta.
Photto by the author.

the coastal town and its art galleries —
if you're not cautious — will absorb all
of your time.

This is not to say that Puerto Vallarta
has ceased to be picturesque. Pigs,
chickens and donkeys still occasionally
tie up traffic. The beaches continue to
offer a seductive invitation, the hills
remain lush and green. Despite the
influx of tourists, the locals are as warm
and friendly as always.

Elizabeth Taylor's living room — now Casa Kimberly.
Photo by author.

ringer with four gold bullets
engraved with the names of the
other recipients.

Years later he would recall,
"There were more reporters on
the set than iguanas — I don't
know of any picture I've made that
called forth such interest." Reporters
and photographers from around the
world flocked to the sleepy town — not
an easy task. What they found was a
village of 5000 linked to the outside
world by an unpaved road and a narrow, dirt airstrip. There were no telephones. Residents kept track of the
outside world by radio.

Actually, the stars got on "famously"
and a generation later, the once
unknown fishing village projects the
image of a cultural center that rivals
San Miguel de Allende. Artists flock to

The primary change is that there's more
variety from which to choose, many lifestyle opportunities. Once one was considered lucky to get into the Oceana
Hotel. This landmark — Burton made
it his headquarters, drinking raicilla,
mind-bending Mexican moonshine still
available at some of the older bars outside town — well located as it is, continues as a tourist mecca. Today most
will prefer more quiet havens at the
north and south of town, many sugges-
tive of the French and Italian Riviera.

Puerto Vallarta is a tropical hideaway
that can't fail to appeal to the most

sophisticated traveler. Huston elected to shoot his film in black and white, believing that the kaleidoscope of color: sea, sky, flowers, birds and beaches, was simply too distracting — thus detracting from his plot line. This is a haven where one can explore old world cobblestone streets lined by pastel stucco buildings with terra cotta tiled roofs that literally climb up the cliff sides.

Add to that the unparalleled beauty of the rugged Pacific coastline. Enjoy twenty-five miles of pristine beaches, the best upscale shopping found in any Mexican resort and the unique charm of hanging bridges, lazy streams and quaint churches alongside luxury hotels. Watch just one blazing sunset from the seaside boardwalk and you'll understand what brings true romantics back again and again.

Natives are justly proud of the new Marina Vallarta which offers all water sports plus golf. Major hotels all feature sports facilities for the landbound and miles of undeveloped surrounding countryside await the hunter, hiker or horseback rider.

But far and away the most romantic possibility is to ask your hotel to pack a picnic lunch for you, then arrange with a water taxi service to take you to any number of deserted beaches returning hours later to pick you up. Jack Rodriguez operates a reasonable and reliable service daily and can be contacted at Los Muertos Beach.

Puerto Vallarta has always attracted artists; now there are discriminating collectors. **Galeria Uno**, at 561 Morelos,

exhibits contemporary art in an airy, whitewashed building with a lush courtyard. Jan Lavender, who opened the gallery more than twenty years ago, features work with a strong element of magical realism which she likens to the fantasy imagery employed by Gabriel Garcia Marquez in his literature. She's excited by the recognition potential of Mexican artists and believes "the art scene is in ferment, explosive, on the verge of breaking out internationally."

Even when just a village, Puerto Vallarta was a mecca for students of serious folk art. Now mask collectors from all over the world seek out Ignacio Jacobo at **Gallery Indigera**, Juarez 168, for some of the most exciting work in the country.

**Arte Magico Huichol** at 164 Corona, is a must-see gallery for anyone fascinated by the legendary culture of the Huichol Indians where art and psychedelic ritual are linked, each revolving about the sacred peyote cactus used as a conduit to the spirit world.

North of town ancient ruins have been discovered. There's talk of extensive excavation, with tours and a visitor's center. A few exotic archaeological relics are on display at the **Cuale Museum** located on the small island that divides the town.

Yet nearby a life-size statue of a more recent icon, the late producer John Huston, is mute proof that some of the most fascinating legends still center around a love goddess of another era. Not only is her home on every city tour but a temple of sorts has been named for her, the movie theater, **Sala Elizabeth Taylor.**

To the south of town, archaeology of a different sort may be pursued. On the Mismaloya beach, ruins of the *Night of the Iguana* set remain to be explored. It's all there — including the bar that Huston constructed and stocked at his star's request. Burton played a defrocked Anglican priest, an alcoholic.

Just down the hill is the lively **La Jolla de Mismaloya,** one of the most charming hotels in town with a perfect beach and a quaint mini village closeby. In the hotel bar, the movie plays nightly by popular request. Hardly anyone comes to town without paying homage.

Cold beer and Burton at his best.

## HOTELS

Visitors still get dreamy passing under the "sin bridge" that connects the two parts of the homes once owned by Taylor and Burton. It was here that Burton confided in his diary: "Elizabeth is now looking ravishingly sun-tanned, though the lazy little bugger ought to lose a few pounds or so to look her absolute best."

Today romantics may enjoy actually luxuriating in the former lovenest which locals persist in nostalgically referring to as the "playpen." The double home, still filled with photographs and other memorabilia has reincarnated as a bed and breakfast now known as **Casa Kimberly.** (1-800-321-6750)

The previously mentioned **La Jolla de Mismaloya** is another pleasant possibility. Besides the hotel, there are a number of mini apartments which afford an opportunity to play house. (1-800-322-2343)

Tucked away in a hidden cove between lush, green jungle and the

*The "Sin Bridge" which connected the homes of Elizabeth Taylor and Richard Burton.* Photo by author.

*Every room at the Camino Real has its own priavte jacuzzi and a sweeping view of the sea..*

*The Camino Real has the best beach in town.*

Pacific is the posh **Camino Real**, where every room has a sweeping ocean view. Many of the private balconies feature jacuzzis where couples can top another day in paradise with a night view of sea and stars.  (I-800-722-6466)

A reasonable downtown alternative, also on the beach, is **Hotel Molino de Agua**, built on the site of a former mango grove.  Besides a virtual botanical garden of tropical plants, the inn has a delightful restaurant, **Lions Court**. (322-2-4385)

**Hotel Posada Rio Cuale**, where the river meets the sea, is an affordable oasis downtown where the action is.  Walk a very short distance to the beach and an even shorter one to the museum and elegant shops on Cuale Island.  Cross the bridge that John Huston built so that he could film it in his movie and you're in the center of everything.  The hotel restaurant is excellent, the gardens charming, the rooms clean and pretty.  Attractive rates make it possible to linger longer or splurge more. (91-322-2-0450)

Puerto Vallarta's hidden treasure is **Los Cuatros Vientos** (the four winds) described by the famous artist Tamayo as the "prettiest hotel in all Mexico."  The 16-room colonial mansion clings to the side of a hill offering breathtaking views of city and sea.  This is the way the town used to be — a hidden haven where you awaken to the sound of church bells ringing, roosters crowing and donkeys clattering down cobbled streets.  Yet inside this nostalgic reminder of yesterday's Vallarta is **Chez Elena,** an eight-time winner of the Holiday fine dining award. (322-2-0161)

Something exciting to check out is the newly opened **Bel-Air Puerto Vallarta** located on the now fashionable Marina Vallarta.  The swank, hotel, is the first of several slated by the Bel-Air chain for Mexico.  The resort has 42 suites and 25 villas with private terraces, jacuzzis and kitchenettes adjoins an 18-hole championship golf course.  (1-800-457-7675)

## RESTAURANTS

Besides the best beach in town, the **Camino Real** has a world class restaurant, **La Perla**.  Not only is the cuisine divine, but the  dining room is a virtual museum featuring the fantasy creations of Mexico's popular sculptor, Sergio Bustamene.  Elegant and expensive, but worth it.

But there are many charming restaurants from which to choose.  By far the most romantic is **El Set**, *the* place to watch the sun set.  The positioning — terraced on a cliff low enough to get a sense of the surf as well — is perfect, and so is the food.  El Set is located on Mismaloya Road in the moderately priced **Hotel Playa Concas Chinas** — very pleasant, simply furnished, but with lovely views of tiny coves, bay and hillside, and the beach is good. (91-322-2-0156)

While downtown, try **Mogambo**, a lobster and steakhouse — don't miss the oyster soup — with a piano bar at Paseo Diaz Ordaz, No. 644; and **Le Bistro**, a jazz cafe on Rio Cuale island.  Don't be surprised if the after dinner margaritas put you in a mellow mood for shopping.   To be expected: the many enticing boutiques remain open in the evening.

Two perennial restaurant favorites appeal to both the palate and a sense of adventure.  After lunching at **Chico's Paradise**, one can splash in a jungle pool. **Chee Chee's** also has a lush setting that calls Tarzan to mind. Beneath the palm thatched dining room is a natural swimming pool tucked into immense boulders where diners can enjoy a pre-lunch dip in the bay.

To pursue the Tarzan ambience even farther, hop the water taxi or excursion boat from Puerto Vallarta to **Yelapa**, a tiny village seemingly from another time.  The adventure starts at the dock, for there are no paved roads to Yelapa.  There's no electricity either or telephones — "just" a tropical lifestyle, hidden waterfalls, and an enchanting village.

You'll think of Gauguin and. . .well, what the hell?  Why go back to Puerto Vallarta with the others after lunch?  Why not stay a night. . .or maybe a lifetime. . .at Yelapa's one hotel, **Lagunita**.  Accommodations are little grass shacks (palapas) with all the basic amenities.

Fish and sea food dishes are popular — marvelous lobster — often you'll see it being caught.  After dinner you'll sit out under the stars drinking coco locos.  At 10, the bar closes and you're on your own with a flashlight.  Yelapa relies entirely on propane gas to generate electricity.

But then who travels to the isolated coast of a tropic paradise to play bingo?


## TIDBITS

Aeromexico offers direct non-stop flights to Puerto Vallarta from Los Angeles and San Diego; Alaska operates daily non stop flights from San Francisco, Seattle, Portland, Los Angeles, Anchorage and Fairbanks.  American Airlines has a daily non stop from Dallas.  Mexicana Airlines flies daily non-stop to Puerto Vallarta from San Francisco, Los Angeles, Denver and Chicago and also has connecting flights through both Guadalajara and Mexico City from other U.S. gateways.  Alaska Arilines also flies into Puerto Vallarta. Canadian Airlines offers flights through their charter service, Canadian Holidays, from Toronto.

**When telephoning,** the city area code for Puerto Vallarta is 322.

**The dress** is casual chic for everyone.  Temperatures hover in the mid 70s year round.

# MANZANILLO
## A FAIRY TALE COME TRUE

Hernan Cortes, the arch plunderer of the Western world, a conquistador with all of Mexico to choose from, liked Manzanillo so well that he wanted to retire there. Today luxury yachts dock at the port city, mogul and movie stars nod hello in the discos.

But a very visible treasure is **Las Hadas**, (on Bahia de Manzanilla. Phone: 1-800-722-6466) a shimmering white, minareted, pleasure palace reminiscent of Kubla Khan. Remember the movie, *10*? Bo Derek and her famous love scene set to the accompaniment of Ravel's *Bolero*? Las Hadas is where it all happened.

*Las Hadas, a modern day Xanadu.*

The attraction? A place where the Pacific plays hide and seek with the Sierra Madre, creating snug coverlets, cliff-hemmed bays and beaches that unfurl like golden ribbons. Small wonder that Manzanillo attracted notorious pirates, among them Drake and Morgan. The whereabouts of hidden treasure remains the subject of endless coffee house speculation.

*A sea view of Manzanillo's famous pleasure palace.*
Photo by Vern Appleby.

Stark, startling white against the vibrant sky, the hotel resembles a fairy tale city. Hence the name: the fairies.

*An Arabian Night fantasy.* Photo by Vern Appleby.

An exotic hybrid of the Moorish, the Mediterranean, the Mexican and the Disneyesque, Las Hadas is unquestionably Mexico's most opulent resort — a ten on anyone's list. *Of all Mexico's many and varied romantic hotels, this one is the most spectacularly fanciful.*

Bolivian tin magnate Antenor Patino built his Xanadu in the late 1960s at a cost of $35 million. Today the full blown vision from the Arabian Nights encompasses chalky domes, ice cream spires, Arabic arches, Eastern statuary and 230 luxuriously appointed rooms. Moorish towers rise from the jungle, cobblestone paths wind upward from the bay where dainty white luxury tents billow along a private beach.

Winner of the AAA 5-Diamond Award, the resort complex includes a golf course ranked by *Golf Digest* as among the world's finest, tennis courts, several excellent restaurants, a dazzling disco, a lagoon-size pool studded with intimate islands and splashing waterfalls, sumptuous rooms with marble baths and ocean views, plus private villas with individual pools.

It's difficult to imagine a more conducive ambience for romance to blossom than among the gentle tropical breezes, the soft warm surf, the buttery gold sunsets, the coos and calls of wild birds, the rustling of palm fronds, the dew of lush ferns and the freshness of blooming hibiscus and bougainvillea that comprises Las Hadas. Yes, it really is that alluring. It's also difficult to imagine any one wanting to wander far from this paradise.

*For those born to wander or at least wonder:* Manzanillo, as a destination, is notoriously short on charisma. Named for the manzanillo (chamomile) trees growing there when the town was founded in 1522, the bay was the push-off point for the conquest of the Philippines by Miguel Lopez de Legaspie. In fact, his ships were built by Indians on the beach not far from where Las Hadas now stands.

# WHEN IN MANZILLO

Today Manzanillo is strictly a no-frills port city—the Mexican Pacific's biggest and busiest harbor.  Docks are downtown and railroad tracks cut through the main street to reach the wharves.  The fleet always seems to be in and the streets are full of sailors attempting to eyeball the local senoritas.  Sometimes they meet at the zocolo which is dominated by a gingerbread cast iron bandstand dating from the Victorian—or rather Porfirian era.

*Romances blossom...* Photo by Vern Appleby.

## SHOPPING

Aside from the the little arcade at **Punta Las Hadas**, Manzanillo is not a shopper's paradise; but when you do happen to spot something you like, prices are apt to be slightly lower than the other Gold Coast resorts.  Try **El Caracol** (Calle Juarez 33) across from the zocolo for shell jewelry and accessories or **Bazar Maria Lidia** (Avenida Mexico 69) for embroidered clothes.  **Tunanta Boutique** on the Santiago-Manzanillo highway is a good bet for fashion running the gamet from beachwear to formal.

*Why would anyone leave?* Photo by Vern Appleby.

## RESTAURANTS

**Osteria Bugatti** (Mexico 200, Crucero Las Brisas), one of the oldest and most popular restaurants in town also has an elegant store.  The restaurant features Italian dishes and a wandering minstrel strumming his way from table to table. The piano bar is a gathering place for late night cocktails.

Another romantic dining spot is **L'Recif** on Peninsula de Juluapan (Vida del Mar) named for an offshore reef.  Surrounded by lovely terraced gardens, L'Recif hangs over the sea.  One tier contains a pool and bar—perfect for lunchtime lounging.  Live Dixieland jazz is an accompaniment to dinner dining.  The French food is excellent, prices moderate.

**Willy's** (Avenida Lazaro Cardenas in the Las Brisas area) is another beachfront, favorite.  An exciting menu features, seafood, spaghetti, homemade paté, duck a l'orange, mango pie and profiterol., a sinful ice cream pastry.

## BEACHES

What to do next?  Consider a drive to **Playa de Oro**.  No, despite all the pirate tales, the beach is not made of gold.  Actually the sand is  grayish, but the beach does promise a walk on the wild side.  The isolated stretch weaves for miles along open sea: low dunes, dramatic cliffs  strange rock formations.  Imagine a time trip to the primeval haunt of a cave man.  Take Mexico 200 twenty miles north of town to a well marked sign.  Turn left and follow the dirt road 4.5 miles.  The beach will be yours to enjoy in solitude.

## HOTELS

Though it would be personally unthinkable to go to Manzanillo and not stay at Las Hadas, there's an alternative that continues to draw raves from loyal return-ees.  **La Posada** (Colonia Las Brisas, Avenida Lazaro Cardenas 201 (2-24—4) known as the "passionate pink hotel by the tropic sea" is smal,l well staffed, and warmly domestic. Stone footpaths meander through tropical landscape as do many cats and kittens. The main sitting room where delicious breakfasts are served, is a charming melange of artifacts.  The 24 comfortable and well appoint-ed rooms face the sea, have brick walls, ceiling fans and heavy wooden doors opened by giant skeleton keys — La Posada's trademark.

## TIDBITS

Manzanillo is serviced by Mexicana Airlines via connecting flights. Temperatures average in the 80s.  The area code is 333.  Dress is casual chic.

## BEYOND LAS HADAS

*Las Alamandas*  is the creation of Isabel Goldsmith, granddaughter of Don Ant-enor Patino, the Bolivian Tin King, who built Las Hadas.   The essence of ro-mance, beauty and style, the hotel consists of nine suites in five villas.  A staff of seventy clean the rooms, prepare and serve the meals and grow all the fruits and vegetables for guests that never number more than 24.   Consider that ratio!

The resort, actually a tiny self-contained village, is situated on 70 acres of beach, lagoons, and exotic gardens.  Reservations and arrangements for a pickup at ei-ther the Manzillo or Puerto Vallarta airports (Las Alamandas is half way between) may be made by calling 1-800-223-6510. The hotel also has its own airstrip.

# ZIHUATANEJO
## WHERE WOMEN HAVE ALWAYS BEEN SPECIAL

"You like cats?" the elderly gentlemen asked.

I shrugged, smiling. "Who doesn't?"

Both he and the tiger tom had come upon me from opposite directions as I sat watching the last rays of sunset fade into the sea. "I have a cat at home," he confided. "A wonderful cat. She is three years old and still a virgin."

*A contended resident of Zihautanejo.* Photo by Derro Evans.

"Really?" The idea was improbable, the implied air of proud proprietorship outrageous, too macho for words. At home I'd have bristled, probably protested. Here in the somnolent serenity of Zihuatanejo, I felt strangely touched.

The tom cat leaped into my lap. The elderly man removed his hat. Could he share the bench, the sea, the sunset with me? Stiffly he sat down, his manner so deferent, so courteous. Cat purr and surf sounds blended as I reflected on words, attitudes, manners of another time.

That time warp feeling is part of Zihautanejo's charm. Still very much a Colonial fishing village, it reminds one of an old photo of Acapulco, trying to catch up but still untroubled.

Situated on the tropical "Mexican Riv-era," 150 miles northwest of Acapulco, Zihuatanejo (see-whah-tah-NEH-hoe) runs along a luxuriant coastline of sandy beaches suited to all the water sports, with lagoons ideal for bird watching, rocky islets perfect for snorkeling and scuba, and coves so secluded that the only footprints are your own.

Despite what's been going on in Ixtapa, just four miles away, "Zihaut" remains untouched. Fishermen still bring their daily catch to the town dock in the mornings, jungle covered bluffs tumble into the bay, small intimate hotels cling to cliff sides and nestle on beaches as much a part of their environment as the tropical blossoms that spill from their balconies. The favorite pastime of resident and visitor alike continues to be a stroll down Paseo del Pescador, or Fisherman's Walk. Note: Travel writers, mindlessly plagiarizing one another, perpetuate a myth. The streets are *not* cobble-stone, but rather decorative brick add-ing not only to the charm of a walk but to its ease.

Four miles away is Ixtapa, a razzle rouser groomed for stardom by the Mexican government as *the* destination for barefoot sophisticates. Cancun's west coast cousin is well cushioned with top accommodations. It's name, pronounced eeks-TAH-pa, comes from the Nahuatl Indian word meaning "the white place." The reference is to two-mile long Palmar Beach where hotels are located seaside, their futuristic architecture counter pointing mountains and coconut palms. It's a lovely place to visit.

Ixtapa, the new kid on the block, was born in the 1970s when FONATUR (The National Fund for Tourism Development) realized the area's potential as a resort utopia. Zihuatanejo's history is quite different. Long before Columbus sailed to the New World, it was called Cihuatlian, meaning "landing of women," and was revered as a sacred sanctuary.

A reminder of those ancient times can be found at the popular beach, **Playa las Gatas**, where a mysterious row of hewn rocks serving as a breakwater can only be explained by legend. It's said that a Tarascan king once built the barrier to shelter his daughter's private beach.

It would appear that women have always been cherished in Zihautanejo.

## HOTELS

Visitors to Zihautanejo may choose from a variety of charming hotels, but its justly touted "three pearls" are surely among the most unique and delightful to be found anywhere in the world.   Like the oyster-grown variety, these pearls are pricey but also priceless, a stay at any truly a once in a lifetime experience.

*The view from the intimately romantic Puerto Mio Hotel.* Photo by Derro Evans.

It would be difficult to find a hotel more sensuously romantic than **Puerto Mio**. (714 427 48) Hugging the hillside overlooking the sea, each superbly appointed room commands a spectacular view. Built in the style of a pueblo— many of Puerto Mio's rooms are split levels — the facility includes a marina, two pools and three tennis courts. The highlight, however, is an al fresco restaurant and bar which may well be one of the world's most romantic. Just below is a tiny, intimate bay flanked by cliffs against which the siren surf crashes and splashes. The view is exquisite. Proposals? Propositions? The results are virtually fail safe.

**La Casa Que Canta,** (1-800-525-4800) reminiscent of an African village with its descending terraces and thatched roofs cascading down the hillside, is the stuff

from which myths are made. Adobe walls painted a muted milk chocolate are laced with straw. The lobby, topped with a soaring roof of dried palm fronds, is open on two sides for spectacular ocean viewing. Furnishings are among the most imaginative to be found anywhere.

*La Casa Que Canta is the stuff of myths.*

Clay icons stand guard in planter boxes. Chairs are brightly painted with arms resembling birds and legs carved to look like feathers, straw coffee tables are fashioned into jaguars with charmingly ferocious faces — whiskers, gleaming

*La Casa Que Canta where the pool meets the sea.*

eyes, et all. But most evocative are the Frida Kahlo chairs—seats that bear the artist's likeness, to the defiant eyebrows.

Each of the eighteen suites has its own living room and terrace.  Red-tiled doors

*Villa del Sol — paradise as you dreamed it.*

are edged with polished pebbles, bathrooms are marble with granite hand basins. These rooms don't have television. They have something better: magnificent sea views and flowers. So many flowers. There are blooms, passionate purple bougainvillea, in soap dishes, blossoms under pillows, even tucked into washcloths. Their effect, against cream colored ruffles, white walls and sheets that seem to shimmer, is stunning.  At night when beds are turned down, there are more flowers, this time red hibiscus, placed between the sheets.

Looking down at the sea is wonderful. There's really nothing to equal it — unless it's literally being on it. Though both the previously described hotels have exquisite views, access to the beach is via a long stairway.    Since what

*Interior of Villa del Sol voted "best small hotel in Mexico".*

goes down must invariably climb back up, the ascent gives one pause when contemplating a moonlight stroll. Guests at **Villa del Sol,** (753-422-39) an elegant and intimate on-the-beach hotel, don't have to think twice. The charming, bungalow style inn faces right on La Ropa, a slender crescent moon shaped beach.

*Villa del Sol nestles in a forest of coconut palms.*

This is paradise just as you dreamed it.  Adobe bungalows with private balconies and jacuzzis, gauze canopied beds and intimate sitting rooms.  Small wonder the Villa del Sol was voted  "best small hotel in Mexico" by the International Press. The encircling enclave of coconut groves — a city ordinance in Zihautanejo forbids any structure higher than a coconut palm  — reminds one that the very first coconuts to reach North America came first to Zihautanejo, brought from the Philippines in Spanish galleons.  Just one more thought to ponder while sipping a coco loco by the pool or on the beach. The call of a tropical bird will be the loudest sound you'll hear.

There are 4000 hotel rooms in the Zihautanejo/Ixtapa area ranging from cozy modestly priced bungalows to splendid Gran Turismo (5-star-plus.)  Besides the previously mentioned hotels, the **Sotovento** (743-427-48) in Zihautanejo has been a long time favorite. Tiny , elegant **Villa de la Roca**  next door has five suites that can be rented individually or as an entire villa.

**Westin Brisas Resort**  (1-800-228-3000) in Ixtapa has its own strip on Palmar Beach and is located  across the avenue from a village style shopping center. There's also a most welcome Adults Only Pool.  Many rooms also have private balconies with jacuzzis.  The most arresting of all the Ixtapa hotels, the Westin is a very special place with architecture that resembles an ancient Aztec pyramid. At sunset, the native colors transform the highrise hotel into a temple of gold.

# RESTAURANTS

Both Zijuatanejo and Ixtapa take pride in their fine restaurants that range from haute French cuisine to traditional home-made Mexican fare.   Ultra fresh sea food such live clams, oysters on the half shell, shrimp, squid, lobser and game fish is a mainstay.   A very special favorite is **Casa Elvira** on Paseo Del Pescador between the pier and basket ball court in Zihautanejo.  There are no "special" recommendations; *everything's* good.

You'll also want to check out **La Sirena Gorda** next to the pier for lunch or a light dinner.  There are no better sea food tacos to be found anywhere in Mexico.  The coconut ice cream is unbeatable too.

As in all the state of Guerrero, Thurday is *pozole* day.  This hearty stewlike dish made with hominy and pickled pig knuckles may be enjoyed at a variety of restaurants, but it's especially fun to check out one of the *pozolerias*  such as **Deotzintle** just south of the Zihuatanejo gas station and another in the village of Coacoyul on the way to airport.  These little gems are open only on Thursdays.

Another institution is **Al Andaluz Expresso,** the rendezvous where everyone in Zihaut goes to just hang out.  Conversation is lively and spirited, food  excellent, in the background classical music. This is the perfect place to come for breakfast. Try the *huevos divorciados* (divorced eggs—one with green sauce, the other red). Later in the day you'll enjoy fresh pasta and pastries, expresso, capaccino or fresh fruit drinks. Centrally located on Paseo Peatonal.

## DAY LIFE

One of Zihautanejo's most interesting attractions is the ***Museo Arqueologico de la costa Grande,*** located at the east end of Paseo del Pescador at Plaza Olof Palme. Inaugurated in 1992, the museum displays murals and maps explaining history and migrations since prehistoric times. There are close to 1000 carvings, figurines and artifacts, a number of them from a pre-Columbian sex cult that flourished in the area. Here you will find female fertility figures, phallic stone carvings, men in bondage.

The ***Ixtapa Golf Club,*** an 18-hole course, designed by Robert Trent Jones Jr. is also a wildlife preserve extending from a coconut plantation to the sea. Also included in the facility, which is open daily, are seven lighted tennis courts and a large swimming pool. For information and reservations, call 3-10-62.

Deep sea fishing ranks among the world's best. Likely catches include trophy-size sailfish, blue and black marlin, yellowfin tuna and dorado. Arrangements can be made by your hotel travel desk or by contacting the boat cooperative.

More than 30 scuba sites range from easy reef dives to 100 ft. depths. Shipwreck exploring is another possibility. Juan Bernard Avila, a NAUI master-diver at ***Zihuatanejo Scuba Center*** (across from Banamex on Calle Cuauhtemoc) offers it all as well as night dives, instruction, certification and opportunities for spectacular still and video underwater photography. The center's staff will also videotape customers and provide them with the cassette complete with titles, special effects and musical sound track.

## SHOPPING

A recent law relocated all beach vendors to special handicraft markets especially set up for them—a mixed blessing. It's true that no one bothers you on the beach, but many of us miss both the surprising variety of the passing parade and the ingenuity of the merchandisers. On the upside, the new mercado stalls are occupied by families. Some have remained un-Hispanicized and speak only Nahuatl. It's fascinating to watch: elaborate-intricate-symbolic-naif-flow designs directly from the imaginations of the artisans onto ceramic bowls, figurines and plates.

By all agreement *Ruby's*, at Cuauhtemoc No. 7, is the most elegant store in town.  Offerings include beautifully crafted jewelry as well as surreal lacquerware that's after the last word.

*Bajo este techo*  (under one roof) is the Spanish spin for mini mall.  *Casa Marina*, at Paseo Del Pascador No. 9 (next to the basket ball court)  is a charming example.  It encompasses three delightful stores, *El Jumil, La Tzotzil* and *La Zapoteca*, all offering a rich and varied selection of clothing, masks, weavings, jewelry and handicrafts, plus *Cafe La Marina,* a  pizza parlor/bookstore.

For more sophisticated fare, there are several tasteful pedestrian shopping malls in Ixtapa, each with top-of-the line boutiques, art galleries, jewelry and handicraft shops.  These are truly charming—cozy, shopper friendly places pleasant for paseo strolling.

## THE BEACH BAZAAR

### (IN ZIHAUTANEJO)

**Playa Principal**—Fishermen return here with their morning catches and store their boats and gear on the sandy beach.  Rimming the beach, the Paseo del Pescador is lined with shops, restaurants and handicraft stands.  At the west end of the promenade is the main pier and, just beyond that, a marina, Puerto Zihuatanejo Maris.  At the east end is the Museo Arqueologico de la Costa Grande with the arresting collection of pre-Hispanic art and artifacts previously mentioned.

*The elegant La Ropa Beach.*

**Playa la Ropa**—("Clothes Beach") is one of the most protected and beautiful beaches along Mexico's Pacific coast.  Its name relates to a cargo of oriental silks which washed ashore from a shipwrecked Spanish galleon.  Along this one-mile stretch of soft white sand, a five minute taxi ride from town, are several open air palapa roofed restaurants serving fresh seafood.

**Playa las Gatas**—No trip would be complete without

a visit to this lively and delightful beach with its excellent palapa restaurants and legendary breakwater. The beach can only be reached by boat. Tickets may purchased at the Cooperativa office on the town pier for $2 round trip.

## (IN **IXTAPA**)

Besides **Playa del Palmar**, Ixtapa's main beach and the location of its hotel zone, there are three other very appealing beaches.

*The Ixtapa beach, an azure cove.*

**Punta Ixtapa** — a point forming the northwest boundary of Palmar Bay. Just off the tip is Isla de a Pie (on-foot island) because during low tide, you can walk to it over the big rocks. Thousands of marine birds make this their refuge.

**Isla Ixtapa** — a wildlife preserve to the north just off Playa Quieta is great for a day on the beach snorkeling or scuba diving. The island has four beaches. Tickets for the five-minute boat ride are $2 round trip.

**Playa Linda**—one mile further up the coast is in a jungle. Horses can be rented here to ride along the sandy beach or through the jungle. There are a number of seafood restaurants along the beach.

## NIGHTLIFE

My special favorite dinner spot in Zihaut is *Coconuts* , an outdoor restaurant which manages to combine lively pizzazz with romantic ambience. The oyster bisque is a special treat. I'd like to share the recipes, but they wouldn't give them to me. Ask and you may receive. Located at Augustin Ramirez No. 1.

Sandal chic is delicious, but at least once in a holiday it's fun to dress up. *Bogart's* , located in Ixtapa's **Krystal Hotel**, is the place. Rick and Ilsa would have enjoyed the sophisticated Moroccan atmosphere and outstanding international cuisine served by attentive waiters, and so will you. An exciting specialty is the boneless duck flamed with Grand Marnier—as delicious as it is spectacular.

The onion soup "with turban" is equally good and reputed to be an aphrodisiac.

But a far more potent one is **Marineros.** It is impossible to exaggerate the appeal of the open air dance floor and gorgeous sea view at this night spot located in the **Puerto Mio Hotel** — the perfect place to cap a romantic evening.

*The Westin Resort, Ixtapa.*

## GETTING THERE

**By air:**  Mexicana and Aeromexico operate several nonstop (40 minute) flights throughout the day between their Mexico City hub and Zihuatanejo/Ixtapa as well as from their U.S. gateways.  They also connect with U.S. airlines serving Mexico City.  These include Continental and Delta flies direct from Los Angeles, nonstop three times a week.  Reasonably priced minibuses meet all flights, though individual taxis are also available.

**By car:** From Mexico City, Highway 95 bypasses Acapulco and joins coastal Highway 200 to Ixtapa/Zihautanejo.  By car the trip is 8 to 9 hours; first class bus 12.

## TIDBITS

**Climate:**  Average annual temperature is 78.8 degrees Fahrenheit.  Summer temperature highs average in the low 90s, with night time lows in the high 70s. Winter highs reach the upper 80s, with lows in the low 70s.    During rainy season (June through September) showers are usually brief, generally in the afternoon or at night—so the sun shines *almost* 365 days a year.

**Dress** is casual chic.  Jackets and neckties are gauche.  Bikinis are best suited to the beach or pool.  Shorts would be out of place at deluxe restaurants.

**Telephones**:  The area code for both Zihauatanejo and Ixtapa is 753.

**Getting around**:  Taxis are plentiful and cheap.    Fares are posted in hotel lobbies. Minibuses run frequently between Zihautanejo and Ixtapa charging less than a quarter.

# ACAPULCO
## EVERYTHING "OLD" IS NEW AGAIN

More than any other Mexican city, Acapulco reeks of sensuality. This is a city that wakes up when the sun goes down, a town where sexiness is part of the legend. *Warning:* There's something languorous in the air and it can prove disastrous to one's inhibitions.

with Monte Carlo. Stauffer's life reads like an old Harold Robbins novel. It began in Bern, Switzerland — the "official" birthdate being 1909. But who knows, at his death in 1991, even Stauffer's closest friends didn't know for certain. Certainly Teddy never told.

*Acapulco has a seductive sizzle all its own.*

Something of a musical prodigy, Stauffer played the violin, clarinet and saxophone with a band he organized as a teenager. Soon Germany's top record seller, the "Teddies" rapidly became the toast of Europe. Then, to escape the growing tide of Nazi repression, the band came to the United States where it was equally successful.

Though Acapulco was "discovered" by Cortes in 1530 nothing much happened until November 12, 1927 at 6 p.m. when the first road was completed and the first car arrived. From then on it was just a matter of time before Acapulco became a mecca for Hollywood film stars and European royalty. Cortes and the pirates that followed him, Henry Morgan and Sir Francis Drake, would have appreciated the scene.

Hollywood stars began to appear on the scene in the 1930's, but it remained for Teddy Stauffer to really turn the place into a jet set destination on a par

*"Mr. Acapulco" Teddy Stauffer with his friend, Frank Sinatra.*

Stauffer was enjoying a much publicized romance with Maria Montez, a highly popular movie star of the day, when World War II broke out. Unable to get a visa, he moved on to Mexico City where he became the band leader at Ciro's, the Hotel Reforma's popular night club.

One day in 1943, an old friend from Hollywood days showed up on Stauffer's doorstep. It was the playboy star, Errol Flynn. At loose ends, the two decided quite by chance to holiday at a small fishing village on the west coast of Mexico. Stauffer had heard the town was lovely.

Acapulco had a population of 8000 when they arrived. Thirty years later, when Stauffer wrote his memoirs, *Forever is a Hell of a Long Time!,* he was pleased to report that the tiny village had grown into a sprawling city-resort of half a million. Unquestionably, much of the growth was due directly to his own very personal efforts.

Stauffer was married to Faith Domergue, a Hollywood actress and former protege of Howard Hughes, when he took over the managership of the Casablanca, Acapulco's pioneer hotel. His love affair with the seacoast city would last far longer than the marriage.

One afternoon as Stauffer watched a few locals dive for coins off the La Quebrada Cliffs, he conceived the idea of building a restaurant-night club on a terrace behind the new El Mirador Hotel. In a very short time La Perla was the "in" spot of Acapulco.

About this time Rita Hayworth arrived with her director-husband, Orson Welles, to film *Lady From Shanghai.* The romance that flared between Hayworth and Stauffer spelled the end of her marriage. Soon the two were off on a much publicized whirlwind tour of Europe.

Back in Acapulco five months later, he met and married his second wife, another film star, Hedy Lamarr, considered by many to be the most beautiful woman of her time. The marriage was short lived as were the next three. Stauffer was far more successful at tennis. For twenty-five years, from 1946 to 1971, he was Acapuclo's number one player.

But Stauffer's equally spectacular prowess as a promoter proved even more enduring. In 1956, he went into partnership with Carl Renstrom, a Nebraska inventor and businessman, to build the Villa Vera Hotel and Racquet Club. From then on Stauffer worked and "played" tirelessly, eventually turning both the hotel and the city into a mecca for such luminaries as Clark Gable, Richard Nixon, Prince Bernhard of Holland, Ali Kahn, Porfirio Rubirosa, Tyrone Power, Brigitte Bardot, Frank Sinatra, Yul Bryner, Bob Hope, Paulette Goddard, Tito of Yugoslavia, Jayne Mansfield, Nat "King" Cole, Lana Turner, Sukarno, Liza Minelli, Gina Lollobrigida, Otto Preminger, Howard Hughes, Ava Gardner, Peter Sellers, Barbara Hutton, Prince Alfonso von Hohenlohe, Tony Curtis, Prince Philip of Great Britain, Diahann Carroll, Johnny Carlson, Roman Polanski, Earl Wilson. . . . .the list goes on and on.

Undeniably, Teddy Stauffer's charm and charisma drew them initially. The "right people" came, saw and talked. Soon everyone else was coming. One man had succeeded in turning both the hotel and the city into the hottest jet set glamor resort in the world.

But what brought them back again and again?

**Scenery:**  Mountains meet the sea in Acapulco affording breathtaking views of bay and beach.

**Weather :**  Superb, at least in winter time.

**Ambience:**  Acapulco has a seductive sizzle that's totally unique. Few places in the world are more permissive. Anything goes, as long as it doesn't break the law. When people claim to have danced till dawn, they probably have.

Maybe they wore a bathing suit till midnight, maybe a ball gown to breakfast. No one will bat an eye at either.

But resorts have a way of falling in and out of fashion. This happened to Acapulco in the 1980s. Now it appears that the grand old lady of Mexican holiday destinations has had an *aca limpia* or facelift. And that multimillion dollar nip and tuck is paying off. Visitors are once again flocking to what is once more a glitz destination. Among those buying or building grand condos at the resort are Pacido Domingo, Julio Iglesias and Elizabeth Taylor.

The glamor town where a couple of soon to be headliners, Jack and Jackie Kennedy, once honeymooned is "in" again. Take a good long look at the face across the pool, the bod on the next balcony or blanket—it could be *anybody.*

## HOTELS

Almost every hotel balcony offers an unforgettable view. The most romantic time is at sunset when the lights begin to twinkle and the first stars come out. Don't miss it. With literally hundreds of hotels in Acapulco, it's impossible to find one that's not to your taste and pocketbook. Here's a random sampling of the most unique:

The **Villa Vera Hotel and Raquet Club,** the first to entertain the "in" crowd, is now an intimate alternative to the many  mega resorts that crowd the beach. This is the place where Liz Taylor married Michael Todd—with Eddie Fisher and Debbie Reynolds as attendants, where Pat and Richard Nixon celebrated their 25th anniversary and President Eisenhower visited while Elvis Presley filmed *Fun in Acapulco.* Lana Turner liked the Villa Vera so well she stayed three years.

Today the hotel maintains its status as a world class resort and magnificent year round retreat. Sitting, lovely as ever on a quiet hillside away from the bustle of town, the Villa Vera's deluxe amenities include eighty units, each different; twenty pools, eleven of them private; three championship red clay tennis courts, and two championship paddle courts.  Thick trees and lavish gardens provide privacy and seclusion.  Four luxurious homes on the grounds are available for rent either by the week or day and come fully staffed with maids, cooks and gardeners.  The Beauty and Fitness Center provides good equipment and trainers.  Bodies are pampered and muscles soothed by cosmetologists and masseuses who come to your room or to your private pool.  Lomas de Mar 35.

Villa Vera's charming younger sister is the **Maralisa Hotel and Beach Club.**  This "boutique" hotel is located on a secluded part of Bahia de Acapulco with just ninety rooms, making it one of the smaller beachfront properties.  Guests have access to the prestigious Villa Vera, including use of the tennis, dining and health spa facilities.  And the Maralisa has something Villa Vera doesn't have—a great beach.  There are also two pools, an open air cafe and palapa bar.

*Pink jeeps are a Las Brisas signature.* Photo by author.

If you haven't yet met your lover — and want to — consider an intriguing possibility:  *savvy singles think pink.* What better way to troll than in one of Las Brisas's pretty pink jeeps? Everybody looks twice at the driver of one of those snazzy little vehicles. And one needn't be clairvoyant to realize that the man or woman at the wheel not only knows how to have a good time but possesses good taste.

An elegant grande dame more than forty years old **Las Brisas Hotel**, one of the *world's* most romantic, remains the loveliest in Acapulco.  It's also the only hotel in the world with 250 swimming pools,  besides a huge free-form freshwater pool and two natural salt-water swimming pools hewn out of the rock. The Las Brisas grounds contain more than 110 acres of pink fuchsia blossoms, pink hibiscus bushes, lush trees and feathery vines which cascade down a hill overlooking the sea.  Clinging to the sides are small white bungalows—casitas—most with their own private pools.

The hotel pampers its guests, luring many back year after year.  They're greeted each morning with a "magic box" ( a basket placed in the wall with a double opening) containing a breakfast of fresh fruit, sweet rolls and steaming coffee. The hotel has three restaurants, a private seaside beach club at the bottom of the hill, and a variety of boutiques and tennis courts.  At the very top, the Chapel of Peace

*Las Brisas, one of the most romantic hotels in the world.*

sits 1,300 feet above sea-level — a romantic place for a wedding, as hundreds have discovered over the years.

Signature pink jeeps are available for rent and Las Brisas also offers sunset cruises and jeep safaris to a jungle picnic ground.

Carretera Escencia Clemente Mejia 5255.  Phone: 1-800-228-3000.

*Las Brisas pampers its guests.*  Photo by Derro Evans.

*Camino Real Acapulco Diamente is new and elegant.* Photo by the author.

The newest hotel is the **Camino Real Acapulco Diamente.** Each of the 144 rooms has a patio or balcony with a view of Puerto Marques Bay. Gardens are particularly lovely. Amenities include two restaurants, a beach club and health club. The hotel is both elegant and tranquil with an intimate location away from the madding crowd. You won't want to leave. Phone: 1-800-228-3000.

**Hotel Los Flamingos** was built in the thirties, when Acapulco's few visitors sailed there by yacht, but it wasn't until the fifties that it became Shangri-la for the Hollywood set. That select group included Cary Grant, John Wayne, Johnny Weismuller, Roy Rogers, Errol Flynn, Red Skelton, Richard Widmark who loved the hotel so much that they once bought it. Fond memories of the old gang are kept alive in the lobby's photo gallery. The hotel is still charming and boasts one of Acapulco's most beautiful gardens. The food is good, the rooms clean, the ambience quiet with a warm nostalgia that appeals to all ages. In its day, Los Flamingos was the epitome of luxury, today it's still a good bet if you desire both tranquility and a spectacular sea view at a reasonable price.

**Hotel Plaza Las Glorias El Mirador.** When Teddy Stauffer began inviting his Hollywood cronies to come discover Acapulco, El Mirador was another hangout of the stars. Over the years much of that luster faded leaving only a glamorous history and a great location overlooking the rocks and cliffs of La Quebrada. Happily—thanks to extensive renovations by the Plaza Las Glorias chain—the hotel has staged a glamorous comeback. Quebrada 74. Telephone: 3-1155.

# RESTAURANTS

**Acapulco Princess** is a lovely place to visit. It's just too far out, a bit too large (1,019-rooms), and a little too country clubby, for my taste.  Still it *is* a charming place to go for lunch.  The seaside dining room is lovely with a menu guaranteed to appeal to everyone. The grounds are serene and lush, the boutiques beguiling. Expensive, but well worth checking out. Playa Revolcadero. 1-800-223-1818.

It you don't choose to stay at Hotel Plaza Las Glorias, be certain to go to **La Perla** for lunch or dinner, watch the divers and have a margarita for "Teddy." The Mexican food is good too.) Be sure to get there at least 15 minutes early to insure a good table. Within the Hotel Plaza Las Glorias. Quebrada 74.

**Coyuca 22** — yes, it is pricey, but eating in this converted villa is like visiting an elegant friend who just happens to fix divine lobster especially for you. The steaks are great too and fish lovers can look forward to the best red snapper in town. Four open terraces overlook the lights of Acapulco. Expect to see the shades of Fred Astaire and Ginger Rogers do a torrid tango round the pool. It's that kind of place. Coyuca 22.

You'll see two friendly lions snoozing or playing in front of **Beto Safari.**  Tear yourself away and walk down the stairs almost to the beach level for a good ocean view. You'll enjoy the seafood and live music from noon to midnight. For a different treat, try *quesadillas de cazon* (tortillas stuffed with shark meat). Costera Miguel Aleman on the Playa Condesa.

The **Crazy Lobster** (Longosta Loca) isn't a bit crazy. They take their food very seriously here and it's good.  The sleekest, best and quietest of the seaside restaurants along Costera Miguel Aleman. Try it.

**Paraiso/Paradise** really is crazy. If you don't know how to dance, you'll do it here anyway.  At Paraiso/Paradise guests check their inhibitions at the door. At this pleasantly zany place anything goes and waiters go wild if there's a birthday or anniversary to celebrate.  Surprisingly good seafood here, but remember the food is loud, the waiters insane, the salsa hot.  Costera Miguel Aleman.

Another one with good food and frantic atmosphere is **Carlos 'n'Charlie's Bar, Grill & Pawn Shop.** Be prepared for generous portions of shrimp and ribs and more crazy waiters. Costera Miguel Aleman.

After all that razzamatazz you'll be ready for something calm, something  serene, something elegant, and—above all—something *quiet* . The perfect place is `La **Concha Beach Club and Restaurant** in Las Brisas Hotel. White tents catch the ocean breeze and protect the skin from the hot tropic sun.  Excellent salads, sandwiches, pastas and Mexican seafood specialties are served a few steps from both pool and sea.   For a delightfully refreshing treat, try the iced Jamaica tea. On Wednesday nights, the public is invited for a special steak and lobster dinner. Reservations are suggested.

Another romantic must is the **Belle Vista**, a sterling and crystal filled hilltop dining room also at Las Brisas.  If you aren't staying at this lovely hotel, you'll surely want to go for lunch or dinner.   Choose from a gourmet menu that offers prawns ravioli with ginger or fresh oysters with beluga caviar—and that's just for starters.   An exciting main course is lobster and artichoke flamed with vodka.

## DISCOS

The disco scene is what launched Acapulco in the first place.   Expect to see it all: Balloons, confetti, light shows, video screens.   Acapulco defies any place to outglitz it.    Being outrageous is what it's all about and, during the season, you might not be able to get into the most popular ones.  A clue:  Looking both classy and sexy will definitely help.    Remember, it's the doorman's job to fill the place with the best looking people possible.  Here's a rundown on the Big Five:

**Baby 'O**—a perennial favorite remains imaginative and fashionable despite or because it looks like a stylized mud hut from the outside.  Opens at 10, the beat goes on until 4. Costera Miguel Aleman.

**Boccaccio**—the momentum never seems to stop here.  Electronic boards that personalize welcomes, birthdays, etc. add to the pandemonium.  The alabaster building resembles a work of modern art.  Lots of action centers around the bar. Costera Miguel Aleman.

**Cats** is the new kitty on the block.   It's pretty with stylized "trees" and sparkling lights. Costera Miguel Aleman.

**Midnight**—With few gimmicks, people are the show here.  Maybe that's why this one is the big favorite with the sophisticated Villa Vera crowd. Very "modern."

**Midnight Fantasy** is considered the creme da la creme for good reason. Floor to ceiling windows overlook the bay.   An inside glass elevator takes you to the the "Sex Shop" where you can buy very exciting lingerie.  Fireworks spill over the ceiling in the early a.m. adding to the excitement.  Beside La Vista Mall in Las Brisas.

For something very different and possibly far more romantic, drop by the **El Fuerte Nightclub.**   Best to arrive early to insure a table before the clicking heels begin their tattoo on the hardwood floor.  Flamenco singers and dancers perform to highly emotional guitar music capturing the drama of old Spain.  Monday through Saturday, shows at 10 and 11:30 p.m.  Costera Miguel Aleman 239.  Reservations recommended.  Phone: 3-7746.

## BEACHES

Next to the nightlife, going to the beach is what Acapulco is all about.  Happily, bathing trunks and bikinis are great levelers.  The golden sands are shared by everyone.   There are no private beaches in Mexico; all are federal property and the hotels, no matter how glitzy, have no jurisdiction over them.

Here's a brief rundown from left (facing the sea) to right:

**Revolcadero**, extending beyond the Acapulco Princess and Pierre Marques hotels, is a favorite of the rich and the beautiful.  Open to the Pacific, Revolcadero has the rough waves that most body surfers seek.

**Icacos** is the first stretch of true Acapulco Bay beach as you drive in from the airport. Here the sheltered waters are calm and quiet and the beach a little less hectic.  La Palapa and the Hyatt Regency hotels share the sands.

**La Condesa**, extending from the Continental to El Presidente Hotel, is considered the most fashionable beach.  You'll see the scantiest bikinis there along with everything else imaginable.   Waves are gentle until late afternoon.  There are a number of nice luncheon spots that also offer music for dancing.

**Hornos and Hornitos** beaches run from La Condesa to San Diego Fort.  Mexican tourists who know a good thing when they see it come here.  Trees provide shade, swimming conditions are good.   Pleasant restaurants closeby.

**Caleta** — Back in the "old days" the Caleta, known as the morning beach, was *the* place to be seen by anyone who got up early enough.  Though the old cachet is missing, the Caleta still attracts traditionalists and those who like calmer waters. It's also the departure point for **Roqueta,** an uninhabited island.   Boats ferry bathers to and from Roqueta throughout the day.  There's a direct route as well as the more scenic one which takes 45 minutes.  Tickets are on sale at the kiosk on the beach.

## SIGHTSEEING

**Plaza Juan Alvarez** (the zocalo).   If you can tear yourself away from the beach or your hotel balcony, this is the heart of Acapulco proper.  The main plaza, located near the piers and docks for deep-sea fishing boats, is dominated by the Acapulco Cathedral (an oddity built in 1930 with Byzantine towers and a mosquelike dome). Opposite, at the waterfronts, stands a monument to  national heroes:  Guerrero, Morelos, Hidalgo, Juarez and Cuachtemoc.   Aged ceiba trees provide welcome shade.   Local women gossip, children play tag. It's a world apart from the glitz of "new" Acapulco.

Nearby and clearly marked is the **Flea Market** where crafts and curios are sold. An interesting place to browse and bargain.  Handicrafts and Mexican curios are featured.  Open daily.

**El Fuerte de San Diego** (Fort San Diego).  The most historic spot in Acapulco was built to protect what was once a highly strategic port from  pirate attack.   Having conquered the Americas, the Spaniards went on to subdue the Philippines and by 1565 a trade route was established between Manila and Acapulco.  Cargo from China and Japan was unloaded in the thriving port city and then reloaded on mules to be carried across Mexico to Veracruz for shipment to Spain.  Vast fortunes were made, for the cargo aboard each ship was valued at what today would amount to tens of millions of dollars.  Naturally, before long pirates were lurking in the waters closeby.

By 1616 what was to be the San Diego Fort was under construction.  According to legend, it was a victim of the pirates — a Chinese princess — who gave the women of Mexico their national dress.  Captured by sea rovers, the princess was eventually rescued by Spanish mariners who brought her to Acapulco. From there she made her way to Pueblo, where tradition has it, the princess spent her life doing good works among the poor.  Scorning the elegant fashions of the day, she wore simple, full skirts and a loose blouse.  The style — probably much cooler and more comfortable than the fashions of the day — caught on.  Today it's referred to simply as *china poblana*, which translates to Chinese Puebla style.

In1818, the San Diego Fort was besieged by Mexican troops during the War for Independence.  The Spaniards made a desperate stand but were finally forced to retreat to their ships. Eventually they sailed away forever and the Orient trade went with them.  A century later Acapulco had all but ceased to exist.   Until a road was built in 1927, the journey to Mexico City was made on horseback and took a week.

The fort, now a very interesting museum, is located a few blocks to the left of the zocalo, just across from piers and customs house.  Pre- Columbian relics found in the area as well as other historic items relating to Acapulco's history are displayed in a manner as interesting as the exhibits themselves. Open 10 a.m. to 6 p.m. Closed Mondays.

The **Acapulco Divers** or *clavadistas* who leap from the cliffs of La Quebrada are world famous. The 150 foot plunge into a shallow inlet must be perfectly timed to incoming waves or the divers will be crushed on the jagged rocks. There's no trick involved, nor are they in any way faking it. After kneeling and praying at a small shrine, each man in turn stands poised on the cliff's edge, arms pointing down, muscles tense with concentration as he studies the rush of crashing surf below. At the perfect moment (hopefully!) he leaps forward and hurtles downward in a graceful swan dive, slipping into the water as it rushes into a small cove. One wrong move could prove fatal.

*The Acapulco divers are legendary.*

The dangerous spectacle has been performed by a select fraternity of trained divers since 1934. But who's to say when it really began. Perhaps the early Indian inhabitants tested their strength against the cruel sea in just the same manner.

The exhibition takes place on the cliffs adjoining the El Mirador Hotel.  Whether you watch from the terrace or in the hotel's La Perla nightclub, don't miss it. Shows currently begin at 1:15, 7:30, 8:30, 9:30 and 10:30 p.m., but it's wise to check with the concierge at your hotel.


## SHOPPING

Aside from the discos, the three favorite pastimes in Acapulco are sunning, snoozing and shopping.   In the golden days it was fashionable to arrive with little more than a toothbrush and pick up the rest as needed since resortwear is an Acapulco specialty. Life today isn't quite that casual, but don't kid yourself, shopping is still very popular.  You might even call it a sport.

Choose from native markets, intimate boutiques or glittering malls.  Most stores are located just a few feet from the beach, on the Costera or just off it.   Open-air souvenir stalls dot the sidewalk and itinerent vendors will bring the the market to you, but *beware:*  their merchandise isn't necessarily cheaper.  Look for the 9.25 sterling stamp if you're buying silver.

The truly fabulous jewelry and sculpture of Mexico's adopted treasure, **Pal Kepenyes,** (he's an Hungarian refugee) is on display for viewing and sale in his gorgeous home overlooking the sea. A visit there is well worth your time. Of particular interest are the necklaces, bracelets and earrings made from *milagros* (miracles), brass offerings cast in gratitude for healings. The only other places you can see them are in exclusive hotel shops at twice the price.  Call 4-37-38 for a viewing appointment.

Next to Pal's, the most comfortable place to shop in Acapulco is at **La Vista** across from Las Brisas Hotel.  This upscale mall that looks like a Mediterranean village overlooks the bay.  Fitting rooms are large and air conditioned, service more knowledgeable.  Check out **Ore, Girasol, Marietta's** and **Antheus** for resort wear; **Gucci** and **Aries** for leather.

**Acapulco Joe's** is where the best Mexican T-shirts come come (with the exception of the place on Isla Mujeres, but that's in another chapter).   Acapulco Joe's also features a variety of other good lookings sports items for both men and women.  Costera Miguel Aleman 1999 and the Hyatt Regency.

**Antonio Pineda** offers an outstanding collection of fine Taxco silver.  Downtown at Hialdo 9.  After browsing (or buying)  go to the back of the shop to yet another, the **Bazaar de Arte Mexicano** and find a wide selection of arts and crafts.

Some other excellent silver shops — remember Taxco, Mexico's silver capital, is nearby — to check out are **Ronay**, at Costera Miguel Aleman beneath Carlos 'n' Charles restaurant; **Plateria San Francisco** , Costera Migue Aleman; and **Tane** in the Acapulco Plaza.

## TIDBITS

Airlines servicing Acaplulco are Aeromexico, Alaska, American, Continental, Delta, Mexicana, and United.  The airport is 14 miles from the hotel zone.  Frequent van transfers are available at reasonable rates.

Acapulco, now a city of more than one million inhabitants, is too spread out to see on foot.  Fortunately, taxis are convenient and relatively inexpensive.  Hotels generally post a price list at the entrance showing the authorized fares to various areas of the city.

The telephone area code is 748.

*World class tennis courts plus a view of Acapulco.*

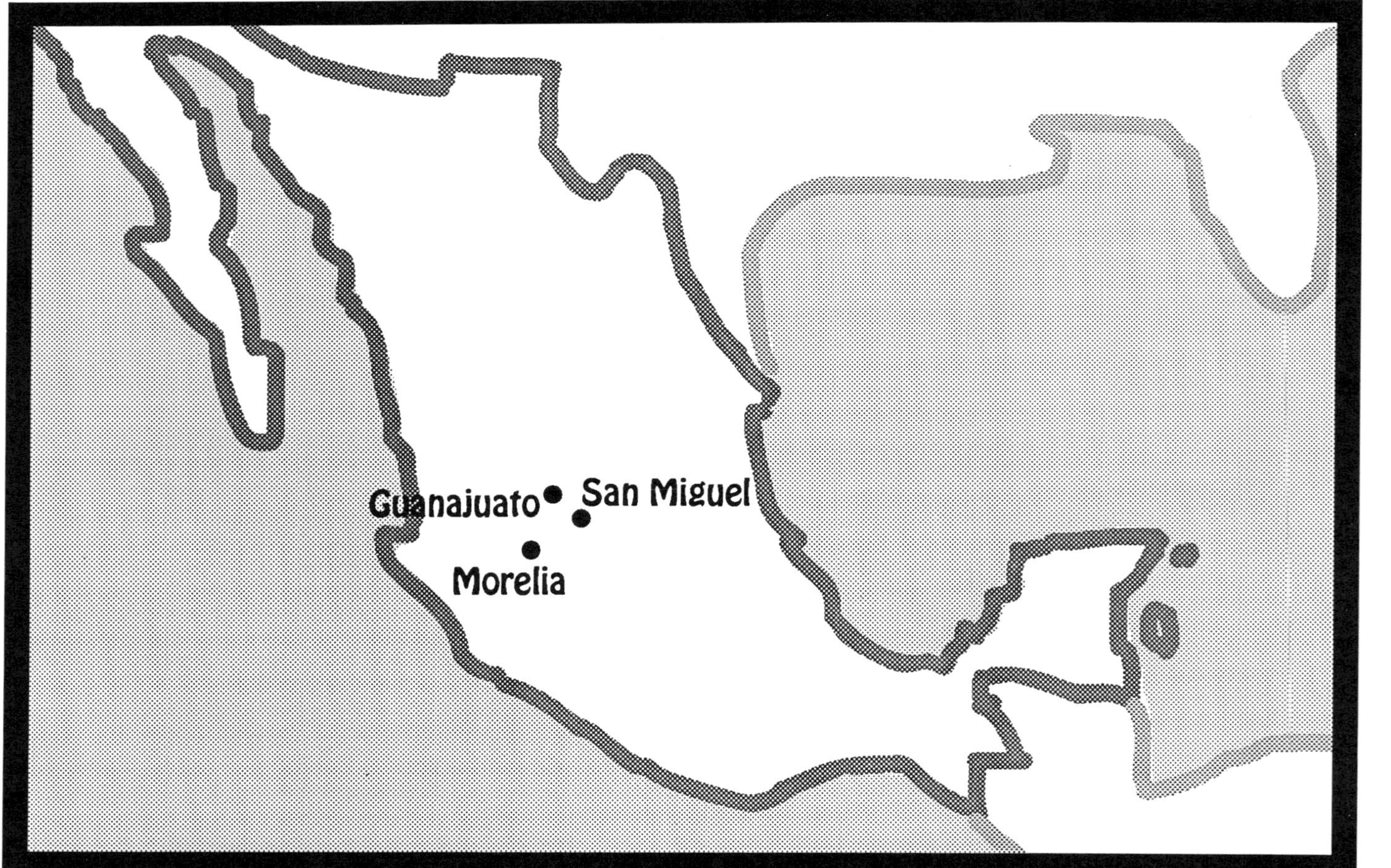

Guanajuato
San Miguel
Morelia

# THE COLONIAL CIRCLE

## SAN MIGUEL DE ALLENDE
### THE PRETTIEST TOWN IN MEXICO

Possibly the most "lover friendly" of all the colonial cities, San Miguel de Allende, with its glorious architecture, lies nestled in the protective arms of encircling mountains. Being *simpatico* comes naturally to a town steeped in colorful history and gracious traditions.

Small, quaint and picturesque, San Miguel is like no other place in Mexico. Casually so-phisticated, highly intellectual, this is Cape Cod South.

In 1542, a Franciscan friar, Juan de San Miguel, named the town for his patron saint, then proceeded to parcel out land, mark off streets, and most significantly, establish a tradition of artisanship and artistic sensibility that has grown increasingly through the years. Today San Miguel is an arty town, a cosmopolitan town where almost any social gathering will include at least one writer, a concert artist, a sculptor, a score of painters and possibly an actor or two.

*Since colonial times San Miguel de Allende has been a gallery town.* Photo by author.

The city sits at an altitude of 6,500 feet, surrounded by the majestic Sierra Madre, the very same mountains where silver was discovered early in the 17th century.   Soon San Miguel was filled with posh palaces built by the silver rich Spaniards and surrounded by their vast plantations or haciendas, fiefdoms measured in square miles not acres, on which a thousand or more families lived as virtual serfs.  Before long the flourishing city came to be known as San Miguel el Grande — to distinguish it from the host of other towns named in honor of Saint Michael. The new appendage tells it all, San Miguel el Grande was the biggest of these and one of the most important communities in what had become the   wealthiest area in New Spain.

Society in those days was a totem pole with the Spaniards on top, their heels firmly imbedded in the shoulders of the Criollos — Spaniards born in the colony

*The cobblestone streets of San Miguel de Allende.*
Photo by E. Monroe.

usurper. In many places in the colony of New Spain "discussion groups" met.

The independence movement was born at one of them — in nearby Queretaro — launched by a woman. Josefa Ortiz de Dominguez, wife of the Corregador or mayor. Josefa, a Criolla, would go down in Mexican history as La Corregidora. Her closest confidants were a young royalist officer, Ignacio Allende, and a parish priest, Father Miguel Hidalgo, from the nearby towns of San Miguel el Grande and Dolores. They and others — essentially an upper class Criollo group — gathered regularly at Josefa's home to plot the overthrow of the Spanish government.

The Corregador was proud that his wife was brainy as well as pretty and boasted of her literary "salon." But, not being very literary himself, he always managed to find pressing duties elsewhere when her guests arrived. Inevitably, the true nature of the meetings was eventually discovered. Though the Corregidor locked Josefa in a room in the municipal palace, she somehow managed to whisper a warning through a keyhole to a fellow conspirator. A messager galloped off to San Miguel and then to Dolores to warn the others.

rather than in Spain itself. Well below were the *mestizos* — those of mixed ancestry — and at the bottom, the native Mexicans or Indians.

Revolutions, first in North America and then in France, telegraphed the remote possibility of change. Then Napoleon invaded Spain and installed his brother there as king. Suddenly colonists who could never have brought themselves to rebel against the legitimate king were ready to take up arms against a

The time had finally come to stop talking and start fighting. In the early hours of September 16, 1810, Father Hidalgo tolled the bell of his church, a clarion call to his parishioners to rise up and fight for freedom. The war for independence had begun.

Soon an army of insurgents led by Hidalgo and Allende launched an attack on the region's largest city, Guanajuato. A year later both men were dead, captured by royalists and then executed in Chihuahua. The movement they'd started was only just beginning.

When Mexico finally achieved independence in 1821, her first patriots were honored by naming the town of Dolores "Dolores Hidalgo" and changing San Miguel el Grande to San Miguel de Allende.

One hundred years later Mexicans were divided in yet another revolution. Among the many things that resulted from the ensuing social upheaval was the breaking up of the huge haciendas. Many of the great palaces were destroyed in the fighting and stand today as ruins.

But one of them became a school. When Sterling Dickenson founded the Instituto Allende in 1938 it made an immediate hit that Depression year with students from the United States who could no longer afford a junior year in Europe. A decade later enrollment was swollen with former soldiers who found that the funds available to them under the GI Bill went much farther in San Miguel then they did at home. Today the Institute continues as an intellectual center, attracting students of all ages.

It seems appropriate that the most widely known art and English language school in Latin America would be centered in San Miguel, historically a patron of the arts. In 1781, when Mexico formed its first official art academy, the town donated more than its annual budget for city government. Today, in any given week, as many as 400 students are enrolled in classes. The Instituto awards a Master of Fine Arts degree and its ceramics department is associated with the Rhode Island School of Design. Many students have permanently relocated to San Miguel, lending new life and energy to ancient crafts and culture.

Protected by the government as a National Monument since 1926, San Miguel appears frozen in time. There are no neon signs or stoplights and controls on renovations are strict. But the brisk tourist trade (more than half of which is Mexican—many make the drive from Mexico City for a long weekend), is what really keeps the town such an architectural gem. The ambitious restorations projects of the some 3000 North American expatriots who reside there permanently can't be discounted either. People fall in love with this town and refuse to leave!

The result is a self-contained and perfectly maintained universe of sienna facades, magnificent carved doorways and gazebo-like squares. Narrow cobblestone streets lace up and down hillsides dotted with lovely old buildings, many bearing stone coats of arms. San Miguel de Allende is an international town in a colonial setting.

Known for its exquisitely restored houses, many delightful small hotels, award winning restaurants and top quality shopping, there is no place in Mexico quite like it.

## SIGHT SEEING

San Miguel de Allende is the prettiest town in Mexico, although many others are more spectacular, imposing or exotic.  Despite the inevitable modern growth it's still a simple place to see, to manage, to navigate.  Starting at the *jardin* , the central square otherwise known as **Plaza Allende,** the whole town may easily be explored on foot.

The jardin's affected Frenchiness is a decided clue to its age.  The dictator, Porfirio Diaz, who dominated Mexico from 1876 to 1911, developed a progressive case of Francophilia as the years passed. Historian Robert Somerlott suggests that the dictator's wife and social mentor — the rough neck rogue was badly in need of one! — was a distinct influence.  A member of her family owned the ironworks from which those ubiquitous filigreed benches and bandstands were made.

*La Parroguia is unique among churches —anywhere.*
Photo by author.

Suffice  to say that, though the jardin is laid out with the formal logic of a French public garden, its ambience is rich, intimate, colorful — thoroughly Mexican.

Across the street is the **Parish Church (La Parroguia).** This extraordinary structure — would you say "Gothic Grotesque"? — was built in 1880 by Ceferino Gutierrez, a self-educated architect.  An Indian who  drew his inspiration from postcards of European churches, Gutierrez sketched his blueprints in the dust for workers to follow.  There's nothing quite like La Parroguia anywhere in the world.  The church comes in handy too:  should you get lost, you've only to glance up.  The sight of the central spire of the pink-stone edifice will immediately reorient you.

Once inside, observe the murals which depict the Indian heritage of the populace.  A descent into the eerily beautiful crypt is worthwhile too.

While you're at it, consider the fate of one who walked before you.  The Emperor Maximilian, in town for a futile good will tour, exclaimed over the beauty of the vault, "This is fit for a king."  Within a year he was executed in nearby Queretaro.

**Ignacio Allende's Home** —The birthplace of the young Spanish army captain who led the revolution has recently been restored and opened to the public as a museum.   Above the door is a plaque proclaiming, "He who was born here is known everywhere."  Surely the independence movement's great hero and martyr is known and revered everywhere in Mexico where possibly thousands of streets and parks have been named for him. Allende's home is visited with the same reverence that North Americans feel for Mount Vernon.

The patriot's parents were Spanish born, upscale and clearly fashion conscious. Stately and graceful with sunlit patios, their late 18th century home was built in the transitional style popular at the time, a blend of neoclassic design with baroque decoration.   Cuna de Allende 1, on the corner of the *jardin.*

Mingling with the rich landowners of Spanish colonial times were the wealthy miners from Guanajuato.  The best known of these were the Counts of Canal. Today the **House of the Counts of Canal** is one of San Miguel's most imposing buildings.  Though occupied now by Banamex, the galleries are open to the public.

One of the most interesting features of the building must be seen from the outside. The mansion's magnificent entrance provides a lesson in Spanish heraldry. Carved above the massive door is an eagle perched on the arch's keystone.  It proclaims the lofty station of Don Mariano de la Canal y Hervas who completed the unfinished building he'd inherited.  Above the columns, you'll see something slightly unusual — the coats of arms of two noble families, Canal and Hervas. Obviously in this case the wife's line was at least as good as her husband's and their heirs weren't shy about broadcasting it to the world.

The plumed helmet, also prominently displayed, signifies service to the Spanish crown in the wars against the Moors.  This tells us at a glance that the owners, on both sides of the family, fought as Spanish knights   prior to 1492.  The rather stubby figure in the main niche is the Virgin of Loreto, patroness of the family, who holds her holy child.

Pacio de los Condes de Canal, at the Northwest corner of Plaza Allende facing Calle Canal.

The campus of the **Instututo Allende** was once the country estate of the de la Canal family who began building there in 1735.  But in 1809 — virtually on the eve of the revolution — and possibly in anticipation of it — the property was sold to the Descalced Carmelite Sisters, an order of barefoot nuns.

Today the converted hacienda standing on the edge of town is home to the institution that instigated yet another kind of revolution — much milder — but nonetheless responsible for transforming forever the population, economy and way of life of San Miguel de Allende.

Throughout the year, courses are given in painting, sculpture, ceramics, photography, writing, Spanish, Mexican and Latin American literature. Summer programs for teachers and MA and MFA degrees are also offered, all of them in English.

Even if you're not interested in taking classes, the historic  building and beautiful grounds are worth a visit.  Sculptors and jewelry makers, ranging in experience from beginners to veteran professionals, work in the patios and studios.  Potter's wheels hum, shuttles fly through looms.  Scores of painters create at easels indoors and out.  It's an exciting place to be.  The results can be seen at regular exhibitions of both student and faculty work in two galleries on campus.

**Biblioteca Publica,** San Miguel de Allende's public library, has a checkered history. It was once a quasi-nunnery and later a slaughterhouse. Today it's Mexico's largest bilingual library outside of Mexico City. Built in 1790 as an orphanage and a hospice "for pious women," the building was commandeered by the government following the Revolution of 1910 for use as a municipal slaughter house.  It was a strange use for such a lovely edifice, but not uncommon during this strongly anti-clerical era when former religious property was pressed into less than sublime service.

When the slaughter house was eventually moved to a more practical location, the old building remained empty until rescued by the organizers of the fledgling library. Today the Biblioteca serves as a community center, a clearinghouse for the hundreds of exchanges that take place between the Mexicans and the North Americans who, enviably, call San Miguel de Allende their home town.

The library has become a kind of town study hall as well as the repository for thousands of books — an amount that grows daily.  The library also sells publications, cards and reproductions. This is where you can  buy *San Miguel de Allende,* the delightful city guide by novelist and historian, Robert Somerlott.

It's also the place where you can purchase tickets for the **House and Garden Tour** which takes place every Sunday at noon.  Small groups leave from the library to tour some of the town's beautiful homes and gardens.  It's a rare and delightful opportunity to see inside a Mexican home.  In the Spanish tradition, houses are least imposing from the street, for, following what was originally a Moorish custom, Mexico lives behind walls.  One of the delights of San Miguel is the opportunity to explore another lifestyle.  A brief talk and refreshments are included in the tour. The proceeds go to fund the library. Calle de Insurgentes 25.

## HOTELS

When you enter the heavy oak doors of the **Casa de Sierra Nevada**, and find yourself in the central patio, confronted by thick, terracotta- toned walls, verdant ferns, wood-slatted furniture and burnt-orange tile floors, you'll feel as though you'd stepped back in time and entered a 16th century manor.   And that's exactly what you have done.

This splendid structure was built in 1580 for the archbishop of Guanajuato (the state in which San Miguel is located) and later acquired by Jorge Palomino, marquis of Sierra Nevada.   The historic hotel contains l8 suites, most of them with fireplaces, terraces and antique colonial furnishings. You can't turn around without viewing some treasure or other — paintings, ceramics, sculpture, textiles, tilework — but then that's true of the entire town! Each suite is a jewel, but El Caracol has a spiral staircase leading to a private terrazza with breathtaking views of distant mountains and valleys.   The Casa Sierra Nevada is located on an ancient cobblestone street just a few blocks above the cathedral and town square.   It's pricey but worth it. Hospicio 35.  Phone: 2-0415.

*A stay at the Casa de Sierra Nevada is a trip back in time to the 16th centruy.* Photo by the author.

*Charming shops on side streets.* Photo by E. Monroe.

Many argue that **Villa Santa Monica**, once the home of the Mexican opera star, Jose Mojica, is San Miguel's prettiest hotel.  Indeed it is lovely.   Originally built in the 18th century by the Conde de Baeza, a wealthy silver baron, the mansion was badly damaged by the revolution. During the 1930s, Mojica acquired the delapidated building which had stood empty for years and before long had restored its former elegance.

Among his many famous guests at the villa were Dolores del Rio and Ramon Navarro who planted a tree in the lovely garden. You'll find a plaque commemorating it.  When Mojica's adored mother died a few years later, he gave away all his worldly goods and moved to Peru where he was accepted into the Franciscan order.  In 1970 the delightful home became an inn.  Each of the eight elegantly appointed suites has a fireplace and private patio overlooking the well kept grounds. The hotel can arrange to have a driver meet your plane. Baesa 22. Phone: 2-0914.

Another personal favorite is the **Villa Jacaranda**, formerly a grand mansion, which offers comfort, cordiality and excellent food.  Fifteen delightful rooms surround a pretty patio which in turn embraces a Roman plunge and solar heated hot tub for guests to enjoy.  A fanciful gazebo provides charming vistas for breakfast, lunch or sunset viewing at cocktail time. Aldama 53.  Phone:  2-1015.

The **Posada La Ermita,** the former home of Mexico's beloved comedian, Cantinflas (Mario Moreno), has 25 lovely suites, an excellent restaurant and lovely grounds.  On the Queretaro road above town.

The **Hotel Aristos**, conveniently located on the grounds of the Instituto Allende, has pleasant rooms and a lovely garden setting.  The restaurant and cocktail lounge are very popular. This is the perfect place to get acquainted.  Phone: 2-0149.

*An outdoor market is a common scene.*  Photo by E. Monroe.

**Posada Carmina,** an 18th century mansion, has ten pretty rooms each different.  The pleasant restaurant overlooks a beautiful courtyard lush with orange trees and flowering vines.  Reasonable and charming. Cuna de Allende 7. Phone: 2-10-36.

**La Puertecita Boutique'otel** has introduced an innovative 14-day Spanish-language workshop that combines formal instruction with guided activities throughout the area.   Claudia and John Kay, the proprietors of this charming gem, are now adding a bird sanctuary and outdoor performance area on the grounds. Each of the eight hotel rooms is a delight, but Bugambilia is highly recommended.  Phone 1-800-336-6776.

## RESTAURANTS

The elegantly appointed restaurant at **Villa Jacaranda** has been featured on the cover of *Gourmet Magazine* and for several years has been honored with *Travel/ Holiday Magazine's* coveted Fine Dining Award as one of the outstanding restaurants of the world.   As you find yourself returning again and again during one trip you'll understand why.   It's also fun to attend the hotel's English language movie after dinner.  An excellent champagne brunch is served on Sundays.   Aldama 53.

Among the residents, **Pasada Carmina** is a favorite gathering place for a quiet lunch under the orange trees in the hotel's pretty courtyard.  The paella Valenciana is outstanding.  Try also the Spanish-style tortilla.  Cuna de Allende 7.

**Bugambilia**, Hidalgo 42, is a charming patio restaurant serving marvelous traditional Mexican food accompanied by romantic guitar music.  Guitar music also adds to the intimate ambience of **La Bodega de Marquez** is an old 18th century wine cellar with stone walls and dim lighting. Calle Recreo 5.

**El Jardin**, just off the main square, features international cuisine in a charming old mansion.

**El Pullman** at Canal 154, is a refurbished Pullman coach where you can enjoy good steaks, chicken and pasta dishes.

Musical accompaniment ranging from flamenco to marimba to Andean livens the ambience at **Mama Mia's,** a lively and popular beer hall which specializes in pizza. For good food and conversation, try the restaurant **Hotel Aristos,** a good place to make new friends and exchange information.

*Finally,* it would be a travesty to leave San Miguel de Allende without enjoying lunch or dinner at the **Casa de Sierra Nevada.**   Mexico's first member of the Felais et Chateaux, the hotel is owned by Peter O. Wirth, whose family owns the Hassler Hotel in Rome.   Wirth is a fifth generation of one of the oldest Swiss hotel families who have been catering to the rich and famous since 1850.  In 1990 he was joined by Maria and Markus Odermatt who currently operate the Casa de Sierra Nevada under their own supervision.  It's a curious coincidence that Wirth's and Odermatt's great grandparents befriended each other and came from the same Swiss town — an area of Switzerland associated with the independence movement much in the manner of Colonial Mexico.

Markus confided that the only request he'd not been able to fulfill in recent years was for strawberries in February, but that doesn't mean that  won't find fantastic delicacies in the Casa de Nevada's gilt-trimmed dining room. The hotel *does* fly in duck breast, special wines and foie gras from France, as well as seafood, selected by the hotel's French-trained Mexican chef.  Expect a divine meal and be prepared to pay for it.  Reservations are required for dinner; coat and tie are recommended. Hospicio 35.  Phone: 2-0415.

Markus was kind enough to share three of his most popular delicacies to try out in our own kitchens.

### COLD VEGETABLE SOUP WITH BASIL

**Ingredients**

200 grams peeled tomatoes, coarsely chopped
100 grams  peeled cucumber, cut into small pieces
 30 grams onion, finely chopped
 30 grams red and green peppers with core removed and
     coarsely  chopped with some finely chopped garlic
 15 grams  white breadcrumbs
  5  cl red wine vinegar
  5  cl olive oil
     some oregano and 6 basil leaves
  5  cl single cream
  salt, freshly ground pepper

**Method:**

• Mix together the tomatoes, cucumber, onion, peppers, garlic
  and bread crumbs.
• Add the vinegar, poultry stock, olive oil, oregano and 3 basil
  leaves.
• Season with salt and pepper.
• Marinate for 12 hours.
• Liquidize to make a fine puree and strain through a sieve.
• Finish with the cream and season again.
• Add the remaining basil leaves cut in thin strips.
• Keep cold.

**Note:**  it is important that this soup be served very cold (possibly on ice.)

**Serves 4.**

## SALMON TROUT WITH LEEKS

### Ingredients
1  salmon trout (2 lb)
3/4 oz. butter
salt, freshly ground pepper
2 fl. oz. white wine (chalis)
1/2 fl oz. melted butter, to pour over

### Method:
- Carefully fillet the salmon trout, removing the skin.
- Cut into four equal portions.
- Butter a suitable dish, put in the seasoned fish pieces, add the white wine and fish stock.
- Bring to a boil, cover and poach in the oven; the fish must remain pink.
- Remove the fish and keep warm.
- Reduce the stock to half its original volume, strain and reserve for the sauce.

### Sauce:
8 fl  oz. fish stock
4 fl oz white wine
3 fl oz Noilly prat
2 g finely chopped shallot
4 oz butter, to finish
Salt, freshly ground pepper

### Garnish:
5 oz young, tender leeks, well washed and cut into pieces 2 inches long.

### Method:
- Reduce the fish stock, white wine, Noilly Prat and shallot.
- Add the cream and reduce to the required consistency.
- Strain and add the fish stock which has been used to poach the salmon trout.
- Blanch the leeks for a short time and add to the sauce.
- Season with salt and pepper.
- Arrange on a suitable dish and place the pieces of salmon trout on top.
- Sprinkle the fish with the melted butter and serve immediately.

**Serves 4.**

## STRIPS OF BEEF IN CREAM SAUCE WITH GREEN PEPPERCORNS

**Ingredients:**
  640 g beef fillet, well trimmed and cut into thin strips
    2 cl peanut oil
    2 cl cognac
  10 grams finely chopped shallot
  15 cl red wine
  30 cl brown veal stock
  20 cloves double cream
  50 grams butter to finish
    5 grams green peppercorns
    Salt, freshly ground pepper

**Method:**
• Season with the pieces of fillet and saute them rare in hot oil.
• Flame with cognac.
• Discard the fat and remove the meat from the pan.
• Add the finely chopped shallot and red wine and reduce.
• Add the brown veal stock and reduce to half its original volume.
• Put in the cream and melt with butter.
• Remove the sauce from the heat, add the green peppercorns
  and season with salt and pepper.
• Mix  the meat with the sauce and serve immediately.
**Serves 4.**

# SHOPPING

Good shoppers when they die must surely go to San Miguel de Allende, but that doesn't mean that you can't enjoy a little of that heaven while still on earth.  As might be expected, a town famous for art sells art.  And that means art of every kind.  Weaving remains one of the most spectacular traditional crafts and is still done on the upright looms introduced by Friar Juan in 1542.  But San Miguel is also known for its paintings, sculptor, tin work, handcrafted jewelry, ceramics, and wrought iron.

Where to begin?  The delightfully zany **Casa Cohen**, located just off the plaza, is the obvious choice.  Not only does it offer the best of the best (furniture, cast brass, paintings, all types of exquisite furnishings) but the building is itself an art form. The founder, Isaac Cohen, migrated to San Miguel from his native Damascus in the late 20's and worked as a peddler.  As his business prospered, Cohen's family grew.  Now he wanted a home large enough for everyone, something grand and a bit *different*, a veritable "Noah's Ark" to house everything and everyone.  Not only that but he wanted it completed in time for his adopted city's 400th anniversary.

Beginning with a foundation of ancient ruins, Cohen employed 90 carpenters, masons and artisans.  By working in three shifts around the clock, they met his deadline.  Like Ceferino Gutierrez before him, Cohen could neither read nor write and had no training in architecture or construction.  Nevertheless he knew what he wanted and got it.  Eighteen fanciful animals support the balcony.  Other whimsical creatures carved in the round stand atop the structure while above the remarkably carved eaves spouts, a hundred more fantastic animals march across the facade presumably bound for the safety of the Ark. The effect is delightful madness. The builder's family have been living and working in the building since its completion in 1942.

Nothing can top Casa Cohen for whimsy, but my own special "heaven"  is **Casa Maria Luisa** at Canal 40. I've not only lost my heart there a time or two but also my mind — imagine carrying a chandelier home!   Fortunately, the store does have smaller items: everything lovely that you can imagine.

On the same street are a number of other charming shops that threaten to break either your heart or your bank.  **Casa Canal**, at Canal 3, features original furniture, antiques and elegant clothes for men and women.   **Josefa**, at Canal l6, has charming crafts and excellent art.

**Galeria San Miguel,** on the main plaza, has exciting contemporary paintings, sculpture and graphics. **Galeria Atenea** (another favorite) on Cuna Cuna de Allende, has impressive Mexican and contemporary art.   **Josh Kligerman's Art Gallery**, just off the plaza on Umaran, is known as San Miguels "small museum."

One-of-a-kind hand printed clothes are featured at **Sidell**, Jesus 21, two blocks east of the main plaza.  Both **Artesanias Bufalo**, Zacatecas 23, and **Vilar**, Recreo 5, carry fine leathergoods. Vilar also has a wide selection of shoes. And at **El Pegaso**, across from the post office, one can enjoy coffee and pastries or browse through a unique collection of masks, jewelry and clothing.

## TIDBITS _________________________________________________

San Miguel de Allende is located 180 miles northwest of Mexico City, a four hour bus ride.  First class express buses — clean, comfortable and very reasonable — leave several times daily from the Central del Norte terminal in Mexico City. At the end of your stay, they will pick you up where you are staying. To phone San Miguel, prefix the numbers with 011-52-465.

Instituto Allende, a private art and language school, offers nine four-week language sessions and two three-week sessions.  Classes are Monday through Friday .  Telephone: 2-01-90.

# GUANAJUATO
## A TOWN OF LIVELY SPIRITS

Nowhere in the Americas is there more of a sense of duality than in Mexico. The extremes of night and day, birth and death, plenty and poverty, light and shadow are interwoven into every aspect of the culture.

In ancient times both priest and peasant were painfully aware of the  effects of the gods and goddesses on not only fertility and abundance but death and destruction.  From the deep wells of the subconscious came not only gifts of prophecy and creativity, but also dark visions of disaster.  Those twin images of birth and death are equally prevalent today.  The tree of life is a perennially popular motif, but so is the skull.  Children play with dolls in the likeness of skeletons; confectioners make little skulls of sugar.

Nowhere is that striking manifestation of duality more apparent than in Guanajuato, a city whose turbulent history is rooted in birth, death and inevitable transformation.  Guanajuato's macabre proclivities are best expressed in its greatest attraction — a collection of mummies at the local cemetery.

Here in a crypt, down a flight of circular stairs, are the withered remains of some 170 of the city's former citizens in a macabre display  unmatched anywhere in the world.  Corpses recline in two tiered compartments:  a pullman car going nowhere.  A guide points out the "attractions": the oldest mummy, there for more than a century; and a woman who died in childbirth, her tiny baby beside her.  With few exceptions the mummies, most naked, a few wearing boots and remnants of bygone finery, seem frozen in eternal composure, hands folded, dead eyes staring vacantly.  But for sheer ghoulishness one stands out: the contorted, horrific remains of a woman obviously buried alive.

Guanajato has another unique feature, an underground expressway running through what was once the municipal sewer.  An eerie ride this,  amid the foundations of an ancient city.  To encounter Dracula hitch-hiking in this grotto would come as no great surprise.

So much for phantasmagoria.  There's a lilting lively side to Guanajuato as well; a multi-faceted side that glitters like an elegant diamond — most probably a cherished heirloom.

To history buffs, this is Mexico's first city.  Haughty and elegant, Guanajuato is certainly one of the most European cities in Latin America both in attitude and architecture.  A labyrinth of winding streets that blossom into plazas or fade into alleys and steps, Guanajuato might easily have been lifted from the hills of Tuscany or Andalusia.

Though the population is now a modest 80,000, for many years this was the richest city in Mexico.  Shortly after the original land grant was bestowed upon Rodrigo Vazques, a Spanish conquistador, silver was discovered in the surrounding mountains. Soon Guanajuato was a boom town; and, as more and more veins were uncovered, the city's coffers and influence grew to unprecedented proportions.

The original village that would soon be the source of more than one third of the world's silver was wedged into the mountainous terrain of the Sierra Madres at the bottom of a narrow canyon along the banks of the Rio Guanajuato. The meandering river created a ground plan of winding mazelike streets that quickly blossomed into a hilly confusion of opulent dwellings constructed by newly rich mine owners. Their tastes were eclectic: baronial German mansions, Spanish castles, Swiss chalets, Italian palazzos, Moorish citadels.

Not only was theirs a material competition but a spiritual one. Churches sprouted up all over town as the mine owners, having won titles of nobility from the king, sought places in the affection of God. One of the most beautiful of the churches, considered one of the most splendid in Mexico, is La Valenciana, built by the first Count of Valenciana next door to his mine.

La Valenciana was completed in 1788 about the time that two dams, Olal and San Renovato, were constructed by the Marquis de Rayas. The latter's generosity provided the provincial city with a pair of luxuries: a reservoir and a park. Another possibly greater one, the university, had already been opened by the Jesuits in 1732.

No wonder Guanajuato, a gem of royalist grandeur, was the first major target of the rebel clergyman Father Miguel Hidalgo and his band of revolutionaries in 1810. Fifty thousand strong, the rebels — mostly farmers and miners — came armed with sticks, pitchforks, hoes, hope and hatred. Spanish royalists were forced to flee to the Alhondiga de Granaditas, a recently constructed granary. The building was made entirely of stone, except for one large wooden door that seemed impenetrable. The city fathers, convinced that the warehouse was impregnable, quickly launched a counter attack. With balls of fire raining down from the parapets onto the attacking army below, the battle seemed decided in favor of the Spanish mine owners.

A teenage boy had other ideas. Juan Jose de Loys Reyes Martinez, a young miner, who would go down in history simply as "El Pipila," found a loose piece of flagstone and tied it to his back as armor. In the face of gunfire and fire balls, he grabbed a torch and ran to the building. Somehow the youth was able to reach the front door and set it on fire before he was killed. The building was opened and the revolutionaries poured in, killing their enemies and taking the city.

The insurgents won the battle, but the war was just beginning. Within months, royalists recaptured Guanajuato. Hidalgo, Allende, Aldama and Jimenez — the leaders of the revolt — were executed in Chihuahua and their heads sent back to dangle for ten grisly years from the four corners of the Alhondiga. A grim warning. Today, the hooks may still be seen, a reminder of the city's passionate history.

A monument to El Pipila stands guard

over Guanajuato.  At the summit of a scenic drive, it provides a stunning vista of the city below.  From here can be seen the tiny plazas and twisting streets that comprise this charming city. These streets — mere walkways really — lined with flowerpot trimmed houses,

*Internacional Cervantino.*  The Festival turns the town into a major international art center with a nonstop schedule of plays, symphonies, opera, traditional and classical dance, film retrospectives and art exhibitions.  Events range from Spanish flamenco and French chamber music to Turkish whirling dervishes and Slovakian puppet theater.  The international art exhibition, spread over three museums, features art from Asian cultures as well as European and New World.  Past Cervantino Festivals have included such luminaries as the Bolshoi Ballet, the Royal Shakespeare Company and the New York Philharmonic Orchestra.

*Teatro Juarez is the centerpiece of the famous Cervantes Festival.*
Photo by the author.

bear quaint names such as the Five Gentlemen, the Nosegay, the Little Birds, and, most famous of all, the Kiss.

With its tiny plazas, jutting balconies, streets that often become steps, and alleyways so narrow that neighbors can lean out a window to exchanges kisses, Guanajuato has a dramatic flavor — almost as if it were a stage setting. And sometime it is.

For three weeks every October the city — so exquisitely preserved that it's been declared a national monument — extends its preoccupation with culture to the world by presenting the *Festival*

The Festivals began in 1972 as a way for Guanajuato to maintain its traditions by presenting *entremeses*, classic one-act skits written as humorous interludes between the acts of more serious dramas by Cervantes and other sixteenth century Spanish writers. These action packed playlets — often performed in armor with galloping horses — are most frequently presented in pantomime. The acting of the university students who perform the *entremeses* is extremely entertaining even for those who can't understand a word that's being said.  Even for experts, the language is difficult for it is, in a sense, Shakespearan Spanish.

The international festival's high culture glamour could easily overwhelm most towns of 80,000 people. But Guanajuato more than holds its own. Not only does it provide a perfect setting for the works of Cervantes and the others, but the charming city is itself the star of the show.

## HOTELS

**La Casa de Spiritus Alegres** (House of Good Spirits) not only qualifies as one of the most romantic inns in Mexico, but is possibly *the* most fanciful. Perhaps it's inevitable that a city so alive with history and myth, a paradise for artists and photographers—for anyone with an eye for beauty and a heart for romance—would attract a couple like Joan and Carol Summers.

Joan Ward Summers, a weaver, and her printmaker husband, Carol, were traveling through the country collecting folk art when they happened upon a seventeenth century hacienda and heard its story. The grand mansion, which once adjoined a silver processing center, had been restored by Giorgio Belloli, an Italian sculptor. Belloli had combined Italianate touches— Roman columns, Baroque masonry, terraced gardens—with the stately and monastic colonial architecture of Mexico. He imported a number of structural details from surrounding areas such as the stone entranceway and plank doors from a crumbling chapel outside San Miguel de Allende.

*The House of Good Spirits is truly enchanting.* Photo by the author.

For the Summers it was a case of love at first sight. The couple who "wasn't looking for a house at all" made an offer that very day. The hacienda's transformation continues. In the dining room Joan's vivid tapestry *Naughty Cats* accents an ancient stone wall. A papier-mache skeleton crowned with a headdress worn by the Tarahumara Indians sits in a Huichol Indian's shaman's chair. When interviewed by *Architectural Digest*, Carol remarked, "We're quite happy with the

*The Room of Miracles at the House of Good  Spirits.*
Photo by the author.

house. It's still unusual, full of jarring and beautiful contrasts, mysteries and surprises.  Just like Mexico itself."

And most particularly like Guanajuato itself.  Fortunately, the Summers don't keep their "good spirits" to themselves.  What was originally their private home and studio has incarnated once again — this time as a bed and breakfast.  In addition to **La Casita**, a separate apartment, there are six charming rooms.  A favorite is **Los**

**Milagros** (The miracles), a light, airy, romantic room with a fireplace and a profusion of lace and flowers.  The walls are decorated with antique hearts and silver milagros.  An angel keeps watch over the bed.

And then there's **El Nagual** (An Animal Spirit)—a room for animal lovers filled with animal dance masks and carvings of animals.  Even the fireplace is a goat.  **El Quetzal** (The Plumed Serpent) is a bright sunny room alive with birds and paper flowers which opens onto a terrace overlooking the garden.  The magic and mystery of Mexico is encompassed in **El Mago** (The Sorcerer) which is filled with ritual artifacts that include a Huichol shaman's chair.  **Los Tecuanes** (The Tiger Dance) is rich and exotic with its tiger masks, baskets and flowers and **Las Munecas** (The Dolls) has a cosy fireplace and dolls from all over Mexico. (La Casa de Espitus Alegres, La Ex-Hacienda La Trinidad, No. I; Marfil, Guanajuato. Telephone/Fax: 473-3-10-13.)

*The House of Good Spirits is not only an inn of romance and fantasy but a folk art museum.*
Photo by the auhtor.

The two most convenient hotels in town, **Hotel Museo Posada Santa Fe** and **Hotel San Diego** both have interesting histories and delightful restaurants.  Each faces onto Jardin de la Union, a diminutive little plaza with the distinction of being one of Mexico's smallest.

The **Santa Fe**, once the grand residence of the Prussian consul during Maximilian's reign, became a hotel in 1862.  It's elegant and charming— shiny brass beds and wonderful colonial art. (Reservations:  473-2-00-84)  The sidewalk cafe just in front is a perfect place to enjoy the passing scene.

But then so is the San Diego's balconied restaurant.  The **San Diego**, originally a seventeenth century convent has beautiful views of the city and its surroundings mountains.  (Reservations: 473-2-14-99).

Just up the street from the plaza, at Avenue Juarez 116, is a tiny gem that could easily be overlooked.  The **Casa de las Manrique** is an exquisite colonial mansion with all the modern amenities transformed into that small hotel that romantics write songs about.  (Reservations 473-2-76-06.)

*One of several lovely views from the Hotel San Diego. Festival.* Photo by the author.

*Hotel Castillo Santa Cecilia.* Photo by the author.

**Hotel Castillo Santa Cecilia** is a wonderland built like a castle with high stone walls, turrets, towers and gorgeous gardens.  Inside the Gothic labyrinth, torch-lit corridors lead to lovely rooms with vaulted ceilings, arches, fireplaces, antiques and rich tapestries.  Located just over a mile from town on Rte. 110. Phone: 1-800-223-65l0.

## RESTAURANTS

With few exceptions, the best restaurants in Guanajuato are found in the hotels. You'll dine in regal splendor at the **Casa de las Manriques.** The appointments are charming, service excellent and continental food delicious.

It's also great fun to sip margaritas at one of the sidewalk tables in front of the **Hotel Posada Santa Fe.** This is the perfect place to people watch, and the Mexican cuisine is very good. So good it promises to prove habit forming. There are so many good things on the menu that you'll find yourself returning day after day. We did. Special treats are the mole dishes and the pozole.

The balcony of the Hotel San Diego's restaurant, **Cuatro Ranas**, is romantic, a little removed from the scene, but still a part of it. The restaurant is deservedly popular and the service excellent.

Three other favorites are **Restaurant Insurgentes** (Avenue Juarez 228) a tiny place with only six tables — always full because the food's so good; the **Miners' Club** (Valenciana, next to the church), a hearty meat and potatoes place; and **Venta Vieja** (Plaza San Javier No. I) intimate and romantic with good food and "atmosphere."

## SIGHTSEEING

Guanajuato is unique among Mexican cities in that it has no main square. Instead, there are seven little squares the **Jardin de la Union** (Garden of the Union) being the most important. Trees form a canopy over the tiled pavement of this enchanting little park and in its center is an old-fashioned bandstand where concerts are performed on Tuesdays, Thursdays and Sundays from 7 to 9 p.m.

Facing the square is the **Juarez Theater,** (Teatro Juarez) — a magnifcent rococo opera house that serves as a monument to both the power of silver and the glory of the Porfiriate. Eight

*Jardin de la Union is the center of Guanajuato.*
Photo by the author.

carved muses crown the edifice, gilt carvings and velvet fabrics adorn the interior and graceful art nouveau railings line the various tiers and balconies throughout.

Built in 1875, the Teatro Juarez continues to welcome the great opera, theater and dance companies of Europe and is the main site of the annual Cervantino Festival. The *estudiantinas,* now popular all over Mexico, got their start on the theater steps. *Estudiantina* refers to student minstrels, young men who, in times gone by, dressed up in finery — black knee britches, ruffles and swords of the vice regal times — and, with a guitar or mandolin, went forth to serenade the ladies. For their efforts they were rewarded with ribbons — prizes proudly displayed on their cloaks.

University students in Guanajuato have revived the custom and now go about on Friday and Saturday nights entertaining not only the señoritas but everyone. Part Pied Pipers, part court jesters, these minstrels lead a lively 90-minute "free" walk through narrow passageways between multicolored adobe homes with stops in tiny plazas. There are love songs and colorful ditties and brief pitches for dona-tions to support the "starving musicians."

The **San Diego Church** next door is noted for its beautiful and highly ornate doorway, an outstanding example of Churrigueresque art. Originally built by Franciscans friars in 1693, the church was partially destroyed by flood and then rebuilt by the wealthy and pious Count of Valencia in 1784. Directly behind the church is an excellent **arts and crafts center** offering a wide variety of top quality merchandise.

**Alhondiga de Granaditas** —the grain warehouse central to the revolutionary history of Guanajuato has been con-verted into a state historical museum. Of special interest is the chamber dedi-cated to the heroes of the indepen-dence movement which is lit by an eternal flame. Exhibits of local cos-tumes and crafts are colorful, the murals by Chavez Morado striking. (Corner of Mendizabal and Cinco de Mayo. Closed Mondays.)

*The San Diego Church was built in 1693.*
Photo by the author.

**La Parroquia**, also known as the Basilica of Our Lady of Guanajuato, dates from 1671. This church, with its lovely coral and gold facade, houses the famous wooden image of the Virgin Mary, "La Virgen de Santa Fe de Guanajuato," which was sent from Granada in 1557 as a gift from Felipe II of Spain. The image is thought to be the oldest piece of Christian art in Mexico.   Seventeen chandeliers illuminate the interior. (Plaza de la Paz)

**Diego Rivera Museum** — One of Mexico's greatest muralists, Diego Rivera spent his early years in this charming building.   Furniture from the period, including the brass bed in which he was born in 1886, fills the ground floor.   The second floor houses 97 of his works, including a large sketch for his controversial mural in New York City's Rockefeller Center.   The third floor is reserved for rotating exhibits. Calle Pocitos 47.  Closed Sundays.

Nearby is the **Callejon del Beso** (Alley of the Kiss).  Here, according to legend, a rich girl, Dona Ana, would secretly meet and kiss her boyfriend,  a poor miner named Carlos.   Dona Ana's father had forbidden her to see Carlos, but she didn't listen.  One night as they leaned across the narrow alley from their respective balconies, Dona Ana was stabbed by her father.  She died just as Carlos kissed her.

Tradition dictates that if you don't kiss your love as you step on the third step of the alley stairs, you're doomed to bad luck.  Nobody seems to know whether it's the third step from the top or the bottom.   Why not play it safe by kissing every three steps?

**Mercado Hidalgo** — the best bet for souvenir hunters is worth seeing even if you're not in a shopping mood.  Another example of Porfiriate architecture, the two story glass and iron structure is a picaresque monument to another time.  Inside, the many balconies and fancy grillwork reminds one of a French railroad station. The main floor is devoted mainly to fruits, vegetables and flowers, but the balcony area is highly promising.  Among the ceramics and straw work are copper pots, pans and vases from Santa Clara del Cobre at prices scarcely higher than Santa Clara itself.  Avenue Juarez.

**University of Guanajuato** — one of Mexico's most important universities has been functioning continuously since 1732.   A labyrinth of open-air hallways and interconnecting patios, the main wing is especially beautiful with its glass roof and sweeping grand staircase.   For residents as well as visitors, the university is a cultural focal point offering symphonies, theater performances, a library, art gallery and choir. This is also the center for the famous *entremeses*  (students' comic skits.) Lascurran de Retana 5.

**Museo de las Momias** (Mummy Museum) — No one can agree exactly why, but bodies buried in Guanajuato's municipal cemetery don't decompose; they mummify.  Vaults are rented out by the year, and by law every corpse must be interred for five years — even if the payment has not been made. However, if at the end of that period a permanent resting place has not been purchased, the body is removed to a common grave.

As a result of this practice, more than one hundred men, women and children may be seen displayed in glass cases lining the walls of a crypt which is open to the public. There they are resting just on the other side of the glass — skin, hair, beards intact. As previously stated, there's just nothing like it to be seen anywhere. Possibly for this reason, the mummies have been on tour to Japan. Open daily. The small admission fee goes to a charity.

**Christo Rey,** (Christ of the King) — ten miles west of the city is the 82-foot high statue towering at the 8000 foot summit of El Cubilete. The monument rivals the Statue of Liberty in size. The site itself is said to be the geographic center of the Mexican Republic.

# VALENCIANA

Once a dowager city, living in genteel poverty, Guanajuato is again thriving. Mines closed for years, have reopened and an increasing amount of gold and silver is being produced. Today it's particularly worthwhile to take a short bus or taxi ride to the suburb of Valenciana. The **Valenciana Mine**, one of seventeen still operating in Guanajuato, is the largest and richest in Mexico. Until the early nineteenth century it was estimated that one third of the world's silver came from this one source and today one can still see miners at work bringing its incredible wealth out of the earth.

Across the road is **La Valenciana**, otherwise known as La Iglesia de San Cayetano, a church in use since 1788, built by Don Antonio de Obregon y Alcocer, the first Count of Valenciana and owner of the mine. It's said that he had silver dust mixed into the cement that binds the stones of the foundation. True or not, it's obvious that he spared no expense in decorating the church's interior—among the most spectacular in Mexico. The ornate altars, heavily trimmed in gold leaf, are prominent examples of Mexican chromatic art.

From the church steps, look across the street at what was once the Valenciana mansion and imagine the daughter of the proud family on her wedding day walking on a carpet that had been created especially to span that distance—a carpet that was actually a tapestry woven entirely of gold and silver threads.

There's an excellent craft store next door with museum quality masks.

Three miles northwest on the Dolores Hidalgo Hiway, Rt. 110.

## TIDBITS

Guanajuato is serviced by both Continental and Mexicana airlines which fly into the nearby airport outside Leon.

The Guanajuato telephone area code is: 473.

Festival tickets may be ordered by phone from the Ticketmaster office in Mexico City: 011-535-325-9000. For more information, write to Festival Internacional Cervantino, Alvaro Obregon 273, Colonia Roma, Mexico, D.F., Mexico. Telephone: 011-525-514-7365.

*Countryside scene.* Photo by E. Monroe.

# MORELIA
## AND THE SEARCH FOR THE ABSOLUTELY PERFECT MARGARITA

"Never fear being lost," a wit once advised me. "Even in the midst of the Amazon jungle or the trackless Sahara, all you need do is take out the ingredients for a martini and instantly some wise guy will appear — seemingly out of nowhere — to advise on the perfect proportions."

like proportions, I can attest that perfection is not easily attained. Inevitably the search led to the source: the town of Tequila some thirty-five miles from Guadalajara, where Mexico's best known export is manufactured. On the way one sees endless fields of blue maguey cactus which supply the raw material.

*Morelia — a mountain town with a strongly Iberian feeling.* Photo by author.

And isn't that true?  More ice, less vermouth, a chilled glass, etc., etc., etc. Everyone thinks he or she knows the secret of the quintessimal martini. Be assured, the perfect margarita is equally elusive.

Having traveled the length and breadth of Mexico in a quest that took on grail-

The distilleries have a Willy Wonka Chocolate Factory quality — bubbling, boiling vats of fermenting tequila. Naturally, for the complete experience, one must sample the goods. Most are familiar with the Mexican ritual of licking salt from the fist and biting a wedge of lime. I knew I'd had enough when I licked the lime and bit my fist by mistake.

The people at the Orendain distillery have their own version of the perfect margarita:

*Mix I and I/4 oz. of white Orendain tequila, I/2 oz. fresh lemon juice and 3/4 oz. cointreau in a cocktail shaker. Shake lightly and strain into a cocktail glass, the edge of which has been moistened with a slice of lemon and frosted with salt.*

And it was very good.

Since that pleasant afternoon I've sampled margaritas from Tijuana to Cancun, discussed technique with master bartenders in the Chiapas rainforest and on Acapulco Bay. I even learned to mix a mean one myself. In fact, I *thought* I'd found perfection in my own kitchen.

And then I discovered **Villa Montana**. It was here that I not only experienced the Absolutely Perfect Margarita but one of the most totally delightful and romantic hotels in all of Mexico tucked away like some precious gift in one of the country's oldest and most beautiful cities.

Maybe you think that's a long way around to introduce Morelia, but it *is* part of the whole experience. And perhaps, too, you *have* to have been around the block a time or two to find and appreciate this off-the-beaten track city with its hidden treasure hotel.

First off there's Morelia itself—a stately, regal city that also had to go around the block a bit experience-wise before it even became Morelia. In 1541, Antonio de Mendoza, Spain's first viceroy to the new colony, conquered only 20 years before, named this town in Mexico's central highlands Valladolid—after his own home town. Mendoza encouraged patrician families from the Old Country to settle there—a pattern that continued through 300 years of Spanish rule.

The era ended when Jose Maria Morelos, a muleskinner-turned-priest, seized the banner of independence following Hidalgo's execution. A philosopher as well as a patriot, the theories of Morelos continue to influence Mexican political thought. Not surprisingly, in 1828, just seven years after Mexico won its independence, the town's name was changed to honor its most illustrious son who is frequently compared to Thomas Jefferson.

Though on the cutting edge of the revolution, the mountain town remains strongly Iberian. A soft, alluring city with its pink sandstone buildings, Baroque architecture, broad boulevards and endless arcades, Morelia is a wonderfully restful place. It's also the perfect base from which to explore the towns and cities of Mexico's charming state of Michoacan. The name, which means "land of the fisherman," is highly appropriate since the state has more lakes than any other in Mexico. The Indian word is also the origin of the U.S. state of Michigan.

> As for the perfect margarita, try it for yourself—courtesy of the Villa Montana:
>
>     2 Tbs. lemon
>     2 Tbs. contreau
>     2 oz.  white tequila
>     4 ice cubes
> Blend everything and pour into a chilled glass with a salted rim.

## HOTELS

Few hotels enchant so immediately and completely by their beauty and tranquility as Morelia's **Villa Montana.**  Set on a gentle hill overlooking the entire pink stone city, the villa is a quiet enclave of sixty  exquisite rooms and suites, each with a wood-burning fireplace, marvelous Mexican antiques, rustic ceiling beams, gleaming terra-cotta tile floors and great bowls of fresh flowers.  Artwork and the tasteful use of local handicrafts collected by the owners, Count Philippe and Countess Eva de Reiset, complement the elegance that pervades every nook and cranny of the magnificent colonial inn.

*Villa Montana has a tranquil elegance.* Photo by author.

The grounds — all five acres of them — contain a veritable menagerie of whimsical animals: a three foot high elephant, monkeys, a tiger, a fish, a quartet of lions. Some are antique sculptures, others creations of talented local artists. Their guardian is an imposing statue of St. George with sword drawn. The sculpture garden is enlivened with bougainvillea, jacaranda, orchids and floripondio.  A cafe terrace is framed by "dancing" cypress trees.

The Villa Montana has been a romantic getaway offering seclusion to many famous for their faces, fortunes or politics.  During the past twenty years all of the

*Each room at Villa Montana has a wood burning fireplace.* Photo by author.

Mexican presidents have been guests at least twice while in office. The late director, Henry King, fell in love with the place while filming *The Sun Also Rises* and returned again and again until at last Room 15 was created in his honor. Tyrone Power, while on location for the epic film, *Captain from Castille*, was so entranced that he tried to buy the hotel.

Reservations for the Villa Montana, located at Patzimba 20l, may be made by calling:  1-800-223-6510 or locally:  4-02-31.

Exceptional as it is, Villa Montana is by no means the only game in town. Two delightful, well situated hotels in convenient downtown locations are **Hotel Virrey de Mendoza** and **Posada de la Soledad**.

The former, at Portal de Matamoros 16 on the corner of the zocalo, was built in l744 as a private home. The impressive building extends around a courtyard covered by a beautiful stained glass ceiling. Appointments are authentic and lovely, the excellent restaurant and bar much frequented by locals.  Local phone: 2-00-45.

Posada de la Sole, Zaragoza 90, began life in 1719 as a convent and later became a *posada* (resting place) for mule skinners and their animals.  In the 18th and 19th centuries, it was a coach stop for travelers to and from Mexico City — then an eight-day journey. The posada is built around a huge open courtyard embraced on all sides by three stories of arcaded galleries aflame with cascading bougainvillea.  The Saturday buffet of *ranchero*  food is festive and fun. Local phone: 218-88.

# RESTAURANTS

**Fonda Las Mercedes** (Leon Guzman 47).  Brace yourself for the most eccentric decor in town (maybe in any town!)  A Dali-esque nude female statue greets you in the 17th Century courtyard as does a life-size raffia figure of a formally dressed matron with a Day of the Dead skull.  Inside, expect to enjoy Mexican cooking at its best.  Whitefish is a specialty as well as breast of chicken portugesa (filled with cheese and wrapped in bacon), and *sabana mercedes* (grilled filet with *chimichurri*) or my own favorite:  calves' brains Grenobloise.  For starters, try *chipotle* chicken soup or ham and *poblano* chile crepes.  Expect marvelous food, not modern technology.  A seventy-five-year-old National Cash Register from Dayton, Ohio, totals your bill and if you need a receipt, it'll be handwritten.

**Las Morelianas**, an elegant restaurant, in a colonial manor house offers excellent red snapper as well as barbecued ribs.  A specialty is the *ensalada caranza* with lettuce, shrimp, chicken, aparagus and mushrooms —delicious.  (Portal Galeana 149)

**Las Bugambilias**, Ave las Camelinas 514, has an interntional menu sparked by zesty game dishes—among them *venada* (venison) and *jabali* (boar).

Also not to be missed is **Meson San Diego** with its charming pink tablecloths, palm and papyrus plants shading a blue pool around which award winning food is enjoyed.  Local delicacies include *trucha a la Parrilla* (trout seasoned with dijon mustard), *pescado blanco de Patzcuaro* (white fish) as well as marvelous pastas such as *ravioles gigantes* and *canelones* with bechamel sauce.

*Villa Montana overlooks the romantic city of Morelia.* Photo by author.

Even if you aren't staying at the **Villa Montana**, don't miss a lunch or dinner there.  Within the dining room's wealth of colonial anti-ques, old paintings and fresh flowers — or on the terrace overlooking the city — you'll enjoy memorable food and service.  For a divine treat, indulge yourself with Serrano ham and melon.  Among the other specialties is chicken *mole* (an unsweetened chocolate sauce) served with almonds.

# SIGHTSEEING

The Tarascan Indians who inhabited the area fifteen centuries before the birth of Christ were a fiercely independent lot who'd successfully resisted the Aztecs. Those who managed to survive the Spanish conquest have retained much of their culture. Today they are still "doing their own thing"— earning just what they need, raising just enough food for themselves—much as they did in pre-Columbian times.

That the uniquely beautiful artistic creations of the Tarascans may be seen, appreciated and purchased today can be credited largely to the efforts of Vasco de Quiroga, the first bishop of the state of Michoacan.  Arriving in 1540, Quiroga — one of the few good guys in a brutal scenario — came, saw what had been conquered and set about restoring the economy that had been virtually destroyed by Nunez de Guzman, a conquistador who has the distinction of being the cruelest and most greedy of them all.

Quiroga assumed the role of protector to the spirited Tarascans who'd  been nearly destroyed but never totally conquered spiritually.  He established the College of San Nicolas, the second oldest university in the Americas, then set about teaching crafts to the Indians who were eeking out a meager existence as fishermen and farmers.    Traveling from village to village, he encouraged the development of non-competing cottage industries so that each village could be assured of a unique independence.   In this manner Indians learned wood carving, weaving and ceramics—skills which the bishop then helped them market.

Today **Casa de las Artesanias**, located in what was once the Convent of San Francisco, showcases elaborate displays of traditional handiwork. Tucked away in a former nun's cell one can see and buy lacquerware from Urapan, copperware from Santa Clara del Cobre, guitars from Paracho, green pottery from Patamban, brown pottery from Tzintzuntzan, ceramic cartoon figures from Ocumicho, chairs from Opopeo, and woven reeds and textiles from Erongaricuaro. Often the artisans themselves may be found working at their craft.  (Plaza Vallodolid.)

**Plaza de los Martires** (Plaza of Martyrs)—the local zocalo—  honors rebel priests executed there in 1810 for their part in the revolt which eventually resulted in the overthrow of Spain. Today, with its flowers and fountains, the square is a focal point for downtown socializing.   People chat and read on its benches, lounge on its grass. Free concerts take place there Sunday and Thursday evenings at 7.

On the plaza's east side is the rose stone **Cathedral**,  considered one of Mexico's best examples of "plateresque" architecture—the name derived from the intricate engravings of a *platero*, or silversmith.  A marvelous example of tender loving care, the cathedral, begun in 1660 wasn't completed until 1764.  Combining majesty and delicacy, the twin 200-foot towers are an esthetic triumph — massively based but pleasingly graceful.   The entrance is composed of three leather and wood doors, leading to a majestic interior with a a great 4600-pipe organ.

The main altar, dominated by a tiled dome, is a copy of St. Peter's in Rome, and has a reliquary dedicated to the Sacred Heart of Jesus — a silver and gold masterwork weighing eight hundred kilos and fifty-three meters high.

**Casa de Morelos**—the home of the famed Mexican patriot, Jose Maria Morelos — now houses a museum that contains many manuscripts and memorabilia, including the blindfold Morelos wore when executed.  In the courtyard are two contrasting carriages.   One of them was used by the revolutionary priest to carry the Holy Host on sick calls.  The other — once the property of the town dandy—is extravagantly furnished and decorated with solid-gold tacks.  Think of it as an 18th century equivalent of Hugh Hefner's Flying Bunny.   (Closed Sundays.  Aldama and Morelos).

**Mercado de Dulces**, on Calle Valentin Farias, is a large market selling candies, including Morelia's specialty, *ate,* a very sweet candied fruit product that comes in a variety of flavors.  If you're leery of sampling here, head down the street to the small candy store, **La Estrella Dorada** at No. 265, where everything is carefully wrapped and labeled. Don't miss the marvelous caramel flavored pancake-shaped *obleas,* made from goat's milk.

Many travel to Morelia just to visit the **Church of the Christ of Health** (Iglesia del Nino de la Salud)—which contains an image of the Christ Child thought to possess healing powers.  According to the story, the image once belonged to a poor woman who was unable to keep it in clothing.  The image apparently grew!  Word of the miracle spread and ailing visitors began to appear.  So many reported healings that a church was eventually built to house the statue.
Half a mile beyond the State Penitentiary on Rte. 5.

# LAKE PATZCUARO

Morelia may be the official capital of Michoacan, but Patzcuaro is its spiritual capital.  A town, a lake, a way of life, Patzcuaro lies thirty miles southwest of Morelia — a little more than an hour by bus or car.   Clearly this is where the heart of the Tarascan people lies.

It's also the birthplace of two remarkable heroines.  The first was Erendira, a Tarascan noblewoman, believed to be the first Indian woman  to mount a horse.   She rode off to rally allies against Nunez de Guzman — the brutal Himmler of the conquest.  Erendira is featured in the striking mural by Juan O'Gorman in **La Bibiloteca,** the town library.

The other is Gertrudis Bocanegra, executed by firing squad nearly three hundred years later for her support of Mexican independence. The gallant woman who refused to reveal the names of her co-conspirators is remembered by a plaza which serves as the marketplace. This Indian market overflows with lacquerware, wool serapes, decorative iron work, carved wood furniture and hand-hammered copperware.

Facing the plaza to the west is the **Casa de los Once Patios** (House of Eleven Patios)—an ex-convent framed with Romanesque arches and stone ramparts. Today's incarnation is a kind of mini mall where some of the best handicraft shops are located — family owned and operated boutiques where one can buy any number of lovely things.

**El Oasis** on the Plaza Vasco Quiroga also has beautiful antiques — clothing, jewelry and religious art. At the nearby **La Galeria Dos** one can find the work of Juan Orta, one of the best known mask makers in Mexico. Orta's fanciful creations — devilish variations — are carved on *copalitto* wood.

The local cathedral has a madonna (the **Virgin of Health**) made from cornstalk paste and liquid extracted from orchids. Legend has it that if one passes under her train a miracle will occur.

Patzcuaro has a charming colonial hotel, **Los Escudos.** The food is excellent there. Balconied rooms look very inviting.

A country village rooted in the sixteenth century, both in tradition and design, Patzcuaro is anchored on the southern end of the long lake. At 7000 feet, Lake Patzcuaro is one of the highest in the country. The famed butterfly fishermen still ply the waters, their nets like the wings of insects as they dip on first one side of a canoe and then the other. Nowadays, these nets are rarely used for work but remain as a tourist attraction.

A boat ride out to the island of Janitzio is almost obligatory. It's said that this was the home of the mysterious Purepechan Indians. Never linked to any other people in the Americas, these gentle people whose language contained no swear words appeared briefly in the fourteenth century only to be totally annihilated by the Spanish.

The island is dominated by a monolithic statue by Morelios which affords a splendid view of the area.

Up the mountain a few miles further just beyond a lovely pine forest is **Santa Clara del Cobre**, a town famed for its copperware. Products range from striking handcrafted jewelry to pitchers, vases and candlesticks made on primitive hand-operated forges. The "factories" are in homes. Though there's a tendency in other parts of Mexico to spray ironware with copper paint, this is never done in Santa Clara where artisans are justly proud of their famous product.

The **Casa Paz Sanabria** on Pino Suarez No. 90-A operates the oldest factory in town. Their wares are truly spectacular. Lovely things are also found at **Galeria Tiamuri** on Obregon 141, a co-op.

## TIDBITS

Home to some one million people, the rose and beige city of Morelia, has been designated by UNESCO as a World Heritage Site.  The 6000-foot high state capital is located midway between Mexico City and Guadalajara, roughly a 4-hour drive or 25 minute flight from either.   The climate is mild, the pace relaxed. Dress is slightly more formal than the beach resorts.

Both Aeromar and Taesa fly to Morelia from Mexico City.  An alternative is the ETN which departs Mexico City from the Central Bus Station. The bus is very reasonable, first-class with airline seating, movies, free coffee and cold drinks.

*Looking for that special gift.*  Photo by E. Monroe.

*Drawing by Nancy Brannigan.*

# FOOD
## FROM THE SWEET TO THE HOT

## CHOCOLATE

For those of us who are chocoholics, it's hard to imagine a world without our favorite treat, nor does it come as a surprise that its origins are both romantic and delicious.  The Aztecs believed that cocoa made the men who drank it more virile and attractive to women. Today dieticians speculate that this ancient belief may be related to the modern day theory that chocolate can chemically stimulate the body to produce those endocrines that make us feel so good when we fall in love.

The New World's secret was introduced to the old when Columbus placed the black cocoa beans at the feet of Queen Isabella.  Later the Aztec ruler, Montezuma, offered a foaming elixir, *chocolatl,* to the conquering Cortez.  The Spaniards kept the secret, and the cocoa bean monopoly, to themselves for one hundred years.  It took a royal wedding to introduce chocolate to the world.  Not until Maria Theresea married Louis XIV did the French learn the delights of hot chocolate.  From then on it was just a matter of time--and not very much of it!--before elegant "chocolate houses" opened in France, Flanders, Italy, Austria and England.

* * *

## VANILLA

Originating with the Aztecs, vanilla comes from the seed pod of an orchid called "vanilla planifolia."  Legend has it that the plant is the result of a long ago sacrifice. According to the story, the beautiful princess, Tzacopontiziza, fled to the mountains to escape sacrifice to the god Tonacayohua, caretaker of harvests, bread and drink. When sudden volcanic flames threatened to engulf her, the princess was forced to descend  only to be captured by waiting priests.

Months later, in the place where Tzacopontiziza's blood was shed, a bush appeared covered with orchids that filled the air with a beautiful aroma.

Later when the Spaniards tasted vanilla, they found it not only delicious but an aid to digestion.  Members of the Spanish court kept the secret to themselves for years.  It wasn't until 1610 when a pirate raided a ship carrying the precious cargo, that the secret was leaked to other.

Today Mexico is the primary vanilla producer to the world for it is the only country where the small stingless bee lives which is needed to pollinate the orchids.  Growers in other countries must pollinate the orchids themselves.

* * *

## CHILI PEPPERS

The average Mexican citizen consumes more chili peppers each year than onion or tomatoes and has more than l00 varieties from which to choose. Chili peppers are found in every part of Mexico, from coast to coast and border to border, making their way into all manner of delicious foods.

## SALSAS

Accompanying virtually every meal in Mexico, *salsas*, or sauces, lend an enormous variety and easily liven most meals. Surprisingly, not all are hot. A major ingredient in many salsas is the *tomate verde* (green tomato), which is not a true tomato but a small lime-green fruit. The tart taste of the *tomate verde* blends well with other ingredients used in salsas, such as chiles, onions and garlic. The assortment of Mexican salsas is as diverse as food itself. Here's a sampling of the tastiest:

***Salsa Costena*** —a table salsa made of searing hot chile costeno or dried chile de arbol which complements fish, meat or chicken.

***Salsa de Tomate Verde*** — made of green tomatoes, onions, garlic and cilantro, this is one of Mexico's most popular sauces. Bits of avocado added to the sauce makes a richer condiment.

***Salsa de Molcajete*** — a combination of roasted chiles and tomatoes which intensify the flavor. This sauce is made in the traditional stone bowl called a *molcajete.* The salsa's texture is chunky and complements any of the corn-based chips and hors d'oeuvres.

***Salsa de Cacahuate*** — ground peanuts and chiles are the basis for this unique table salsa which is used on grilled meats and eggs, and adds special flavor to plain rice.

***Salsa Endiablada*--this picante, or hot salsa can be found in bottles throughout Mexico. It's commonly sprinkled on beans, broiled meats or any dish needing extra zip.

***Salsa Mexicana*** — a classic salsa made with sweet field ripened tomatoes, onions, garlic, chile and cilantro, this is a perfect complement to a wide variety of dishes, and is served at virtually every meal.

***Salsa Chile Guajillo*** — a simple salsa made from *guajillo* chile with tomato and garlic. Guajillo accentuates grilled meats and tacos.

# MEXICAN FOODS
## ITEMS YOU RE LIKELY TO FIND ON THE MENU

**Ate:** A jellied paste made from various types of fruit, usually quince or guava.

**Cabrito:** Broiled goat, popular in northern Mexico.

**Cajeta:** Carmelized and flavored milk (usually goat milk) used as a spread.

**Cevice:** A cocktail or salad made of raw marinated seafood (usually mackerel) with chopped onion, tomato, peppers, oil and often diced avocado.

**Chia:** A beverage consisting of lemonade with tiny native seeds.

**Chile:** There are unending varieties, from mild peppers to the almost incendiary *jalpenos*. Eaten whole or used to spice up sauces.

**Chile rellenos:** Peppers stuffed with cheese or ground meat, fried in egg batter, then placed in hot tomato sauce.

**Chongos:** A custard of curdled milk, mixed with egg and with most of the moisture boiled out, syrup and cinnamon added.

**Cochinita pibil:** A Yucatecan specialty, consisting of suckling pig cooked in banana leaves.

**Enchilada:** A tortilla in which other things have been rolled up (meat, fish, cheese) fried, cooked or covered in sauce. Swiss enchiladas use a sauce made with cream, hence the name.

**Gazpacho:** A soup of Spanish origin, made of raw vegetables, blended and served cold.

**Guacamole:** Mashed avocado mixed with lime juice, onions, tomatoes and spices. Served with tacos and as a spiced dish.

**Horchata:** A milky white beverage made from pulverized cantaloupe seeds, rice, nuts and fruit.

**Mixiote:** Mutton, accompanied by a somewhat piquant sauce and spices, cooked in the membrane of maguey spikes, in corn husks or banana leaves.

**Mole:** A dark sauce, with numerous ingredients, principally chocolate, chile and spices, and served with meats and chicken, or as a sauce for enchiladas.

**Paella:** A Spanish import, popular in Mexico. Rice cooked with just about everything imaginable: pieces of chicken, pork, sausage, shrimp, crab claws, clams.

**Picadillo:** Minced meat, mixed with tomato and onion, and seasoned. Used in rolled tortillas, in chiles rellenos and in quesadillas.

**Pozole:** A highly seasoned soup or stew containing hominy kernels, chickpeas, pork, radishes, sausage, tomato and whatever else is in the kitchen.

**Quesadilla:** A tortilla folded once over and stuffed with just about anything-- cheese, meat, mashed potato, squash flower--then fried in deep fat.

**Sangria:** Lemonade colored with red wine.

**Taco:** a tortilla rolled and stuffed.

**Tamales:** Corn meal stuffed with pork or chicken, with chile sauces, then steam-cooked in corn husks. Regional varieties use banana leaves and finer meal.

**Tepache**: a cidery beverage made from pineapple rinds with brown sugar and cloves.

**Torta:** A sandwich made with a roll of bread (*bolillo* or *telera* ) cut in half.

**Tortilla:** A thin cake of corn meal (wheat in the northern states). Used in countless ways as a staple in the Mexican diet. Served with meals, spread with relish and sauces and rolled to hold meats, and cooked in sauces.

# MEXICAN WINES

Every day in every way Mexican wines are getting better and better. Some of them are already quite good. Sample these:

*Red Wines*___________________

**Domecq:** Cabernet Sauvigon, Chateau Domecqu, Zinfandel

**L.A. Cetto:** Cabernet Sauvignon, Petite Sirah, Zinfandel

**Monte Xanic:** Cabernet Sauvignon

*White Wines*___________________

**Domecq**: Blanc del Blancs XA, Riesling

**L.A. Cetto:** Chardonnay, Chenin Blanc, Fume Blanc, Riesling

**Monte Xanic**: Chenin Colombard, Chardonnay

**Sparkling**

**Saile Vive**: Brut

# MEXICAN BEER

The delights (and varieties) of Mexican beer (cervesa) are hardly a novelty to North Americans. Corona is the second largest beer import in the United States, but all are inexpensive and readily available.

It all began with Spanish conquistador, Alfonso de Herrera, who received permission from King Carlos V to produce beer in Mexico. Herrera recruited brewmasters from Flanders and by 1554 the first brewery in the Americas was prospering.

Today, Mexico has seventeen breweries throughout the country. Some of the brand names you'll encounter — most excellent, but each a little different — are Carta Blanca, Corona, Superior, Dos Equis, and the author's special favorite, the dark and rich Negra Modelo. Bohemia, which is more like an ale, is also very popular.

*The perfect margarita.* Photo by Vern Appleby.

## MARGARITA

If Margarita Sames had been just anybody, Mexico's favorite drink might never have gone beyond the four walls of her home. Luckily for millions of margarita lovers, the drink's creation has some very powerful friends.

A rich, young socialite in 1948, Sames was celebrating the Christmas holidays in her Acapulco home. Looking to create a good daytime cocktail that "you could have several of, "she took two of her favorite drinks, contreau and tequila, and mixed them together. She then added lime juice, rimmed the glass with salt and brought a tray of samples to her poolside guests. Among the movers and shakers who sampled those first cocktails were Nick Hilton, founder of the Hilton Hotel chain; Joseph Drown, who owned the Hotel Bel-Air in Los Angeles; and Shelton McHenry, who owned the popular Tail O' the Cock restaurant in Los Angeles.

Margarita's Drink made a big hit with her friends, who began introducing it into their own establishments in the United States. Eventually the popular cocktail went "home" to Mexico to the delight of South of the Border citizens who claimed it for their own.

# BIBLIOGRAPHY


Cannon, Ray. *Sea of Cortez*. Menlo Park, Calif.: Lane Magazine & Book Company, 1966.

Guzman, Martin Luis. *Memoirs of Pancho Villa* . Austin, Texas: University of Texas Press, 1965.

Herrera, Hayden. *Frida: A biography of Frida Kahlo.* New York: Harper Colophon Books, 1983.

Heymann, David C. Poor Little Rich Girl, the Life and Legend of Barbara Hutton. Secaucus, N.J.: Lyle Stuart Inc., 1984.

Kandell, Jonathan. *La Capital: The Biography of Mexico City.* New York: Random House, 1988.

Krutch, Joseph Wood. *Baja California and the Geography of Hope.* San Francisco: Sierra Club, 1967.

Lansford ,William Douglas. *Memoirs of Pancho Villa..* Los Angeles: Sherbourne Press, Inc. 1965.

Macado, Manuel A. Jr. *Centaur of the North* Austin, Texas: Easkin Press, 1988

May, Antoinette. *The Yucatan, A Guide to the Land of Maya Mysteries.* San Carlos, Calif.: Wide World Publishing, 1993.

May, Antoinette. *Passionate Pilgrim, The Extraordinary Life of Alma Reed.* New York: Paragon House, 1993.

O'Connor, Richard. *The Cactus Throne.* New York: G.P. Putnam's Sons, 1971.

Paz, Octavio. *The Labyrinth of Solitude: Life and Thought in Mexico.* Translated by Lysander Kemp. New York: Grove, 1961.

Quintana, Patricia. *The Taste of Mexico.* New York: Stewart, Tabori & Chang, 1986.

Rivera, Diego, with March, Gladys. *My Art, My Life: An Autobiography.* New York: Citadel, 1960.

Smith, Gene. *Maximilian and Carlota.* New YorK: Thomas Morrow & Company, 1973.

Toor, Frances. *A Treasury of Mexican Folkways.* New York: Bonanaza Books, 1985.

Van Rensselaer, Philip. *Million Dollar Baby, An Intimate Look at Barbara*

# INDEX

## INDEX

## INDEX

Other books by Antoinette May

- ***The Yucatan**—A Guide to Maya Mysteries plus Sacred Sites at Belize, Tikal & Copan*

- ***Passionate Pilgrim***

- ***Witness to War***

- ***The Annotated Ramona***

- ***Helen Hunt Jackson:** A Lonely Voice of Conscience*

- ***Psychic Women***

- ***Different Drummers***

- ***Haunted Houses of California***

# ABOUT THE AUTHOR

A writer who has traveled extensively all over the world, Antoinette May is repeatedly drawn to Mexico.  As a psychic researcher whose work has been the subject of such TV documentaries as *In Search Of* and *The World of People,* she's particularly intrigued by the dark mysteries of this remarkable land.

May is travel writer, a biographer, a former newspaper editor, and the founder and publisher of a women's magazine.  She writes a weekly column for the *San Francisco Chronicle* and lectures on parapsychology at universities and colleges.

*Antoinette May emerging from ruins*

May is the recipient of the prestigious *Pluma de Plata* award from the Mexican government.